TRANSLATION AS A TOUCHSTONE

TRANSLATION AS A TOUCHSTONE

RAJI NARASIMHAN

SSAGE www.sagepublications.com
Los Angeles • London • New Delhi • Singapore • Washington DC

First published in 2013 by

SAGE Publications India Pvt Ltd
B1/I-1 Mohan Cooperative Industrial Area
Mathura Road, New Delhi 110 044, India
www.sagepub.in

SAGE Publications Inc
2455 Teller Road
Thousand Oaks, California 91320, USA

SAGE Publications Ltd
1 Oliver's Yard, 55 City Road
London EC1Y 1SP, United Kingdom

SAGE Publications Asia-Pacific Pte Ltd
33 Pekin Street
#02-01 Far East Square
Singapore 048763

Published by Vivek Mehra for SAGE Publications India Pvt Ltd, typeset in 11/13 pt Adobe Garamond by Diligent Typesetter, Delhi, and printed at De Unique, New Delhi.

Library of Congress Cataloging-in-Publication Data

Narasimhan, Raji.
    Translation as a touchstone/Raji Narasimhan.
        p. cm.
    Includes bibliographical references and index.
    1. Translating and interpreting. 2. Literature—Translations—History and criticism. 3. Criticism. I. Title.
PN241.N37418'.04—dc23   2012   2012042656

ISBN: 978-81-321-0954-9 (HB)

The SAGE Team: Neelakshi Chakraborty, Shreya Chakraborti, and Sanjeev Kumar Sharma

To all those interested in
the creative aspects of translation

Thank you for choosing a SAGE product! If you have any comment, observation or feedback, I would like to personally hear from you. Please write to me at <u>contactceo@sagepub.in</u>

—Vivek Mehra, Managing Director and CEO,
SAGE Publications India Pvt Ltd, New Delhi

Bulk Sales

SAGE India offers special discounts for purchase of books in bulk. We also make available special imprints and excerpts from our books on demand.

For orders and enquiries, write to us at

Marketing Department
SAGE Publications India Pvt Ltd
B1/I-1, Mohan Cooperative Industrial Area
Mathura Road, Post Bag 7
New Delhi 110044, India
E-mail us at <u>marketing@sagepub.in</u>

Get to know more about SAGE, be invited to SAGE events, get on our mailing list. Write today to <u>marketing@sagepub.in</u>

This book is also available as an e-book.

Contents

Introduction: Some Possible Approaches to Translation

Let me begin by setting down a gut feeling I have had—and still have—about the nature of translations. This gut feeling is that a translation ought not to read like original writing. At the risk of immodesty, let me quote from my preface to my English translation of Rajee Seth's Hindi novella, *Nishkavach*[1], '... translations should never read like original writings. A translation should sound and read like a translation, that is, like a rendering in another language. It should have a bi-cultural and consequently, a bi-lingual note and feel.'[2] And here, the corroboration, heart-warming, straight from the formidable portals of academia:

> The translated text exists through its difference from the original, and the original makes known and legitimizes its own existence only in and through the translation. Each refers irremediably to the other. Neither exists completely separately: the existence of each is interwoven—*metissage*—with that of the other.[3]

My own belief, which has a somewhat defiant, back-to-the-wall stance in those lines written more than a decade ago, has by now matured into a sturdier rationale, reasonably confident of clearing a viva.

—'Do you mean to say a translator should ride two horses at the same time?'

I hear the indignant voice of the examiner at this viva.

'Yes'. I hear myself saying in even, unflappable, regulated tones. 'For, a translation is a sustained exercise in transiting from one language to another, and back, and back again *ad infinitum*. This unceasing motion to and fro, fro and to, is the essence of translation.'

My examiner is only partly convinced. But he is not dismissive. And I dig in my heels, sensing my chance, and say the D-word with emphasis. 'A translation is a product of Difference,' I state, slowing down now, wanting to highlight the D of Difference. 'The Difference of two cultures, the Difference of two traditions of thinking and thought: the pre-existence of Difference is what gives character, meaning and validity to the genre of translation.'

Character. Meaning. Validity. Words that are a little too general, everyday. I feel the need for a more technical sounding, clinching word. My examiner would be happy too, if I supplied it. He is encouraging of look, expectant.

'It is *dvaitic* (dualist) in spirit. It is not *advaitic* (non-dualist). It must reflect its *dvaitic svabhaav*.' I stop short. The Sanskritic terms take me by surprise. My voice sounds strange to myself. Why didn't I say 'dualist nature' for *dvaitic svabhaav*? I know the answer, even if I stand amazed at myself. It is a reflex at acculturizing English: creating a morph of Indian face and features in an English physique. 'Anglo-Indianize it'—I can hear the snorts and sniggers from those with sour memories of contacts with the Anglo-Indians of British days.

But that was the colonial era. In our post-colonial, post-modern days with their upsurge of translation activities, a healthier, more creative convergence of English and the particular Indian language(s)—or source languages—is necessary. It is a literary-aesthetic need now, an imperative, I would even say, requiring craft and sensibility, in contrast to the exigencies of circumstance from which the amalgams of the colonial age came about.

Several implications of practical and professional relevance for the translator arise from this need for a more electric contact with English, which I have adopted as the criterion for my analyses of the translations considered in the pages that follow. One of these is to keep transliteration as not only a viable but often preferable approach in translating into English. The viability aspect has been largely accepted by now in the guidelines of translation. Glossaries are put in only in exceptional case, as Rimli Bhattacharya says in her Introduction to *Katha Prize Stories*, 'when they bring alive the context of the story.'[4] Translating terms like 'kundelu', 'udumu' into their English equivalents of 'hare' and 'monitor lizard', would, Bhattacharya says further, 'draw undue attention and even defamiliarize the reader from the situation.'[5] They are glossed for this reason, and not translated. In a similar attitude, disfavouring italicizing Indian words, she says that many Indian words 'belong and should belong to the English language as spoken and used in different parts of India.' The incorporation of Hindi words into the English prose evolving from operations of the English media ('aam aadmee', 'baithak', 'dharma', and so on) is another now accepted practice that stamps the language with our élan.

However, stronger reasons than those of viability exist for transliteration. These are reasons of bare aesthetics thrown up by the resurging of dramatic weight that occurs in the course of a story, novel or play. These reasons need not arise in all writings. But when and as they do, as they do in the musical interludes of Vijay Tendulkar's play, discussed in the essay concerned, transliteration may well be the best means of reflecting the original. The translator has to be aware of this option and an established recognition of this method might help raise the translator's level of awareness.

▌ Exceptions

Transliteration, in other words, is a means, *one among others*, of highlighting the factor of Difference, of Otherness, that is the hallmark of a translation. It is *one* means of effecting the creative juxtaposition and interaction of two languages and their two traditions that a translation has to deal with. The stress is on the creative aspect. And even in *Silence! The Court is in Session*,[6] it should be pointed out that transliteration does not seem to be the perfect answer to the other musical or lilt-laden interludes and their unfinished-seeming translations.

One interlude, for instance, runs as follows in Hindi: *bulbul sey sugnaa kahey/kyon geeley terey nain/kahaan rahoon sugnaa daadaa/ kahaan bitaaoon rayn/kahaan gayaa mera rayn baseraa/chiv chiv chiv/ chiv chiv chiv rey/chiv chiv chiv.*[7] The English translation is: The parrot to the sparrow said/why, oh why, are your eyes so red?/'Oh, My dear friend, what shall I say/some one has stolen my nest away'/Sparrow, sparrow, poor little sparrow.[8] A straight comparison with the Hindi turns out highly damaging to the English. For instance, instead of 'Eyes so red?' for 'geeley terey nain', would not a straight 'eyes so wet?' have sufficed? And then the repetition of 'kahaan' in three successive lines of the total eight; and of the eight, the last three are only articulations of the calls of a sparrow: 'chiv chiv chiv/chiv chiv chiv re/chiv chiv chiv.' This charges the poem with the pathos that is its strength and central feature. Should the English translation not have made special note of this tonal register in the verse, studied its make up and strived to capture it the translation? Should not the strength of alliteration supplied by the word 'kyon' to 'kahaan'—*kyon* geeley terey nain?/ *kahaan* rahoon sugnaa daadaa/*kahaan* bitaoon rayn?'—and some tactic mirroring the complimentarity be adopted?

Is it because of these initial omissions that the concluding onomatopoeic lines—chiv chiv chiv...—which fill the verse with a compelling resonance have also been omitted in the translation? *And*, no sparrow figures in the Hindi version. The parrot's confidante is the 'bulbul', that is, nightingale. 'Bulbul se sugnaa kahey...' Could this be because the word 'nightingale' is too long and out of proportion to the word 'parrot' that it is meant to counter-tone, as 'bulbul' counter-tones 'sugnaa'? Even so, other means could have been found for conveying proportion The last line, 'Sparrow, sparrow, poor little sparrow' is practically a mockery of the plaintive tone of the Hindi: 'chiv chiv chiv...' The onomatopoeia subsumes and personifies the factor of bird-call: parrot or bulbul. The English is the intrusive, lament-expressing voice of the narrator.

However, when you shut your ears to the Hindi, and read the English, a certain lilt does become apparent. For instance, there is the rhyming of 'said' and 'red'. And then there is the beat: 'The pa-*rrot* to the spa-*rrow*/said/Why-oh-why are your-eyes-so red?/Oh-my-dear-friend, *what* shall I say?/Some one hassto-len my nest-a-way/ Spaa-row, spaa-row, poor-little-spaa-row....' It's like a nursery rhyme in English, yes, with its clap clap clap staccato beat. But the point to note here, despite—or because of—the rudimentary attempt at poetic diction, is that a poetic parallel in the English to the Hindi is the only solution possible for working in the former language into the latter. Transliteration is ruled out because unlike the example discussed in the chapter on the play, an appropriate mood for a lingual leap or transfer does not arise in the present case. There, the dominant mood is that of inconsolable grief exploding from Benare at the verdict of the court. '*Benare bilakhtee huee abhiyukt kay vakeel kay stool kay paas jaatee hai. Bayjaan see uspar baiththee hai. Dukh kay aaveg sey baithaa nahee jaataa hai. Maiz par sir rakhkhar rotee rahtee hai.'*[9] (Sobbing inconsolably, Benare goes to the defending lawyer's stool. Drained, grief-stricken, she sits on it. Waves of grief rock her, and she is unable to sit. Placing her head on the table she cries away) [Author's translation].

This state of breakdown demands articulation in a language that is one's own, for it demands intimacy of expression and a certain privacy. English, for Benare at this point, cannot sustain her emotional load and give it the anguished, lyrical expression that the Hindi does. This kind of emotional overload is not the setting in the verse under discussion. Here are the lines denoting her overall state of mind at this point: *'napkin sey moonh ponchchtey hue kuchch gungunaatee huee Benare aatee hai. Ek-dum fresh hai…dahinee taraf manch par rakhkhee apnee dolchee main saabun, napkin aadee rakhtee hai aur gungunaatee hai.'*[10] (Wiping her face with a napkin, humming a song, Benare enters, washed and fresh looking. Puts back soap, napkin etc. into the bag left of stage and hums…) [Author's translation]. It is a light-hearted Benare we see here, a Benare who *can* break into humming in English, in the teasing, burlesque she's been shown in earlier sections in the play. And precisely because English is a natural choice here, ruling out transliteration, it was incumbent on the translator to have moulded it, chiselled it, to refract the immediate context.

It is, to cut a long story short (also, to repeat what can still stand repetition!), a creative adaptation of language—English or Hindi—that is called for in a work of translation. The word 'transcreation', that flashes into our mind here, is hardly unknown to us, thanks to the pioneering works of P. Lal and the Writers' Workshop, with whom the term has come to be more or less being synonymous. We could well afford to apprehend that word with the still greater fullness it demands in these late post-modern, post-colonial times of ours.

| Refurbishing Links with English

The target or translating language that has come in for a considerably more detailed examination in this collection is English. Two of the books considered—*Chemmeen* and *Samskara*—have been translated into Hindi and Tamil, and possibly in other languages as well in addition to English. In both cases, I have rated the Tamil translations as more evocative and reflective of the milieus portrayed in the parent texts. This, I imply, is due to the nearness of the language to the milieu concerned: Malayalam in *Chemmeen* and Kannada in *Samskara*. This might seem to contradict the definition of translation I have adopted that it is a genre of writing thrown up by the factor of Difference, and that, it has to highlight this factor in as creative a way as possible.

Here, further explication of this view is called for. Both the English and Hindi translations of *Chemmeen* are found wanting in so many respects that the Tamil, admitting its quality and worth, shines in splendid isolation. Very unlike *Samskara* where the English rendering of A. K. Ramanujan not only excites compare-and-contrast studies with the Tamil, but also awakens the reader to the greater ingenuity and inventiveness called for by the English. The significance and implication of Difference awake anew in the reader, and thence, to the weight that accrues to a translation from its efforts of bridging the Difference inhering in it.

A point of objection can be brought up here, voiced among others, by writer–translator Prasenjit Gupta.[11] He questions whether it would not further privilege the already privileged position that English holds in India, no matter all the drives to unprivilege it. Certainly, when Ramanujan writes: 'In full view of the frightened Brahmins I'll stand exposed like the naked quick of life: and I, elder in their midst, will turn into a new man at midnight,'[12] we see a certain spin-off from the Tamil. It is possible that no spin-off is felt in English when set against Kannada, Ramanujan's own language. But what the language translated from is, does not matter in the reasoning behind the fears being examined here; the reasoning that recommending the method of poetic paraphrase for the English translation of any Indian language text is to further enhance the already enhanced standing of English among us. The Tamil of those lines has a certain explorative feel to it. Praneshacharya is shown crystal-gazing, in a mix of reading and envisaging, the process of becoming that lies immediately ahead of him. There is a conscious, careful selection of words which slows to a heavy ponderous gait of zero speed as it reaches the corresponding climactic lines for 'will turn into a new man at midnight.' This halting, uncertain deciphering by Praneshacharya of what should and has to transpire in the coming hours fades in the English rendering. The poetic sweep gives the lines the distinctive, sovereign quality of poetry. Also, the image of Jesus risen from the dead, which is distantly discernible in the Tamil of those lines, becomes pronounced in English. Undertones become overtones, overtones of the Bible. This, along with the assured poetry of the lines in English, can well direct the critical attention towards the appropriative nature and history of English, and our resistance to this psychic invasion. The indisputable cultural insider-ness of Ramanujan, plus his personal standing as an Indian poet in English, of course rules out any exclusive, adulatory considerations of the language. But a better argument in defence of the poetic-paraphrase approach to translating into English is that we have to stop seeing the language exclusively as the 'other', stop having chips on our shoulders about it. Our sense of otherness is also accompanied by a sense of closeness: a closeness that at its best manifests itself in poetry, and in the by now well-established, fully conceded practice of writing in English. Attitudes of otherness and closeness, of distance and proximity, have kept pace with each other, grown side by side, each in its own space. Otherness thus need not gainsay closeness. It is an acculturization of the language that has taken place among us, impelling us to shape the language our own way, say, as the African writers do.

Any language finding favour with individuals or with groups as their medium of expression—written or spoken—has to be boldly claimed as one's own. Inhibitions bred by whatever factors—colonial, anti-colonial—have to be overcome. The spirit of takeover has to come into play at some stage. Let us then, claim English. And here, how much more telling the single Hindi word 'apnaanaa' is, for 'claiming as one's own'! Let us make English 'apnaa'. If English is a world language—global language in the current terminology—it is everyone's, every country's. A global presence implies the freedom of every member of the globe to claim the language: not just the freedom of the global language, to claim the members of the globe. We could learn this precept anew. We could, deep-reading Raja Rao's remark about English in his Preface to *Kanthapura*,[13] emotionally claim it, not just concede it the position of the intellectual pace setter. Further, this healthier, self-assured accommodation of English into our semantics does not rule out noting its inadequacies. The erasures occurring in Prasenjit Gupta's English translation of Nirmal Verma's 'London Kee Ek Raat' are examples of these inadequacies. A generic trait of the original has got wiped out in the translation. This trait has to do with bilingualism. In the first place, the English speech lines in the original Hindi text stand out understandably enough. But more pertinent than this expression of a natural apartness of languages, is that the English interjections are signifiers of the intense sense of alienation that afflicts the narrator/protagonist. The alienation is a result of tensions bred by conditions in his society, compounded by first hand experiences of the ugly realities of race and colour prejudices bred in western societies. It is this bitter knowledge which echoes in the English interjections of the Hindi text. The bilingual quality of the story, thus, is not just an attention-seeking writing ploy, but an outcome of its narrative push, of its narrative steam. The problem for a translator translating 'London Kee Ek Raat' is, thus, that of conveying the symbolic quality of the English interjections through his medium. He lacks the advantage of having two languages at his command—of having more than one arrow in his quiver—at these points of the story.

Take this paragraph, for instance. The Hindi is:

> *'damn him if he doesn't' Willi ney ajeeb kheejey svar mey kahaa. 'mai to kal kisee haalat mey naheen aaoongaa ... please come tomorrow' manager kee nakal uttaratey huey usney muh sikod liya. 'Tomorrow be damned. Tum kal aaogey?' Usney pahlee baar meyree taraf unmukh hokar poochchaa.*[14]

The swing of language from Hindi to English and back is of course the obvious, immediately noticeable factor. But more than the narrative's bilingualism is the narrator's bilingualism. Each switch that he makes from his mother tongue to English defines the nature of his ties to the two languages: the psychic waves they cause within him determine his mode of being. From the mooring that his mother tongue gives despite his conflicts with his motherland, to the border-line state he is relegated to in using the language of the land, which marginalizes him; this is the trajectory of the alternating languages in the abovementioned paragraph. This back and forth motion is what gets lost in a monolingual rendering. And thereby a key nuance of the Hindi's discourse is lost. The text is flattened. Here is the English:

> 'Damn him, if he doesn't!' Willie said in a strange, irritated voice. 'I'm not going to come back.... Please come tomorrow!' He imitated the manager's tones, twisting his mouth. 'Tomorrow be damned! Are you coming back?' He asked, lifting his gaze towards me for the first time.[15]

The absence of bilingual play is particularly damaging in the line 'please come tomorrow,' spoken by Willie. He is caricaturing the manager who has told them to come the next day for possible vacancies. The Hindi-speaking narrator's usage of English here is thus not just a direct transcription of the speech of a person speaking on the spot, but of a person not on the spot, invoked by the person on the spot. This double distancing on which hinges the comedy of the caricature gets ironed out in the English rendering. '"Please come tomorrow," he imitated the manager's tones, twisting his mouth,' is how the English renders the Hindi, ' *"Please come tomorrow, " manager kee nakal utaartey huey usney moonh sikod liya.'*

Both versions resort to a narratorial statement of the fact that the speaker is caricaturing the manager. But in the Hindi there is an 'othering' of the manager, a third-personing of him which makes the racial tangle more complex. This complexity is lost to the English, bereft as it is of the sound play of varying phonologies. To some extent, the flat effect of the English can be traced to the choice of words. 'He imitated the manager's tones, twisting his mouth' does not have the barbed, pictorial quality of *'usney manager kee nakal utaarte huey moonh sikod liya.'* We see the 'moonh sikodna'—facial distortion—in the words. But the Hindi is only putting its natural advantage to the best use. And the English goes under by not being fully heeding of its natural disadvantage.

A Third Approach

In addition to transliteration and transcreation, there is one more approach possible to the task of highlighting Difference that is incumbent on the translator. This approach, which I think, can be called the creative juxtaposition or the creative aligning, of the two languages comprising a translation, does not operate in any of the works discussed in the essays. However, in view of the thoughtful—I cannot really think of any other word—translation of Sunil Gangopadhyaya's stories by Nilanjan Bhattacharya,[16] where this method seems to have been the guiding principle, it can be included in this consideration of methods of translation. No word flourishes mark this method. The tone and pace are unhurried. A patient, unflagging effort to comprehend and grasp the essence of each story, each incident, and make the words of the translating language move in pace with the eddies of the text being translated, mark the translation. Here is a sample from the title story of the collection, 'A Bowl of Steaming Rice or a Mere Ghost Story': 'Nibaran, Pawan's youngest son, came out with a small jug of water. Nitai held the jug above his mouth and swallowed nearly half its contents in one gulp.'[17] The reading attention focuses on the second of the two sentences there. It portrays a form of cultural behaviour alien to the culture of the translating language. But the alien-ness has been worked into the muscles of the language, giving the reader a sense of the familiar. Difference stays live and valid amidst harmony. How has this equidistance, or proportion, been achieved, you wonder. Not knowing Bengali, the language of origination, you do not have a firm basis for comparison. But the unbroken and unhurried flow of the English translation seems too deliberate a writing mode to seem the translator's own choice of style. Would, wouldn't, the Bengali be having this feature, you wonder. You cannot decide. Your monolingualism does not let you. Nor does asking a Bengali or Bengali-knowing friend seem a satisfactory alternative: personal corroboration is what you feel in need of.

However, on some reflection, the issue of the real style of the Bengali original seems dispensable. The issue, over and above that of the style of the original, is the factor and feel of Difference conveyed by the translation. And these, so pronounced in the translation, are rooted in the events present in the story, in the irony ascribable to the narrating voice present in the events, and carrying the seeds of Difference. Expressed in another language, the Difference shows up more through the veils of irony, and becomes a feature of the prose of the translation. Winning this much bona fide, the translation gains a presence of its own, separable from the issue of the style of the original. The translator's skill is felt in his tireless-seeming transcribing—his reportage—of the details of every event in a voice held neutral despite its obvious inclinations.

This stolid-ness unfolding into a vista of Difference is seen at its best, perhaps, in its grappling with the mythological references made in the original. Consider, for example, these few lines:

> On the night of ashtami, Surendra danced like a madman in front of the altar. It was easy that he was quite drunk. With his dark skin, stocky build and thick curly hair, he resembled one of *Nandi-Bhringi*, Lord Shiva's mythic pair of sidekicks. Holding an earthen censer in each hand spewing clouds of incense smoke, he was dancing wildly and yelling, 'Mother, Mother!' at the top of his lungs.[18]

On first reading, the choice of words could seem uneven, jarring at some places, pleasantly apt and fitting at others. Take the word 'altar', for instance. The word comes with strong Indian connotations, rousing anew the reading attention here. So, why not 'Surendra had danced like a madman in front of the "vedi"'? But the steady, hasteless rhythm and fall of the sentence—its *taal*—comes as an emollient, a peacemaker, and fixes the attention on the setting and import of the line: the religious ecstasy of Surendra in a formal, sacral setting.

This mediation of the basic rhythm of the prose style does not take place in the case of the word, 'sidekicks': '…Lord Shiva's mythic pair of sidekicks,' occurring farther down the passage. It is just smart, trendy—qualities neither present in, nor associated with the translator' prose style. The word stays stuck in the throat. Funnily enough, the mediation happens with the term *Nandi Bhringi* in the same sentence, just some half a dozen words before 'sidekicks'. The solid, physical description of Surendra that precedes *Nandi Bhringi* bears down on the word, thinning its exoticness, its oriental-ism. Likewise, the word 'censer'—'Holding an earthen censer in each hand'—sheds its anglicized avatara for *dhoopdan* and merges with the picture of a devotee's possessed dancing that the writing creates. Similarly, the cry—'Mother! Mother!'—in the last sentence could well have been 'Maa, Maa!' with suave naturalism. But again, the Anglicism falls off in the overall, powerful image of religious indigenousness that is created.

This grassroots quality of the scene owes a lot to the even, good humoured and closely observant tone of the narrating voice. It is a tone that, in its turn, is a construct of *(a)* the narrator/translator's position as a neutral insider to the scene, and *(b)* his gentle, minimal-seeming adjustment of the language, to which he is an outsider, to the pressures of the scene. The whole segment, thus, becomes an exposition cum composition of Difference.

The same blend of minimal manipulation of language and close observation of the given scene is seen even more vividly in this one line—the scene is of Surendra rescuing a woman being tortured by exorcists—'...like Lord Shiva at the court of King Daksha, he lifted Shanti off the ground with his strong arm and slung her across his shoulder.'[19] The action of manly arms flinging a woman's inert body across his shoulder breaks into the reader's awareness on the wings of the slow, rhythmic gait of the language, with all the mystique of mythology. The story of Shiva circling the universe with the dead body of Sati (Parvati) flung over his shoulder flashes into the mind, and lingers as a pictogram over and above the explicit reference to it in the line. The reference fades, and the mythic elation stays amidst the phonology of English buzzing in the ears. The sway and spell of Difference is total.

The pivotal role of Difference is felt even more tellingly when the language of the original is totally unfamiliar to the reader. Take, for instance, Edith Grosman's English translation of Spanish texts:

> After lunch Rome would succumb to its August stupor. The afternoon sun remained immobile in the middle of the sky, and in the two o'clock silence, one heard nothing but water, which is the natural voice of Rome. But at about seven, the windows were thrown open to summon the cool air that began to circulate, and a jubilant crowd took to the streets with no other purpose than to live, in the midst of backfiring motorcycles, the shouts of lemon vendors, and love songs among the flowers on the terraces.[20]

The non-English character of the locale comes across in this paragraph even without the specific mention of Rome. The languor of afternoon hours, the suggestion of siestas, the persistent, lazy play of isolated sounds amidst the arrest of all motion which mark the first two lines of that passage, are giveaways of the non-Englishness. And the Dionysian, un-English stratum of the setting shows up vividly and unmistakably when the standstill breaks and windows are opened to let in the cool air, crowds laying siege to the streets, swept by nothing more and nothing less than the fever of living: backfiring motorcycles, vendors' cries and love songs being sung on the terraces. A Roman might call it exotic. But forgetting subtleties of definition connected with authenticity and so on, the points to note here are: *(a)* the otherness of the narrated material, *(b)* the otherness that comes to the translating language a result of the otherness it is dealing with, and *(c)* the blending of the two other-nesses into a mode of writing that is distinct even if not definable in exact terms.

Roadblocks to Difference

The operation of Difference can get blocked in translation due to factors present in the original, as in the case of Neelabh's Hindi translation of Arundhati Roy's *The God of Small Things*.[21] The underlying reason for this blockade, it seems to me, lies in the genre of the original—the genre known as Indian Writing in English. It is a genre constituted by inputs that are already translated. The Indian English writer, no matter how un-self-conscious in his usage of English, has to make a conscious effort to voice in English, realities that make no echoes in that language. The bare saying of the term 'shishu hatya'— child killing—for instance, invokes a vignette of culture that defines, describes and decodes its essence. The English term, 'infanticide', is neutral and unresonant, in comparison. If the Indian English writer is writing about an incident of infanticide somewhere in his country, he has to bring into it the saga of 'shishu hatya' and its sanctioned cruelty that immunizes and empowers the 'hatyara' or killer. He has to translate the phlegmatic term 'infanticide' into the charged word 'shishu hatya'. The factor of Difference, thus, gets inscribed into the writing.

How is the translator to communicate the factor of Difference already present in the original text, through his language, say, Hindi, which is not at odds with the theme and runs with its grain? He has to capture the particular overtone of shock and outrage present in the English. The danger is that he may identify with the tone so strongly that he can end up writing a novel of protest, his own novel, in effect. He can get carried away, forgetting his real task, his *vaajib* task, as translator: that of evoking the standing Difference between the spirit of the two languages he is dealing with; of imparting tether, coherence and individuality to the translated text by subtextually making it a discourse on Difference.

The danger of over-identifying with the original can arise when the translating language is nearer to the translated language than Hindi is to English. This, as has been discussed in the essay concerned, has happened with Sundara Ramaswamy's Tamil translation of Takazhi Siva Sankara Pillai's Malayalam novel *Chemmeen*. This derangement of the wavelength between theme and narrator, as established and made operative in *The God of Small Things* is what has taken place to a conspicuous degree in *Maamoolee Cheezon Ka Devta*.[22] Take, for example, the following—the context is of the chance meeting of eyes that takes place between Velutha, the untouchable, and Ammu, the touchable—'Centuries telescoped into one evanescent moment. History was wrong-footed, caught off guard. Sloughed off like an old snakeskin. Its marks, its scars, its wounds from old wars and the walking backwards days all fell away.'[23] The language derives its articulating spur and energy from borrowed memory, dressed and presented as its own. And perhaps, because of this wrought, fabricated quality, there runs, side by side with it, a strong sense of transience, of momentary-ness, a seldom-to-be-repeated feel to the event described. The word 'evanescent' in the opening sentence of the passage contains and conveys the full, massed weight of the entrenched power of history, and the doom writ for the event. 'Wrong-footed', 'caught off guard', 'sloughed off like an old snakeskin,' '...fell away', are all phrases denoting both a lapse of history, and a retribution waiting in the wings, biding its time. All these features which highlight the factor of Difference between the language and the usage of the language, thereby heightening the pathos in the situation, have got erased in the Hindi. Here are the equivalent lines:

Ek kshanbhangur pal mey sadiyaan simat aayeen. Itihaas auchak mey nishkavach pakdaa gayaa. Saamp kee puraanee kaynchul kee tarhaan utaar pheynkaa gayaa. Uskey chinh, uskee choton kay nishaan, puraanee ladayyon aur peechchey ko chalney valley dinn kay zakhm—sab jhjhad gaye.[24]

Its careful, crafted quality and the translator's painstaking, dedicated reading of the English text are not to be denied. Nor do we want to make more than necessary reference to the feel of excess and over-statement made by the word 'nishkavach' for 'caught off guard'. The English phrase comes after the term 'wrong-footed', a very mimetic term. It has been substituted by the term 'auchak meyn', meaning at the wrong moment. It is not without its own lilt and evocative power, though one does miss the etched, precise feel of 'wrong-footed'. Could, couldn't, the vocabulary of music have come in handy? 'Itihaas beytaal pakdaa gayaa' or 'betaal huaa', say? But it could seem hairsplitting or pedantic, and you settle happily enough with 'auchak mein'. Where Hindi seems helpless, seems caught in its own tradition and history of relating to that scene of caste infringement, is in its incapacity to creatively distance itself from the scene—sway with its rapture, and at the same time, read the dangerous rootlessness of the raptures. Look at these concluding lines of that passage in the English, after '…all fell away'—'In its absence it left an aura, a palpable shimmering that was as plain to see as the water in a river or the sun in the sky. As plain to feel as the heat on a hot day, or the tug of a fish on a taut line. So obvious that no one noticed.'[25] The rumble of retribution is felt in the last phrase, 'that no one noticed', where a hush enters the narrative tone, the voice seems coming from behind a veil, as it speaks the four innocuous words. They seem code words, which are saying that no human eyes noticed, but the eyes of history did, that history would right its footwork gone faulty, the 'sloughed off snakeskin' would grow again, that the 'aura' and 'palpable shimmer' history left in its split-second absence is indeed split second, 'evanescent'.

This sibylline undertone or aside is what is lacking in the Hindi rendering of those lines. It is a judgmental role that comes a little more naturally to English, in its relating to *our* realities. To echo it, Hindi or any other *bhasha* tradition has to somehow augment its own voice of dissent, make its own heightened contact with the theme concerned, and reflect Difference. Neelabh, whose sense of sound—*dhvani bodh*—is so often seen to advantage in his rendering, as the essay on his translation makes clear, shows himself passive and uncreatively reproductive in his rendering of the lines concerned. The first line of the rendering hits the right note in its end phrase 'sab jhad gayey'— 'all fell off'. But the word for word reproduction of the preceding portion—'*uskey chinh, uskee choton kay nishaan, puranee ladaiyon aur peechchey ko chalney vaaley dinon kay zakhm…*'—does not rise above tautology. 'peechchey ko chalney valley dinon key zakhm', especially, does not make the sharp, electric connection with the custom of the untouchable having to walk back and clear the road if he happened to be closer to a touchable on the road than the prescribed distance, that the English equivalent 'walking backward days' does. There is a caustic note, a tone of mockery in that sharp compression of customary behaviour, a cocking-a-snook attitude at tradition, an instinct for irreverence, that the Hindi has not mustered, cannot muster, one could say. Yet, all these shortfalls lose edge, and the allusions to history lying buried in the words and phrases—'choton kay nishaan', 'peechchey ko chalney vaaley dinon ke zakhm'—reveal their fangs from the sharp, severing act evoked by the words 'sab jhad gaye'. Such redemptive features are not present in the succeeding lines for the English lines quoted above:

apnee khaaalee kee huyee jagah mein voh ek kaifiat chchod gayaa, ek chchoo jaa sakney vaaley jhilmilaahat, jo itnee saaf nazar aatee ththee jaisey nadee mey paanee yaa aakaash mey sooraj. Itnee saaf mahsoos hotee ththee jaisey kisee garm din kaa taap yaa tanee huyee doree par machchlee kaa jhatkaa. Itnee spasht ki uspar kisee kaa dhyaan naheen gayaa.[26]

The words are replicate words, seeking their authentication from no source beyond or higher than the words of the parent language. Surely, a translation needs more than verbal authentication for status, for individuality? Especially when the purpose of a translation is taken to be that of highlighting lingua-cultural differences? And even more so, when the translation is an Indian English writing original, which itself is a product of Difference? What makes the reader particularly unhappy about this and other such instances of literalization in the translation is that transliteration, a close cousin of literal-ness, has been used to advantage, used with a keen ear for the phonology of languages, by the very same translator. Here are the English and the Hindi of some such lines. The context is of the little girl Rahel and the indulgent adult Velutha sporting with each other. 'Rahel lunged at his armpits and tickled him mercilessly. *Ickilee ickilee ickilee… "Aiyo kashtam,"* Velutha said.'[27] The Hindi retains the Malayalam word, creating a music of contrapuntal notes. The translator hears the sounds of the Malayalam words and deliberately leaves them in the body of the Hindi, trusting to the high-breathed feel made by the tug and pull of the action-filled scene, to suck in the southern vocables into its northern body, as 'Rahel uskee bagalon kee taraf jhaptee aur berahmee sey usey gudgudaaney lagee… *"Ayyo kashtam,"* veluthaa ney kahaa.' How did the need for a similar, thoughtfully experimental approach to the lines quoted earlier, escape the translator? Especially when they are lines that speak from a complementary, simultaneous vision, of the golden, visible passing moment, and the steely, invisible reality of History and the Past, in an idiom born of an attitude of a brash-seeming, calculated irreverence, not really native to Hindi, and for that very reason requiring special translational skill?

The answer, it seems to me, cannot be really put down to any lack of awareness by Neelabh. He follows Roy's text word for word, single mindedly like a stalker stalking his quarry, presenting (one is tempted to say 'cloning') Hindi duplicates for every trope and turn of the English: 'That man standing in the shade of the rubber trees with coins of sunshine dancing on his body'[28] is rendered as '*Us aadmee ney, jo rabarke vrikshon kee chchaayaa meh khadaa ththaa aur jiskey badan par dhoop kee asharfiyaan naach raheen ththee…,*'[29] and 'She hoped that under his careful cloak of cheerfulness he housed a living, breathing anger against the smug, ordered world that she so raged against'[30] is translated as '*unhoney ummeed kee ki usney khushmizagee ke apney saavdhaan labadey kai neechey us santusht, vyavasththith duniya ke khilaaf ek zinda, dhdhadakta ghussaa sanjo rakha hoga, jiskey khilaaf khud unkey andar itnaa adamya rosh ththaa.*'[31]

'Dhoop kee asharfiyaan' one admits, is a happy variation of 'coins of sunshine'. 'Asharfiyaan' supplies the effulgence of sunshine that 'dhoop' does not, and the full English phrase does. 'Dhoop kay sikkay', a possible rendering of the English, one in keeping with the word for word style of rendering adopted, does not have the liquid sound that 'asharfiyaan' has, and as does the English phrase 'coins of sunshine'. Neelabh's sense of sound has instinctively come into play here. But alongside, we also see a shortcoming in the Hindi that says more, something different from the happy outcome noted above. I am referring here to the third person pronoun of respect, 'unhoney', for the simple, easygoing 'she' in the English. The reason for the usage in English is not just the absence in the language, of equivalent terms of respect, but an inoffensive informality of manner that English induces, and that Hindi and most other Indian languages do not. Neelabh, for all his meticulous duplication of the English has not been able to say 'usney' for 'she', and has not been able to forget the mother image of Ammu, the woman through whose eye the narrator is seeing his/her narrative.

That apart, the laborious, long-winded seeming, yet devoted Hindi-ization of terms like 'housed', 'smug, ordered world'—'sanjo rakhnaa', 'santusht, vyavaththith duniya'—does compel attention. Each painstaking construction sets the English original ringing in the ear, the Hindi going up again with the ebb of the English, till the ears buzz in a bilingual hubbub. It is a reading experience all of its own.

But is such acrobatic reading any stamp of abiding worth upon a translation? The stamp that comes to it when it is done with full understanding of the role of translation as a means of bridging cultures through a dialogic highlighting of the differences between them? This kind of an amiable playing up of Difference is difficult, if not impossible, with a genre of writing—Indian English Writing—that, as pointed out earlier, is itself a product of Difference, a difference between language and story not operative in any Indian language. And added to this is Roy's irrepressible play with her medium impossible to duplicate in another medium. Given Neelabh's own gifts with his medium, it is possible that he saw this basic difficulty and decided to go in for literal translation. Whatever the reason, the lesson of *Maamoolee Cheezon Ka Devta* is that the choice of the material to be translated is important, that what is to be translated is no less important than how it is to be translated. The essay on Neelabh's translation elaborates this need for the right choice of text, and the bearing this has on highlighting Difference, the main purpose of a translation.

▌ Notes

1. Seth, Rajee. 1995. *Nishkavach*. New Delhi: Bhartiya Jnanpeeth.
2. Narasimhan, Raji. 1998. 'Translator's Note', in *Unarmed*. Chennai: Macmillan India Limited, p. vii. Trans. of Seth, op cit.
3. Nouss, Alexis. 2005. 'Translation and Metissage', in *In Translation: Reflections, Refractions, Transformations*. Delhi: Pencraft Internatonal, pp. 226–27.
4. Bhattacharya, Rimli. 1991. Introduction, *Katha Prize Stories*. New Delhi: Katha, p. 2.
5. Ibid., p. 2.
6. Adarkar, Priya. 1979. *Silence! The Court is in Session*. New Delhi: Oxford University Press. Trans. of Vijay Tendulkar. 1968. *Shantata! Court Chaloo Ahe*. Mumbai: Mauj Prakashan.
7. Verma, Sarojini. 1994. *Khaamosh! Adalat Jaari Hai*. New Delhi: Vidya Prakashan Mandir, p. 39. Trans. of. Tendulkar, op cit.
8. Adarkar, p. 23.
9. Verma, Sarojini, p. 103.
10. Ibid. p. 39.
11. Gupta, Prasenjit. 2002. Introduction, *Indian Errant: Stories by Nirmal Verma*. Indialog Publications.
12. Ramanujan, A. K. 1978. *Samskara. Three Crown Series*. New Delhi: Oxford University Press. p. 135. Trans. of. U. R. Anantha Murthy. 1965. *Samskara*.
13. Rao, Raja. 1938. Foreword, *Kanthapura*.
14. Verma, Nirmal. 2006. 'London ki ek raat', *Jalti Jhaadi*. New Delhi: Bhartiya Jnanpeeth.
15. Gupta, Prasenjit. 2002. *Indian Errant: Stories by Nirmal Verma*. New Delhi: Indialog Publications, p. 22. Trans. of. Nirmal Verma, op cit.
16. Bhattacharya, Nilanjan. 2006. *A Bowl of Steaming Rice or A Mere Ghost Story*. Stories by Sunil Gangopadhyaya. Kolkata: Yapanchitra Books.
17. Ibid., pp. 140–41.
18. Ibid., p. 151.
19. Ibid., p. 171.
20. Grossman, Edith.1994. 'The Saint', from *Strange Pilgrims: Stories by Gabriel Garcia Marquez*. London: Penguin Books.
21. Roy, Arundhati. 1997. *The God of Small Things*. New Delhi: IndiaInk.
22. Neelabh. 2004. *Maamoolee Cheezon Ka Devta*. New Delhi: Rajkamal Prakashan. Trans. of. Roy, op cit.
23. Roy, p. 176.
24. Neelabh, p. 194.

25. Roy, p. 176.
26. Neelabh, p. 195.
27. Roy, p. 177.
28. Ibid., p. 176.
29. Neelabh, p. 194.
30. Roy, p. 176.
31. Neelabh, p. 194.

Chapter 1

Chemmeen: Its Passage through Three Languages[1]

The chance to consider a book in three different languages does not often present itself to a reader. When it does, it is exciting. The play and pressure of each language upon the theme and body of the original, and the product that results from this interaction, underscores a lot about the nature and art of translation. Before coming to that larger formulation, it may not be out of place to consider the special quality of *Chemmeen*,[2] the book which has presented one with this opportunity of seeing it through the sound and sense of three languages. The special quality of *Chemmeen* is its femininity, the kind of femininity that results from a man's appreciation of it. The ability to don the feminine personality seems the hallmark of many notable men of letters. Writers like Sarat Chandra Chattopadhyay, Rabindranath Tagore, Phaneeshwarnath Renu and Pudumaipittan, gain their special poignancy from their ability to pattern their voice to feminine scales and inflections.

Chemmeen is the story of Karuttamma, the daughter of the sea. The sea is maternal, and matriarchal in the perceptions of the fishermen living on its shore. Life-giving, nurturing, it is also rousable to unpredictable fury like a flesh and blood maternal, matriarchal force. Living by the side of this primal force, a particular system of mores and a particular feminine culture is bred among the fisher folk. It stresses almost fanatically the primal male urge to make the female pray for his welfare and longevity, make her his link with God. Perhaps this is a natural distribution of roles between partners, one of whom is impelled to venture out to test his strength against the unknown, while the other, not so impelled, is required to be understanding and empathetic. Empathy, at the best of times, is a bit of a shadow play between the empathizer and the empathized, between the actor and the acted upon. But it becomes a classic existential situation when the

person empathized with is mostly physically absent, away on dangerous missions, and death is a numbing presence in the homestead. It
then inevitably falls to the lot of the partner physically present at the
homestead, to placate death, beg for its mercy, and keep its attention
turned from the one away.

This primary, pre-historic division of roles has been imbued
with gender properties by the fisher folk depicted in *Chemmeen*.
They impregnate it with mythic values for an inner ballasting to
their community life. The fisher-wife is called upon to pray for her
fisher-husband's safe return from the sea. This is the core slogan and
underlying platform of the story. It is not only a slogan spelt out in
words, but given a pictorial reinforcement that becomes a major motif
in the work. The fisher-wife, we learn, does 'tapasya' on the seashore
when it rages, and her husband is out at sea. She stands on one leg in
a yogic posture and does not move till he is back. The powers of her
purity and chastity act as a lighthouse for the man battling the waves,
and steer him to shore. Around and from the ideology condensed
in this figuration, the feminine character and overall femininity of
Chemmeen are built.

The translator has to grasp this feminine orientation. His prose has
to rock with the pain and pleasure, the ethics and passions, battling
each other in Karuttamma's sexual awakening. He has to be alive to
the collision and rebound—like the sea colliding and rebounding
off the shore—that these feelings make in her mother, Chakki. The
femininity of *Chemmeen* is not constituted so much from the love affair
of Karuttamma and the Muslim boy, Pareekutty, as from the struggle
of mother and daughter to domesticate the rearing sexuality of the
latter. Female sexuality is an object of dread in the Indian context (the
mythicizing of it notwithstanding) and in conditions of poverty like
those in which Karuttamma and Chakki live, is even more so, lacking
as it does then, the bare privacies demanded by the processes of growing and becoming. Chakki and Karuttamma, as mother and daughter,
represent in their personalities the drives and counter-drives that come
into play with the sexual awakening of the girl, and it is on this tussle
of the women—a tussle that is joint as well as mutually opposed—that
another aspect of the femininity of *Chemmeen* is built.

A strong consciousness of the body is a major attribute of this
feminine atmosphere. Both Chakki and Karuttamma are beside

themselves with fear and anxiety about the physical manifestations of female sexuality and its animal potencies. Both are seized by a haunting sense of responsibility to harness these potencies to sanctioned and legitimate ends before it is too late. The novel reveals its innermost self—opens its maws, so to say—in these flashes of intense self-seeings by Karuttamma and Chakki, when they curse the external manifestations of female sexuality. The deep transference to the female psyche that Thakazhi makes in this novel shows itself at its clearest in these self-reproachfully roused states of the two characters. The translating language has to rock with the inwardness of these self-seeings. The language must bend to the emotional inflections of the two major female characters, as the Malayalam does.

Of the three translations we have chosen to consider—Tamil,[3] Hindi[4] and English[5]—the Tamil definitely has stretched the language tunefully, making it register the bated breaths and gasped thoughts of Karuttamma and Chakki. Now, Sundara Ramaswamy, the translator, himself is among the finest writers of Tamil today, with a highly developed sensitivity to the nerves of speech. Secondly, Tamil is much closer to Malayalam than Hindi and English, so a certain level of fidelity to the original is assured. The dialect of Tamil that the characters speak in the rendering is more akin to the language of the rustic characters of Thakazhi than Hindi can possibly be.

But such translatability is no guarantee of a translation as we define it. In fact, it can be a pitfall, as Sundara Ramaswamy's work proves. A translation has to be bitonal and bicultural in its effect. It ought not to read like the original, or read original, but should suggest the original as a vastness lying beyond—like the horizon suggesting lands beyond.

This distinction has been so completely erased in the lyrical prose of Sundara Ramaswamy that the special pleasure of reading a translation is taken away. We never experience the pleasure of being carried on two streams of narration simultaneously; we never experience the special pleasure of disjunction. One small passage taken at random, with particular reference to one phrase in it, would be enough to explain this. Karuttamma and Pareekutty meet, as forbidden lovers do, amidst danger. Pareekutty calls her softly by name and asks her to say what he means to her. She holds and raises his face in both her hands, eyes in a semi swoon, drinking in his adored face, and says,

'My king beloved' (*En Asai Raja*). Once again, the narrative goes on, they become two of body one of soul. Swaying on the pinnacle of ecstasy she babbles into his ear all that comes to tongue.

Here is the Tamil of Sundara Ramaswamy:

> *Naan unakku yaaru? Sollu?*
> *Avanadu mugathai tanadu iru karangalilum yendi yeduttukondu arai-*
> *kuraiaai tirandirunda vizhigalal avanadu azhagu mugathai assayodu*
> *nokkiyapadi badil sonnal, : Yaaru? En Asai Raja". Meendum avargal*
> *eerudal oruyirranar.Unarchiyin unnatha sigaraathil aval vaaykuvanda*
> *padiyellan avanudaya seviyil yedai yedayo aratrikondirundirundal.*

The Malayalam original of Thakazhi is not very different from the Tamil translation. The image is the same, of Karuttamma with half closed eyes, unsteady of leg, babbling into his ear, and holding his face in her hands. That gesture of holding Pareekutty's face in the hands is a breakthrough gesture, a shaky enactment of the tremendous unshackling she has achieved, as one can see in the paragraph quoted above. It is the first act of freedom she is performing. The extended arms symbolize a coming away from herself, a decisive leaving of herself, while the gently appropriative act of holding her lover's face between the hands expresses the acceptance by her without fear, of the vastness outside herself. The mime element in that scene is very important, and none of the other translators except Sundara Ramaswamy has transferred and incorporated the full emotional intensity of the mime content so wholly in their renderings. The only common point in all the renderings is the mention of the half-closed eyes, 'ardhanimee-litha…' as it occurs in the Malayalam.

But in Sundara Ramaswamy's prose, the scene, and the particular Tamil equivalent he has used for 'My king beloved' (*En Asai Raja*) take on a near autonomous quality. The phrase is his, not there in the Malayalam. The Malayalam says, 'My pitcher of gold'. The recreation is only the acme of his personal, full and seamless involvement in the stream of emotion present, not only in that scene, but throughout. On closer reading, this feeling of seamless involvement that the rendering gives subsides, and a sense of 'they', of a distinct third person presence *is* felt. 'They' become one of soul, he says. 'They' could not disengage from 'their' embrace. But this suggestion of third person presence has not, by any means, amounted to the purposeful retention and cultivation of otherness, of Difference, making for the bisected quality which we have postulated as the true form and physique of translation. The otherness that seems to surface in Sundara Ramaswamy's rendering is probably more a pronouncement of critical hairsplitting, become permissible in comparative studies, than anything real! In Tamil syntax and construction, subject and action merge. The sentence, 'They become one of soul,' gets compressed to a single phrase, 'oruyiraanar'. It is only by separating the components of this phrase, an exercise which is purely academic, as we said, that the sense of 'they' is felt. It makes it, of course, a linguistic characteristic rather than a conscious strategy of translation.

The story of the women and the femininity of the original have obviously caught the imagination of Sundara Ramaswamy. He himself has these biases in his own writing. Probably he is among the very few writers today who can recapture in the turns and timbre of his prose the unspoken feelings of a woman, feelings that become onomatopoeic through overt inflections and a certain monosyllabic flutteriness. The corroboration that *Chemmeen* provides to this natural bent of mind has sufficed for him, and he has not bothered about cultivating and conveying a matching intimacy with the other characters or aspects of the book. He has left this to the care of his own eloquence and suppleness of language. In addition to the advantage that his like-mindedness with Thakazhi gives him, he has the advantage too, as we said, of dialect Tamil, creating its illusion of speech similarity with the rustic Malayalam of the characters in the original. It is in addition to these enormous natural advantages that his linguistic artistry presents itself. And it seems just too much of a pile up, making for an imbalance in the translation. There is an explicit-ness, a lack of suggestion, come about in much of the narrative sections, born of the very linguistic virtuosity, that we otherwise admire. No, linguistic virtuosity is no guarantee of a translation that is right in its tether with the original.

The Hindi rendering of *Chemmeen* by Bharati Vidyarthi takes several paces deeper afield, the problem of the dark areas in a translation as in

Sundara Ramaswamy's, becoming a fault in the rendering from beginning to end. Neither linguistically nor from the point of insight and deeper understanding has Vidyarthi's translation risen above the pedestrian level. Some redeeming features, of course, can be mentioned, such as the leave-taking scene between Karuttamma and Pareekutty after Karuttamma's marriage with Pazhani has been fixed. The conversation that takes place between them is spare, muffled, almost strangulated by emotional intensity. Stretches of silence intersperse the conversation. There are swift and tremulous oscillations of mood ranging from the urge to pour the heart out, and the simultaneous perception of the futility of it. Karuttamma goes away without saying any or anything of the many things she had planned to say to clear the air between them. The text says, 'This was the only way of taking leave she knew. Paree kept gazing at her. This was the only way of proffering leave he knew too.' [Author's translation.] The Hindi rendering is, '*Yehi uska vidaa leney kaa tareekaa aththa. Paree usko dekhtaa rahaa. Vida deney kaa uskaa bhee yehee dhang thaa.*'[6] Mimesis is a strong characteristic of Thakazhi's writing generally. In that scene, in the Malayalam, which the Hindi recaptures best among the translations being considered here, occurs one particularly mimetic, visual phrase—'kizhakottu nadannu'—or, Karuttamma walking away eastwards. The idea of return contained in the act of taking leave is tellingly recaptured in the term 'eastward', 'kizhakottu'. None of the translations, not even the Hindi makes use of this term. The Tamil, in translation, reads, 'Yes, she had taken leave of him. Unblinking he kept his gaze on her. Yes, he had given her leave.' [Author's translation.] Mime is not as strong a presence here: the translator's voice does quite a bit of speaking. The English simply—and stolidly—says, 'And so they parted.' Whenever and wherever the element of mime gets reflected strongly in the translations, they gain power, it can be said. In the Hindi, in spite of the absence of the term 'kizhakottu' the realm of wordlessness, of feelings and actions beyond the ken of word or voice into which Karuttamma and Paareekutty are shown thrown in the original is best reflected. Like figures seen through binoculars, we see the departing figure of Karuttamma, and the fixed yet animated face of Pareekutty gazing at her. They bring home through the hush permeating and alternating with the sentences, the universality of the situation underlying its particularity in which the two people are caught.

A few more such instances of completion can be cited. But these would not alter the overall conclusion one has to make about the Hindi translation, that it is a passive rendering, never getting anywhere near the springs of warmth in the original.

Apart from such declined readability, the real loss suffered by such boneless renderings is their incapacity to do anything about thinnings or cracks in the original. In *Chemmeen*, there is such a crack, arising from Thakazhi's failure to make a forthright statement on the moral issue involved in the business deal struck between Karuttamma's father, Chemban, and Pareekutty. The point Thakazhi is driving at implicitly, is that sexual morality and general morality are not different from each other. Pareekutty lends money to Chemban for buying his own fishing boat and tackle. The implication is that Chemban takes full monetary advantage of Pareekutty's feelings for his daughter, the very feelings which he opposes as outrageous, not to be countenanced. Karuttamma is wrenchingly alive to this duplicity, and her distress is a direct outcome of the corruption she smells in her father's conduct. How can one form of immorality be taboo, and another not? Thakazhi never formulates the question as plainly as one expects. As against the examining into the nature of femininity that he does with genuine fervour, on this question he veers away into a kind of loftiness, from which position he detaches the human factor from all happenings, tragic or otherwise. Nature, as manifested by the open sea, and the cumulus of impressions it creates in the depths of the human mind, comes in for portrayal as the supreme arbiter, drowning out individual, human efforts and motives.

But this flight to grandeur lacks a firm dialectic base and becomes grandiloquent, gesticulatory. One of the reasons for this, as we said, is the failure of Thakazhi to make plainer the moral conflict and the odour of corruption from which the novel takes form. Again and again, at various points of climax, the underlying reasons for Karuttamma's burden of sadness comes up, begging for unambiguous statement. Her sadness is not caused by separation from Paree, but by her father's exploitation of him, and the sullying of love, of herself, that this exploitation implies. An unequivocal assertion of this from the author, supporting the subconscious perceptions of Karuttamma, is never forthcoming.

The question is how is the translator to get round this inner gap in the text? Simply disowning responsibility for it, turning a blind eye to it, is not the way. The fault only gets reproduced, further entrenched, in language after language. In this age of translations, a creative responsibility has come to be placed on the translator, compelling him to rise to the level of redress when necessary, the qualities of empathy and cooperation he is expected to have.

The Tamil rendering of the novel muffles the fault in the work by sheer lyricism of language, by the translator's own close identification with the characters and the theme of femininity. The Hindi translation does not address itself to the problem at all. It could not have, because the required alertness and in-depth understanding by the translator is not there from the beginning. From the point of view of clearing away obscurities and haziness, Narayana Menon's English translation of the novel scores over both the Hindi and the Tamil. Menon's way seems to be to get to the heart of things without ado, cutting down on the sentiment, and the chronically near-hysterical, agitated states of the characters. Instead, he favours soberly stating the truths embedded in the agitations.

But, as we shall see, the tidying up is not always done with discretion. The abstracting of essence does not always read assonant with the sense of the original. And sometimes the abstraction has not been done at all, when the translation could well have done with it. This results in its own dissonance. The beautiful sentence, 'En Aasai Raja' (My king beloved) in Sundara Ramaswamy's translation, has come in literally from the Malayalam as 'My pot of gold,' in Menon's rendering:

> 'Karuttamma ... what am I to you?' She took his face in both her hands and looking at him with half closed eyes, she said, 'Everything. My pot of gold.'[7]

'Pot of Gold' cannot be called pleasing by any process of reasoning. The term 'gold' has overtones of intimacy in most Indian language not really there in English. In Tamil the common saying 'Tangamaana penn' (A girl no less than gold, or 'as good as gold'), or

'*En Tangam*' (My golden child/beloved) have an intensity—a catch-in-the-voice intensity—that cannot be conveyed in English. Even with the linguistic backing available to him, Sundara Ramaswamy has not used the term 'tangam' in his rendering. Perhaps he could have used it in a gasping, all but inaudible way in keeping with the swoon in which Karuttamma is shown in that scene. But he does not, whatever his reason, and the rejection makes its retention in the other two translations even more glaring. The Hindi version says '*Mere ratnabhandaar*'. It preserves the association of wealth present in the original, but as in the English, the word 'ratnabhandaar' is not in keeping with the swooning state of Karuttamma. It is too long, too double-consonanted and Sanskritized. To the word 'gold', the word 'pot' adds its own absurdity. Its sharp, monosyllabic sound stamps down upon the whispery, tapering notes of the scene, shutting out its soft wash of echoes.

However, this is but one sentence. Let us consider Menon's translation in detail, starting with the quality of otherness, which we have adopted as a ground level of evaluation. Otherness comes in for what can only be called an uneven expression in Menon's translation. The narrative prose gets a quickening, an action-packed quality, which is arresting and pleasantly startling, like a road suddenly swept clear of cosy clutter. Karuttamma's source of unhappiness is not obfuscated, or mystified, and there is a clear attempt at considering the springs and network of her behaviour with the openness and naturalness of a psycho-sociological temper, a characteristically English educated Indian's temper.

Take this passage, quoted here alongside the Tamil:

When their love-making was over, Karuttamma became shy as well as a little afraid of herself. She spoke of all kinds of things, yet the unknown fear remained with her. It was a kind of madness. Something slightly unclean, without morals or decency. Was it becoming of a woman's duty? What would her husband be thinking of her?[8]

The corresponding Tamil lines are:

Paguttarivum chintanai unarvum seyalpadugira inda ulagukku karuttamma tirumbiyapodu vetkam avalai pidungi tindradu. Vetka

*unarchiyodu inam teriyada bayam manattinul uruveduttudu. Taan yedai-
yedayo pesivittadai aval unandaal. Manaattil avasiamillada ennangalai
kilaarivittukondu kuzhaindaal. Appodu aval ullaattil eduvum televaana
uruvam petririkka villai. Yedo pittuppidittadupol irundadu. Maanam,
avamaanam inri, vetkattai turandu…evvalavu abasamana vizhayam…
Oru penn seyyakudiya kaariyama idu? Avaludaya kanavan avalippatri
enna ennikkolvaan?*

There is a world of difference in those two translations. The Tamil's
pitch of voice is higher, much higher, than the English. Passionate
and resonant with the feelings of Karuttamma, it is more descriptive,
more associative. The opening sentence, the English of which would
read, 'To this world based on common sense and mind-awareness,
when Kauttamma returned…' has been severely curtailed in Menon's
rendering, to 'When their love-making was over.' In the Hindi, it
has been translated prosaically as 'jab kaaruttamma hosh ki duniyaa
me aayee….'

In the Tamil, Karuttamma's feelings have been set down with
minutiae, with a sense of discovery, by the writer, impelled by the
original. We understand these feelings, are carried along by the sheer
silvery quality of the prose. But a sense of having outlived and outgrown fears such as Karuttamma's persists in our mind, interfering
with our highest level of reading pleasure. For us, wisened and made
crass by our prolonged, conditioning exposure to literature which
makes erotic passion moral and frankly wanted as liberating by hero-
ines, Karuttamma's self-questioning, her 'being eaten up with shame'
('*vetkam avalai pidungi tindradu*') serve the purpose of recall. But we
would rather have the recall made for us by the author in language
that has a recollective base, making for a montage for Karuttamma's
feelings. Sundra Ramaswamy is too involved in the feelings himself,
his feelings and intensities vying with those of Karuttamma.

A subtle and delicate loosening of the narrator–narrative bond is
what the English performs. It supplies the maturity and a matter-of-
fact diction, based on contemporary realities, which our present day
sensibility demands for a comprehensive reading experience.

However, as we said, this clean-shaven prose does not always have
happy results. We see the best results of it, better even than the passage considered above, in the rendering of the scene showing Palani

caught in the storm at mid-sea. The scene is the grand climax of the story. Artistically it is a bit of kitsch. The sea's fury seems overdone, and Palani's battling it is coloured by the fabulous, the impossible. *Chemmeen*, after all, is not a fable. In the other renderings, the fable element or the impossible has not been sought to be tamed, or brought to more lifelike proportions, in the kind of modifying gestures that the pressures of translation cannot help. We saw this in the Hindi and Tamil renderings of the phrase 'a pot of gold'. In the English, the steering movements of Palani have been set down with a certain nautical aliveness, relieving the super brawn power of the scene with a measure of simple brain power:

> Palani let loose the line. If he held fast the line and the boat stopped the boat would be smashed. He let the fish pull the boat as it liked.
>
> When the head of the boat mounted the crest of the high waves, he balanced himself with the aid of his oar and jumped upward so as to lighten the weight of the boat. When he reached the top the boat again suddenly came down. The boat became almost vertical.[9]

The operative phrases in that passage are about the letting loose or holding fast of the line, and about the agile, squirrel-like, split-second motions of the boatman in balancing and jumping up the oar to lighten the weight of the boat. Above all, there is the short sentence about the boat becoming almost vertical. It is a sentence that stands away from the crowded actions of the preceding lines, and flashes a sudden, clarifying distant view of the scene, freezing it.

None of these actions comes with a like dour recounting or clean-edged outline in the other translations. In the Hindi translation, the sentence about the boat becoming almost vertical does not figure at all, though it is very much there in the original. It occurs in the Tamil, but with its own drawbacks, as we shall see. That apart, the terms 'daand' for oar, 'rassi' for line, in the Hindi, make the whole feel of that passage in the rendering a little off the mark, not seeming associated with fisher-folk culture so much as boat-people's culture, *mallah* culture. On the other hand, 'letting loose the line', 'holding it fast', the very word 'line', carry in their inner systems of sound, standing images of a sea faring tradition. They contain in their terseness and solidity, the sharp, salty words of command uttered on deck, with the whistle of wind and push of water muffling the voice, heightening urgency. This seasoned, occupational authority is not there—perhaps not available—in the Hindi rendering. Palani's precision act of leaving the floor of the boat for the top of the oar and waves, does not register in the reader's mind with the enlargement and enhancement that would have followed, if it had been seen by the translator as a clearheaded, integrated piece of action. It comes as a far off miniature act, as if seen through a peep hole. The Hindi rendering is:

Oonchee tarangon par jab naav chadti ththee tab naav ka bhaar kam karne ke liye voh daand pakade oopar uchchal jaataa ththaa, aur tarangon kee choti par aate voh naav meh gir jaataa ththaa.[10]

The phrase 'oopar uchchal jaataa ththaa' for that central, all-important act of jumping clear of the boat's tether underfoot in the composition of his dance, is not weighty enough, not solid enough, to invest that scene with meaning and rescue it from the kitsch in which it is embedded.

Let us look at the Tamil version of that passage now:

Pazhani meylum toondil kayitrai negizha vittaan. Appodu irunda nila-mayil avan toondil kaitrai izhuttu pidittukondan enraal tanneerin asura vegame toniyai tagarthu erindividum. Suraameen adan pokkuppol toniyai izhuttuch chendrudaan paaaarkathume!

Meley ezhumbi uyaruginra alaigal meedu erugindrapodu toniyin sumayai kuraippadarkaagap pazhani tonikkul kudittuantarangattil ezhumbuvaan, toni alaikootattin sirasil eriyadum meendum pottendru tonikkul vizhuvaan. Appodellaam talikuppura nindrukondirukkum toni...[11]

Compared to the Hindi, there is a greater familiarity with navigational reflexes, and the terms rise from deeper within the language. Not only here but throughout the Tamil rendering, terms like 'sukkan' or 'tuduppu' (oar), 'toni' (boat) occur, which are authentic and impart the firmness and realism of professional phraseology to the narrative.

But yet, as with the passage about Karuttamma's guilt feelings and fears, it is an anthropological interest that we derive from the scene and the overall phraseology. We perceive the boat as a fragile bark, which of course, it is. The fragility of man and his small dexterities against the might of the elements is of course a major part of *Chemmeen*. But a sense of remoteness, of times over, persists in our mind, making the battlings of Pazhani archaic, somewhere needless. Look at the phrase 'pothendru vizhuvaan', meaning 'would come down with a plop'. The point is not that the phrase does not occur in the English, though that too is something to be noted. (In the Hindi, it is '*voh naav meyn gir jaataa ththaa…*'—prosaic, to say the least.) The point is that the phrase suggests a precipitate-ness. It is an uncontrolled onomatopoeic utterance caused by a sudden, admiring over-incursion of the authorial voice, than from a disciplined and creative reading of the scene. Even the base word 'kudittu' for 'jumping' has a homebrewn acrobatic sound to it, as indeed, has that whole passage in its compulsive adherence to the acrobatic quality of the scene, in contrast to the tempering of it that takes place in the English.

The English banishes the sense of the archaic. It contemporizes the action without affecting the otherness of culture, geography and time. Pazhani seems an ordinary man performing extraordinary deeds as ordinary men sometimes do. This ordinary-ness is not there in the vernaculars. It is not there in the original too. But we miss it, and this need felt by us is met by the English. Menon's strategy, then, of going in for bare statements and a weeded prose, has paid off in this and in some other scenes.

On the other hand now, let us look at this passage:

> In those few seconds Karuttamma forgot the sorrows of her life. She felt she had not been vanquished. She had the strength few had. She was under the protection of a strong man, life was secure. Palani would see to it that the world outside wouldn't dare touch her or hurt her. And she also had something else which gave her spirit sustenance. A man loved her as no man had loved a woman. Between these two, her life was full. Now the man who loved her, stood in front of her.[12]

The understanding of herself and her situation that comes to Karuttamma 'in those few seconds' is of a primal, atavistic sort, the sort that brings to mind an unconscious, guiltless feminine freedom associated with matriarchal orders, untouched or unsubverted by the model and ideology of chastity. She is expanding in her perceptions of herself. She is breaking from the bounds of her given identities of name and parentage, towards a consciousness of unconditional feminine worth, emerged clear of social impositions of shame and morality. She is entering that state of amorality which is the immediate result of such a breaking free and is the precursor to a more self-authored, more openly and genuinely need-based morality. According to this morality, a woman can well take from each man whatever he is peculiarly fitted to give her. She can segregate her sensual and spiritual spheres of being, of her body and mind, as ingenuously as the male, and need not reproach herself for disloyalty or fickleness. Nor is she sullied by this impartial, selective utilization of her body for distinct and disparate purposes. Like nature, like the sprawling and immense earth with which she is so often compared, the female body has its hidden springs of purification, recuperation, self-generation and regeneration, which make themselves felt to the woman the moment she is ready to register their vibrations.

The important point about this inner awakening of Karuttamma is that it is taking place at a semi-conscious level. And it is this semi-consciousness that is impaired in Menon's rendering. The English strips the protective layers furnished by the semi-conscious condition of Karuttamma against the full brunt of the unearthings taking place within her, against the awful dare of her coming alive to the multiple nature of femininity, a multiplicity kept hidden from her by society. The English straightens and defoliates the semi-consciousness of Karuttamma's growing, into a self-conscious process. It profiles an order and a sense of ready, extant, social accommodation to the unorthodoxies blooming within her. It seems to be saying, there was Palani, her husband, to look after her on the everyday level. And there, on the subtler, poetic level of the spirit, was Pareekutty, providing completion, contentment. And at this moment, the man from whom she derived spiritual sustenance, stood before her, calling to her. She would, therefore, go to him.

There is a clarity, and a straight, uncluttered passage between thought and action, taking place in the English. There is an attenuation of the time and distance between the two that is characteristic of the original. Karuttamma, in the English rendering, is not thinking. She has already thought, fully and clearheadedly. There is no completed thought in the original, not at any point. There is only thinking, a slow, quaking course of thinking, below the fast-paced writing, that rends selves, emerges with fury and devastation.

Reading those sentences in Menon's English rendering, we are put in mind of western real life adjustments in which such self-accommodations are practised with a certain cold bloodedness. It is almost as though, to make it read plausible in English and to the western sensibilities—an exercise in which the Indian writer in English comes to be engaged inevitably in some form or the other—Menon has, with the best of intentions, yielded to a phraseology already seasoned in the expression of thinkings like Karuttamma's.

There are few works in Indian writing so completely free of the western correlative in their dialectic, as Thakazhi's. He works out the liberation of Karuttamma from the confines of superstition and fear to non-masochistic ideas of self-justice, purely by intuitive readings of her character, by divinings of her mind without the comparative method of having a western model as reference. His reference is always the sea, utilized as a symbol for the rise and fall of Karuttamma's mental processes, and as metaphor for the explosive fury with which they finally break forth, annihilating her, the annihilation spelling the end of her story and pervading it. The factor of historicity—the Then and Now axis—of course, has been incorporated in the work, as is seen in the conversations between the fishermen on such issues as the powers of the headmen, the age of marriage for girls, the castes allowed to be boat owners. But here too, the present is sought to be changed by the fishermen because of the fading relevance of the past in their own minds, because of its erosion by sheer time, not because of inducements from western examples.

It is precious, this intact preservation of a sense of cyclicality of values, unprompted by western norms. And it is this pre-western historicity which has to be maintained by the English rendering, and to which the translator has to be alive. It cannot be said that Menon is not alive to this pre-western historicity. There is a modesty of gesture and inflection in his voice, in the approaches and addresses to the people and their life that he makes through the agency of English. But beyond establishing such a seemliness of manner and deportment, he does not guide the language into the thought springs of the people.

He lets it float on the outside, depending on its conventional expressiveness to have the story told. This is chancy, to say the least. English is a dangerous language; its powers of mental arrest and manipulation almost unlimited, because of its imperial, colonizing past, and its worldwide currency. The pressures made by these blocks to free flow of thought and imagination are most felt in a sentence such as this, spoken by one of the fishermen during their discussion on the customs of fisher folk, 'Are there any instances of any fishermen of the wrong caste getting a boat and net?'[13] The phrase 'wrong caste' is an alien interpolation in this semi-drowsy conclave of insiders swapping data about themselves. It tears away the rings of privacy around the conclave, the unseen fencing that comes around all in-groups, and rudely scatters the atmosphere of unself-conscious privilege getting built in their midst. It is an educated, sociology-conditioned voice that we hear in the phrase, imposing itself on the uneducated but unscattered and well-contained voices of the fisher folk.

This overpowering and counter-creative usage of English has perforated the translation all through. One cannot help recoiling from it. Take, for instance, the English translation of the names of various kinds of fish: 'shrimp', 'herring', 'haddock', and so on. Even the Hindi terms, 'jhinga', for instance, do not sound right in the context of Thakazhi's work. The English positively foreignizes the context, bringing in a dry correctitude in place of the charged evocativeness of the original. The fish names in Malayalam pulsate with the dins and rhythms of the fisher folk of Nirukunnan seafront. Not just any seafront, but this particular one, saturate with Karuttamma's tears, Chakki's scurrying about, Pareekutty's gentle, helpless mooning on its sands, Palani's desperation and feats of boatmanship. Every novel worth its name has certain commonly used words in it, become special and sacred with the emotional saps fed into the work by the author. This sacredness of the local and particular is what gets impaired in the Englishing. The worst instances of these skids on the slopes of English are sentences concerning Karuttamma's femininity. Karuttamma, we are told, was given to 'gadding about' on the seashore, or 'gallivanting about'. She 'puts on a new kind of smile' to tell her husband something she is not sure how he would receive. When Pareekutty comes to her, dumb and suppliant, it is described as, 'The man she had ruined stood before her.' And there are a couple of instances of 'aunty' and 'mummy' as forms of address.

It is tawdry, this usage of phrases lodged on the tips of our tongues by deposits from pulp fiction produced in the West. To some extent, the well-reflected inner context mitigates the tawdriness. The inner context, for instance, in which the line about the new kind of smile occurs, to some extent, rubs off on the line in the heat of reading. The context, one admits, does get built in the spare prose which has been kept as a model by the translator. Writing spare prose is not easy. A lot of judgment goes into the thinning. Just two lines earlier occurs the colloquialism, 'she had no desire to play a game.' This seems all right; but not the putting on of a new kind of smile. English colloquialisms are tricky. The Indian context does not accept them all with equal ease. The sentence irks. It stays undigested in the back of the mind. In the same way, disturbs the sentence, 'the man she had ruined stood before her.'[14] The context is sustained and kept breathing in the paragraph, the cored, essentialized prose making itself felt all along, till the whole thing collapses, tripped by this sentence. Again we overlook it, peering ahead for what happens next. Yet, the irking persists. As for 'gadding about' and 'gallivanting about' these are sloppy, inexcusable.

The English language, as we said, breaks in upon one with a certain glut, an animal abundance, as if in keeping with the climate of mass production and mass consumption powering it. The translator has to exercise frugality in his application of the language to the Indian original. Frugal, Menon is, as we have seen. But a translator also has to play it by the ear, and ultimately a translation is a question of tone, of a timbre and pitch of voice subtly affecting and interacting with the volume of the original. It is, as we have been saying, an 'other' voice. But this otherness also induces you to reread the original. The translation then slides back into our attention on the gravity of the original, replaying its compositions of sound, alongside those of the original, gaining for itself a reconfirmation.

Such a reconfirmation is the highest acclaim a translation can win for itself. It should be so whatever the languages concerned, and more so in English, where the pitfalls are many, the chances of going wrong many, and therefore the challenge greater. Menon's translation does not really gain this highest acclaim for itself. The English has claimed him. He has claimed it too—and very well indeed—in certain passages, in the quick spill of the apt sentence in the momentum of rendering, in the fleeter, practical prose narrative that leaves no room for the kind of indulgent writing for which we have little sympathy today. But the totality escapes him. The language never gains the separate presence, the well-formed and separate body, bearing on its frame the cast and bias of the original, that make a translation memorable, perceptible.

Translation, let us repeat, is a major and extremely meaningful literary activity today. Like some other branches of the communications industry, it is a means to gratify the increasing feelings of fellowship and mutual curiosity among cultures. It need not, indeed should not, be so like the original as to supplant it. To read the original is not an achievement calling for praise. But it has to be itself. And this self is a second voice, a complementing voice, and a harmonious, assonant voice. Above all, it is distinct, even while being all this. None of the three translations, one is forced to state, reaches this ideal.

| Notes

1. This chapter has earlier been published as "'*Chemmeen*'" and its Passage through Three Languages', Indian Literature, Number 162.
2. Pillai, Thakazhi Sivasankara. 1956. *Chemmeen*. National Book Stall.
3. Ramaswamy, Sundara. 1962. *Paari Nilayam*. New Delhi: Sahitya Akadami. Trans. of. Pillai, op cit.
4. Vidyarthi, Bharati. 1959. *Machchuarey*. New Delhi: Sahitya Akadami. Trans. of. Pillai, op cit.
5. Menon, Narayana. 1962. *Anger of Sea-Goddess*. London: Victor Gollancz. Trans. of. Pillai, op cit.
6. Vidyarthi, p. 111.
7. Menon, p. 216.
8. Ibid. p. 121.
9. Ibid., p. 219.
10. Vidyarthi, p. 243.
11. Sundara, p. 341.
12. Menon, p. 215.
13. Ibid., p. 31.
14. Ibid., p. 215.

Chapter 2

Negotiating the Language Divide

This essay takes Usha Ganguly's Hindi stage adaptation of Mahashweta Devi's story 'Rudali'[1] as its ground text. For readers and commentators who do not know Bengali, Hindi could be taken as the closest cousin. The Hindi version[2] differs from the Bengali in some important respects, as we learn from Anjum Katyal's introduction to her English translation of the story in Bengali, and the play in Hindi.[3] But the Hindi has its own power. It makes for compelling, involved reading that overspreads the original without superseding it, and thereby remains a functionally credible source of reference. Katyal's English rendering is not of Usha Ganguly's published text. It is of an unpublished script meant for the actors of the play.[4] However, Katyal's rendering closely follows the published Hindi version for the most part. It can thus safely be taken as the counter-text for translational comparing and contrasting. The places where it departs from the Hindi have been dealt with separately.

The English rendering, by and large, has not bothered with the inner tether of the Hindi. By 'inner tether', one means, of course, the standing realities of Sanichari's story which the Hindi reflects, thereby getting a weight, a mooring, more than the narrative. Such a contextuality, which is more than the narrated story, and which the Hindi commands by birth, is not felt in the English, and understandably enough. This is an old, familiar complaint against, and acknowledged handicap of, most English renderings of Indian language texts. And the ultimate test of the English renderings is the way they deal with this handicap. Katyal's rendering, in common with most English renderings, stations itself on the outskirts of the words and the events, and leaves it to its empathizing energies to give interiority and the dimension of depth to the words and events. However, the pronounced exteriority which the events and the characters get as a result of the translator's bypassing their interiority, gets justified by the end of the play in its last scene.

This vindication lessens the initial impact of the wordiness that marks the translation. The present essay sets out to examine both the wordiness and the vindication. Let us begin with the wordiness. The stage directions in the first scene serve our purpose here. Stage directions, it might be pointed out, have a vital bearing on the quality and unfolding of a play, not only in its enactment but in the reading also. Here, then, are the directions in the two languages:

> *Sanichari ka ghar. Stage right mey sanichari baithee chakkee pees rahi hai. Stageleft sanichari kaa beemaar beta budhua chaarpai par leta ua khai. Budhua ka beta harua charpayee ke neechey peyt ke bal leta khilauney se khel raha hai. Sanieechari kee boodhi saas somri gudadi se liptee sokee hai.*[5]
>
> (Sanichari's home. At stage right, Sanichari sits grinding wheat in the chakki. The monotonous creak of the chakki is the only sound. At stage left, her ailing son, Budhua is lying on a charpoy. Harua, Budhua's child, is stretched out on his stomach under the charpoy, absorbed in playing with a toy. Sanichari's old mother in law Somri, is lying towards the back, wrapped in a tattered covering.)[6]

In the Hindi, the directions are clipped and businesslike in tone, confining themselves strictly to the listing and verbalizing of the items in the setting. This severe economy conveys the stark, flinty poverty of Sanichari's household. The English dispenses with this taut, unadorned statement of facts, of voicing the visual. It ventures into descriptive, adjectival modes that renders the characters into specific individuals: as against the magnified and deindividualized group identity that Mahashweta Devi gives them, as we learn from Katyal's Introduction. Take these sentences that follow the two words— 'Sanichari's home'—that make up the opening sentence: 'At stage right Sanichari sits grinding wheat in the chakki. The monotonous creak of the chakki is the only sound'. The Hindi does not specify *what* Sanichari is grinding. '*Sanichari baithi chakki pees rahi hai*'—that's all. The second sentence in the English, 'The monotonous creak.....' is simply not there in the Hindi. The specifications in the English lessen the sense of the ceaseless weight of poverty, its deadly monotony, and its fixed, grim mien, vivid and faceless like a skull, that press upon the reader in the Hindi. The descriptive words 'monotonous', 'only' and the very use of the word 'sound', wipe out the surrealist compound of voice and silence—a compound in which both are absent and also present—that rises from the Hindi, giving its own articulation of the poverty. Again, the sentence following this, about Harua playing with his toy, has an unnecessary descriptive term 'absorbed in' attached to his play. This narrational insertion erodes the defined and sharp-edged quality that we feel in the Hindi, where the words are left to speak for themselves without aid or prompting from the narrator.

The employment of language in the English translation, we can say thus, from this sample consideration of the stage directions, is more overt, not alive to the suggestive power of the dry, unemotional prose of the Hindi. This lack of ear for the inner voice or inner speech of the text shows up tellingly and distressingly in the casual, self-willed way in which the translator treats the action of the chakki in the text.

In the Hindi the chakki's whirr is a speech form in itself, yoked closely to the dramatic movement. When the whirr stops for some lines of dialogue, the dramatic movement also stops short, held in suspense like a horse rearing up. And when it resumes, the dramatic substance and contents of the play come back refocused, sharper of feel. After-sounds of the dialogue just spoken, containing facets of the grim standing reality of the Sanichari household go up in refrains as from gongs. They butt and tumble against the chakki's whirr, setting up an orchestra of animate speech and inanimate sound. When the chakki does not stop and does not, therefore, resume, when it stays as a relentless, ceaseless sound despite provocations from the persons around, that too is a speech form and comment, telling on the course and impact of the play.

Does the English translation succeed in imbuing the sound of the chakki's whirr with such strong signification? Does the whirr speak in the English as it does in the Hindi?

Let us then consider the places in the opening scene of Ganguly's adaptation where these repercussions of the sound of the chakki are felt strongly. The first break in the chakki's whirring occurs much farther down the scene than in the English. The context is that of making rotis for hungry Somri, Sanichari's mother-in-law. Sanichari won't, can't, till she's finished grinding the wheat for which she'll get aataa in payment. The rotis will be made from it. And in the meantime, why hasn't the footloose daughter-in-law of Sanichari, Parbatia, got back from the market yet?

At this point comes Somri's tart comment, '*Naah voh raand aayegi naa roti pakegee*'[7] (That whore will never return—I'll never get my rotis)[8]. And this is when Sanichari's chakki stops for the first time. It is not expressly stated. We infer it from the last part of the one-line stage direction here: '*Sanichari Somri ko ghoomkar kadee nigahon se dekhtee hai, phir chakkee peesne lagtee hai.*'[9] (Sanichari turns around to glare at the old woman, then resumes her grinding with renewed energy)[10].

The sentence is divided into two distinct, yet related sections. Both are action filled, and charged with a mimetic urgency. The first section consists of Sanichari turning round and staring with fixed, harsh eyes at Somri. A strong, visual quality pervades this section. Of course, the visuality would be real, factual, on the stage. But it is as written text that the play is being considered here, and the bare physical action of Sanichari turning round and staring fixedly at her tormentor photographs itself as a compelling image in the eye of the reader. The story seems to halt here with the halting of the chakki, as Sanichari, seated crosslegged or semi-crosslegged at the chakki, swivels from the waist up to stare at Somri. It picks up the very next moment, in the concluding second half of the sentence, '*phir chakkee peesney lagtee hai*' (emphasis added), (then starts grinding again) [Author's translation]. This momentary pause of Sanichari and the chakki forms a watershed in the movement of the story. It spans two time segments of the story, one representing the static, poverty stricken and problem ridden condition of Sanichari's household; the other, the stoic will and determination of Sanichari to keep things going at all costs. The whole story of Sanichari, the saga of feminine grit and endurance that it is, stands lit in a flash still of the two segments. The break and resumption of the chakki's whirr thus gets deconstructed into statements about the core and substance of the play. Does the English translation achieve this inner articulacy?

To consider this let us examine the bare, linguistic properties in the Hindi of the one line stage direction. As already said, it has two segments. And both are linear, strictly action based, with no commentative intrusions by the author, except for the phrase '"kadi nigaahon se" (dekhtee hai)'. But the adjectival fibre of the phrase gets acted upon by the kinetic energy of the word 'ghoomkar'— turning—that precedes it, and the sustained activity suggested by the words 'dekhtee hai' that succeed it. The steam and sense of action from two sides, thus, press in upon the adjectival phrase, embedding it into their flow, keeping it from becoming conspicuous.

The second segment of the sentence '*phir chakkee peesney lagtee hai*', is laconic in its bare recording of the action of the resumption of grinding. The reader registers this resumption, and goes on with the reading, as images of standing poverty thrown up by the resumed act flit in the reader's mind, buttressed by the blind whirr of the chakki. An important consequence follows the action centric character of that line. The factor of human agency gets diluted, seems to become subject to intangible forces beyond human will. There is not a single pronoun in that whole sentence, a sentence that encapsulates dimensions of time, and profiles the spirit of the story. Not Sanichari but her action and bodily movements come to the fore, making her, the human agent, secondary to the larger, non-human powers that are foregrounded.

A matching linguistic economy that liberates and energizes the symbolism of the sound/action components of that one line does not seem present in the English. 'Sanichari turns around to glare at the old woman, then resumes her grinding with renewed energy.'[11] The operative terms here are the word 'glare' and the phrase 'with renewed energy'. 'Glare' is the translator's equivalent for '*kadee nigaahon se dekhtee hai*'. That this one word does serve, even if not fully, to contain the five words of the Hindi equivalent is, of course, a point to note. But its limitations are as telling. It does not reflect the personality traits of Sanichari in the way the Hindi does. There is a reserve in her behaviour, however aggressive her demeanour. She is never abusive of language, for instance, in retaliation to Somri's free recourse to abuse. However provoked, she does not, cannot, throw conventions of propriety to the winds however provoked.

In the line that we are considering, this innate control is evoked forcefully by the refrains and overtones of the language, the prose that these evolve into. Secondly, the body language of Sanichari is a study in control, of feelings held in leash. Seated flat on the ground, hand clasping the wooden peg of the chakki, she makes just two movements: one, pirouetting from the waist upward to glare at Somri, the chakki stilling; and two, turning round again in reverse motion, the chakki in motion again. Bitter feelings assail her as she pirouettes to and back. But she swallows them. At the conclusion of the line, we see her as a taut, well-behaved woman, her emotions held in check, battling them like the sails of a boat battling the waves. A silence and a seething interiority envelop her. This quality of interiority in her personality is what seems lost in the English. 'Glare' has an open, outward quality to it, while 'nigah'—harsh or soft or whatever—is an eye gesture of a secretive nature, meant to be kept underground. This secretiveness carries over and gets reflected in Sanichari's physical action of resuming the grinding. The whole scene is a construct of eye language and body language uniting into a language of silence given voice by the whirring of the chakki. And it is this emblematic sound of the chakki that invokes the past, present and present continuous of Sanichari, and of the lives of the world's Sanicharis. 'Glare' does not accomplish this mammoth task of projection and consolidation. And because of the different tone of its eye idiom, it cannot, does not, connect with the crucial, concluding part of the sentence in the multiple ways of 'nigah'. Moreover, this concluding section is very different from the Hindi on the bare, lingual level. The Hindi, as pointed out earlier, is sternly action centred, bereft of any pronoun or adjective, with its single adjectival phrase 'kadee nigahen' getting kineticized by the action-based character of the sentence. The English allows pronouns and adjectives without reserve, indifferent to the detached, depersonalized quaiity that the Hindi achieves by its boycott of these forms.

The English rendering of the concluding part of the sentence is, '... then resumes her grinding with renewed energy'. 'Resumes her grinding' sounds far too stated compared to 'phir chakki peesne lagti hai'. That little word 'phir' packs into it a lifetime's weariness and drudgery, a whole way of life made vivid by the sharp image of Sanichari at the grindstone that thc remaining four words of the sentence evoke. Apart from its prosaic-ness, the English employs the adjectival phrase 'renewed energy' nowhere even suggested in the Hindi. It replaces all the heavy hopelessness and changelessness of Sanichari's life that the Hindi evokes, with the image of a Sanichari mercurial and aggressive, not above the retaliatory violence against elders that she seems incapable of in the Hindi at this point. She does not seem yoked to the chakki in the fatalistic way she seems in the Hindi. And thus, the sound of the chakki does not rise to the symbolic heights it does in the Hindi, and thus does not become language.

The link actions of Somri that provide continuity to the dialogue have been omitted. The specific event in this part of the scene is of Somri nagging Sanichari for food. '*Roti de. Ari o Sanichari, roti de na.*'[12] Each sentence she speaks hereafter in this scene is a variation of this opening sentence of hers and the play's. And before each sentence, she is shown making a particular movement or assuming a particular posture that gives a special dramatic impact to the sentence. The movement she makes after that opening sentence is of turning round half-asleep, lying wrapped in the quilt, towards Sanichari. '*(Somri dhire dhire soyee huee, Sanichari kee taraf mudhtee hai). 'Sasuree, tere kaan mey keeda ghus giya hai ka?*'[13] (Have worms got into your ear, wretch!) [Author's translation]. Now she is shown sitting up slowly, the chakki going on nonstop. *(Somri dhire-dhire uthkar baithtee hai).* And from this seated position she yells, '*Ari o daain! Kahe bhookha maaratee hai? Roti de naa*'[14] (Sorceress! Why're you bent on starving me to death? Give me roti quick!') [Author's translation]. All her subsequent sentences are hurled from this seated position. The calculated venom of each gains extra sting from the seated position of her famished, tense body. The English skips these punctuations of body postures and thereby loses a means of added voltage to the abusive one liners flung at Sanichari by Somri. The renderings of the one liners too, seem low key, lacking the carrying, reverberating tones of the Hindi. The English for the first line '*Roti de. Aree o sanichari, rote de na*' is 'I want food. Give me a roti! Arre o Sanichari, give me a roti, won't you?'[15] 'Won't you?' is pleading of tone, carrying none of the confident, curt bullying of 'de na', of which it is a translation. Even in ordinary, spoken English 'won't you?' is a coaxing rather than a coercive term. And why *a* roti? There is a big difference between *a* roti and just 'roti'. Wanting *a* roti implies just that—one roti—being asked for an immediate, specific purpose, whereas 'roti' not preceded by either a definite or indefinite article implies food, food as a collective term, in the sense in which Somri is using the word.

The translation for the second interjectory sentence by Somri, '*Sasuri, tere kaan me keeda ghus giya hai kaa?*' is 'Have you gone deaf or what?'[16] Where is the raucous abusiveness of the Hindi there? It is just a sharp, rude rebuke, uncivil at the most. And it elides the very earthy image of worms burrowing into the ear, evoked by '*kaan me keeda ghus giya hai kaa?*' The third interjection of Somri, examined earlier in a different context, is '*Na voh raand ayegi, na roti pakegee*'. The English is, 'That whore will never return, and I'll never get my rotis'. Again, it is off the mark. The negative note is total and downright in the Hindi. So categorical is it that the tasks augured by the speaker as doomed to remain undone, seem to pale in comparison with the augury contained in it. A pagan glee throbs in the Hindi's negative-ness, a perverse joy at the prospect of calamity, even at the cost of unappeased hunger. This cutting edge is a strongly felt absence in the English. If the complementary pair neither/nor had been used to supplement the term 'will', would it not have been brought closer to the English, 'Neither will the whore (slut? tart?) return nor will the rotis be made'?

Conjecture apart, the point to note is that the phrasing of the English translation once again creates a totally different image of Sanichari, by aligning her with the factor of time in a different fashion. She seems to be functioning only in the present—the present of the play—and seems to be reacting to the provocations of the circumstances in a unidimensional, passing way.

The fourth interjection of Somri, after her assumption of a sitting position, is the point from where the bad blood between her and Sanichari climaxes into a no-holds-barred exchange of words. '*Ari naaspeeti—deygi naheen kuchch?*'[17] The English is 'The bitch won't give me a thing to eat.'[18] Where is the crisp, crackling term 'naaspeeti'? Where is the direct confrontational stance? Somri is throwing the word 'naaspeeti' at Sanichari in a frontal assault without any attempt at concealment. The English rendering seems like a detour. 'The bitch' has a distancing, third person ring to it. 'You bitch', in some way fitted into the rendering, perhaps comes closer to the original's direct, confrontational manner. The rendering might then be, 'You bitch, won't give me a thing, to eat, eh, bitch?', or something along that line; at least the interrogative tone would have been retained! But the main drawback of the English is its flat, non-specific quality. 'Naaspeeti' is a specific colloquial term meaning 'one doomed to destruction'. 'Bitch' is merely abusive, a run-of-the-mill taboo word applicable to anything and anyone not liked, a word devoid of the colourful inventiveness of the Hindi. Somri's aggressiveness mounts steadily from this point. Her interpolations become particularly vicious and calculated, and Sanichari is being driven to breaking point:

> '*Haraamzaadi, dekhna teri lahaas ko geedad khaayenge,*'[19] (You bitch, just watch out. Jackals will eat your dead body);
> '*Haan mai haraamzaadi hoon, dain hoon. Meri lahaas ko geedad khayenge. Aur kuchch kahna hai?*'[20] (Yes, I'm a bitch, a daain, my corpse will be eaten by jackals—is there anything else you want to say?);
> '*Haan, bolna hai. Roti dey,*'[21] (Yes, there is. Give me some roti. (The chakki stops))
> '*Hai meri mayya!* (*Apna sir chakki kee lakdee par dhartee hai. Phir uthkar duguney veyg se chakki peestee hai)—Hai maiyya!*'[22] (She rests her head on the chakki a moment, then gets up and starts grinding wheat from the second bag lying bedside her....)

Again, the absence of the vigour imparted by a live, spoken idiom is felt in the English; a shortcoming, one must hasten to add in all fairness, for which the translator cannot be held accountable. But some ordinary precautions against over-wording could have been taken; some alertness could have been paid to the clipped, incisive tone of the Hindi, so that the basic unlikelihood of Somri, Sanichari and others of their clay speaking English gets blunted, and a *willing suspension of disbelief* is created.

Let us begin our list of 'wish it hadn't been so'—our wishlist—with the old enemy 'bitch'. It does not suffice for 'haraamzaadi', just as it does not for 'naaspeetee'. All the sharp, diabolic sophistication of the term goes missing in it. This apart, why use the long-winded term 'dead body' for the stark, unpadded word 'lahaas'? Would 'corpse' not have done? 'Corpse' is used in the next line. The repetition would have given the exchange the kick it stands lost of. Then, why the passive form 'my corpse will be eaten by jackals'? Would not the

straight, active form make for the tautness that evokes the original
more? And then, this sentence: 'is there anything else you wish to
say?' Again, long-winded, over-worded: why not just 'anything else
you want to say?' Or, just 'Anything else?' That sequence could then
have read: '....jackals will eat your corpse'. 'Yes...jackals will eat my
corpse. Anything else?'

And now a most inexplicable departure from the Hindi comes up,
figuring in the stage directions. Sanichari, spent after all the pounding
of 'roti de' 'roti de' from Somri, rests her head on the chakki, 'then gets
up and starts grinding wheat from the second bag lying beside her.'[23]
There is no mention of any second bag in the Hindi. The sentence
is, *'phir uthkar duguney veyg se chakkee peestee hai'*[24] (then gets up and
grinds the chakki with redoubled speed). Has 'duguney veyg' been
somehow read as 'doosra bag' in a strange and funny misreading?

The next two interpolations from Somri are clinching, for they
lead up to the final outburst from Sanichari, a Sanichari come clear
of all considerations of age or standing or propriety. It is also the last
time Somri figures in the play, except for passing appearances in the
next scene. She dies soon after. All the lines spoken by her in this
interlude, therefore, are of special significance, and should help in
bringing home the event of her death which is not directly or closely
dealt with. The interpolations, then:

'*Tu sabko maarkar jinda rahegi, daain. Sasur, jeth, aadmi sabko dakaare
baithee hai. Ab beta ko khaayegi.*'[25] (You'll kill off everyone else but
you'll stay alive, you daain. As it is you've finished off your father-
in-law, your brother-in-law, and your husband. Now you'll devour
your son.)[26]

'*Zyadaa bakar bakar mat kar.*'[27] (Watch your mouth!)[28]

'*Kaahe na kahoon—sanichar ko janam hua sanichari khaayega naheen
sabko?*'[29] (Why shouldn't I say it? After all you were born on an unlucky
day, Saturday. It's your destiny to devour everyone around you!)[30]

'*Tu kaunsa sukhkh paa gayee, Somri? Tu to somvaar ko paidaa hue
ththee. Are, mangli, budhnee, bisree sabkaa haal dekh liya hamney! Ham
se koi nahee poochchtaa ki khaayaa ki naheen. Din bhar khaau khau.
Jaise baap tumhaare saurey man anaaj dhar gayee hain. Ab ek avvaz bhee
niklee to seedhe tentua dabaa deynge*'[31] (And what great happiness did life
bring you? You're Monday-born, but you didn't get a better deal, did

you? Arrey, I've seen what lives they all live, those born on Tuesday, Wednesday, Thursday. As for you, you do nothing but bitch, bitch, bitch, all day long. Behaving as though your father left you a pile of wealth! Another word out of you and I'll throttle you.) [32]

Stage directions follow this outburst of Sanichari. And the first two lines of the Hindi are omitted in the English. '*Somri sanichaaree ko dekhtee hai. Phir dhire dhire ghoorkar so jaatee hai.*'[33] (Somri stares at Sanicharee. Then, staring, slowly drifts into sleep) [Author's translation].

Again, one cannot help noticing the natural language divide of Hindi and English that the translation does not succeed in making less noticeable. And because of this the standing realities of the Sanichari story do not break into the reader's consciousness with fresh force in the English rendering. The long-windedness is distressing, harmful. The qualifying phrase 'as it is' before the kinship words, the multi-syllabic quality of the words, and the different impact of the future tense between 'you'll kill off everyone else but you'll stay alive', and 'tu saabko maarkar…' soften the English to a speculative, supposition level, as against the grim, foretelling tone of the Hindi.

The difficulty in translating kinship terms into English is a standing difficulty. Nonetheless there is room for making the prose taut and pruning it of props, thereby making the English a noteworthy second to the Hindi. 'You'll kill all and stay alive, daain. Pa-in-law, husband, husband's brother, all you've gobbled and belched out. It's your son you'll belch out now.' That is a sample, and rewordable, without doubt. But the idea is to keep the English weeded of qualifying, auxiliary phrases like 'as it is' or 'kill off' that give it a backward tug, blunting it.

The next line in that sequence is Sanichari saying 'Watch your mouth!' for '*Zyaadaa baker bakar mat karo.*' It seems adequate and the throw of emotion in the two seems to match, overcoming the varying lengths of the two versions. But the very next line spoken by Somri, dispels this euphony of sound and spirit. 'Why shouldn't I say it…?' for the Hindi, '*kaahe naa kahoon…?*' The contrast between the two versions is obvious, hits the mind and the ear straightaway. The questioning stance is sharp and direct in the Hindi, '*Kahe na kahoon?*'

The two questioning words 'kahe na' are so sharp and carrying that the activity they defend—griping—fades from attention. The succeeding words fall like gongs, full throated and kindling a whole cultural vignette founded on beliefs of bad birth and bad omen, exploding into cannibalistic imagery.

The English, again, flounders on words of commonplace defiance, and stepping stone words like 'after all', ancillaries like 'around you', on the adjective 'unlucky' before 'Saturday': all this makes explicit what is implicit in the Hindi. And most damaging of all, it deconstructs the word 'khaayegi', articulating the notion of destiny contained in the Hindi. The word 'devour' for 'khaayegi' is inapt. 'Khaanaa'—to eat—and 'hadapna'—which is what 'devour' means—are different kinds of action. The sensation of chewing, crunching and a full, satisfying mastication evoked by 'khaayegi' is wiped out in 'devouring'.

And now comes the high watermark of the scene that shows Sanichari erupting into bitter but levelheaded plain speaking. The English here, one notes happily, matches the Hindi for the most part and emerges a worthy other: '*Tu kaunsa sukhkh paa gayee, Somri....*' ('And what great happiness did life bring you...?') The differing phonologies of the two languages somehow euphonize. The rhetoric of the two opening sentences achieves a similarity of thrust and pitch overriding their individual acoustics. Look at the trajectories of sound that get homogenized: '*Tu kaunsa sukhkh paa, gayee, somree....*' and 'And what great happiness did life bring you?' The English leaves out the term 'Somri' of the Hindi. The term, through its usage by Sanichari who is hierarchically far below Somri, lays bare the leaps towards deliberate insult and open telling off of an elder that the normally rule-bound Sanichari feels driven to. Yet, those eight words of the English translation, even though unaided by the rebellious usage of name that becomes name-calling, weld into a statement of consolidated insult equal to the Hindi's. They have an unbroken forward momentum not always felt in the translation. No preliminary or ancillary words or terms break the momentum.

The very next sentence, however, cuts into this flow. 'You're Monday-born ... but....' Need 'You're' and 'but' have been there? Would not 'Monday-born, you didn't get....' have been enough, better? But again, the major section of that sentence, '....you didn't get a better deal, did you?' has a fast forward movement; the words lift you on their immediate meaning to the larger context they signify. And similarly, the third sentence triumphs over its speed-breaker phrase, 'what lives they all live, those born on...', and hoists the attention to the superstitions attached to the planets by belief systems, to speculations, however fleetingly, on cultural anthropology.

Of the remaining three sentences in those lines spoken by Sanichari, two and a half are disasters. 'As for you...' is a stepping stone phrase, holding up the momentum. 'And you! You do nothing but...' could have sufficed and maintained the sharp, crackling anger of the speaker. But the insertion of the bedraggled, worn out term 'bitch' cancels out any such redemptive possibility. The word is at best there in the Hindi on the level of suggestion. The focus is squarely, unambiguously, on hunger, food and the voraciousness set off by unappeased hunger— 'Din bhar khau-khau...' The references are specific, factual, without a single abusive term. 'Bitch' wipes out this specificity and hazes the context with commonplace abusiveness. The context of food and hunger is entrenched in the next sentence, *'jaise baap tumharey sau man anaaj dhar gayen hain.'* The English is, 'Behaving as though your father left you a pile of wealth!' Wealth? Money? In a situation where food, 'anaaj' is more precious than money? That whole line of translation seems off track, in addition to being hamstrung by roundabout phrasing: 'behaving as though' where 'as if' could have done; 'a pile of wealth' for simply 'a pile'. 'Another word out of you' in the final line could have just been 'One more word from you...' It is also incorrect. The corresponding word in the Hindi is 'aawaaz'. 'The merest squeak from you now...' is, one would think, nearer it.

But all these lapses vanish and become inoperative in the short swift thwack of the word 'throttle' in 'I'll throttle you'. The word functions at many levels. First, it leaps clear of the mass of fellow words around it. Secondly, it subsumes all the dread and menace of chronic want projected in the word mass, and thirdly, on the heels of this subsuming, rising on its thrust, it appropriates and states in its own right the violence of the chronically hungry. The Hindi is, of course, far more earthy, and comes with a native spitfire force. '...seedhe tentua dabaa deynge', Sanichari hisses at Somri. But 'throttle', despite its educated sounding phonology does evoke the sense of choking and asphyxiation

present in 'tentua dabaa deynge'. Perhaps it has to do with the placing of the word; perhaps the harsh adamantine sound of the double
't' helps it convey the brutal, squeezing action conveyed by 'tentua
dabaa deynge'. Whatever the intangibles, the word binds the whole
paragraph into a unified mood, akin to that of the Hindi. It is one
more interlude of happy reading in the translation.

But this harmony comes undone in the translation of the stage
directions that follow. These directions are important, as pointed out
earlier, for the linkage in the storyline they make with the death of
Somri, soon to follow. The opening line establishes this linkage. The
Hindi says, '*Somri sanichari ko dekhtee hai. Phir dhire dhire ghoorkar
so jaatee hai.*'[34] That sequence of action comprising a staring of high
intensity going down to low, lower intensity, and finally sleep, is a
hieroglyph of death: it can make a strong retrospective effect when the
reader examines the lifecycle of Sanichari and women like her.

The English leaves out this sentence laden with meaning. The omission makes Sanichari the domineering figure she is not. Domin*ant* she
comes out from the clashes she has with other members of the family,
and from her capacity to sink and rise with the tides of circumstance.
But domin*ating*, she is not. This omission makes her so. The opening line of the stage directions in the English is 'Sanichari sits down
and starts the chakki again.'[35] Read along with the last line of the
preceding paragraph where she says 'another word out of you and
I'll throttle you,' she seems a woman marked by economy of movement, decisive, without any of the brooding and silent resignation she
is subject to. Just a few lines before this juncture, for instance, she
is shown saying the heavy, gloom-laden words: 'If there was a god,
your illness would have been given to me instead.'[36] This pessimistic
element of hers is what the Hindi highlights in the stage directions,
and the English overlooks, forgetful of the role of this element in the
story of Sanichari.

These inner fixtures of Sanichari's character that give ballast to
her story and its enactment, are noticeably reflected in the ensuing
and concluding section of the scene. The central motif here is the
open brawl and hand-to-hand of Sanichari and her daughter-in-law,
Parbatia. The snap and bang of the combat get reflected well enough
in the English. The abusive aspect lacks the nuanced finesse of the

Hindi; it can be said that 'bitch' and 'whore' remain the standard epithets, sometimes present even when the abusiveness is not there in the Hindi. *'Kahan se laayee ye chotee aur choodian?'*[37] becomes 'where did you get these from, you bitch? Speak up!'[38] Again, *'paeesaa kaun diya? Tarkaaree kaa paeesaa sey khareedaa. Bolti kahe naheen, kaun paeesa diya?'*[39] becomes 'Where did you get the money? Go on, tell me, you bitch, did you spend our vegetable money on this rubbish?'[40] And then there is the translator's bête noire term 'saalee', belaboured by the sledgehammer terms of 'bitch' and 'whore'. Despite these opacities, the din of the brawl scene does come across as yet another interval of good reading.

However, it is in the aftermath of the brawl, the interval, the trough between the fade out of one storm and the rise of another, that the oversights of the English show up badly. Sanichari here is in the thoughtful, inward state that almost always overcomes her after a showdown. And this inward state, as has been pointed out often in this essay, gives the Sanichari story its dimension of depth, its rounded, three-dimensional quality.

Let us, then, follow the emergence and course of this inwardness in the post-brawl stage of the drama of Sanichari. We first see it in her reply to Dulan's wife, Lachchmi, who enters the scene when the hand-to-hand of Sanichari and Parbatia is at its height. 'What's the matter,' Lachchmi asks the women turn by turn. Stage directions follow, of which the first line is *'Parbatia Sanichari ko dekhtee hai.'*[41] The English misses out the alternating nature of Lachchmi's queries, and thereby the heightened sense of emergency conveyed by the Hindi. The act of seeing, which occurs more than once in the scene is of special importance in the drama as a whole. The seeing is always a retrospective and uneasily futuristic act by the seer whose eyes mirror, condense and give perspective to the immediate present. The reader's or the viewer's eye feels yoked to the seer's eye, the field of awareness expanded. Thus, in that line—*'Parbatia Sanichari ko dekhtee hai'*—are gathered overtones and undertones of the Sanichari–Parbatia relationship, and the tensions woven into the saas–bahu nexus. It is after this deep, meaningful stare that Parbatia, the stage directions say, gathers the cosmetic items spilled out of the basket during the hand-to-hand, and walks away into the kitchen: *'Phir jaakar tokree mein choodee aur chotee rakhkhar rasoi men chalee jaatee hai.'* Her walking away is an unhurried, controlled act. She has spent the fire and rage of her emotions in the fisticuffs and the charged act of staring at Sanichari that she has just carried out.

The English drops the line *'Parbatia sanichari ko dekhtee hai.'* The stage direction consists of just one line 'Parbatia snatches up her trinkets and stomps off stage in a rage.'[42] Rage? Stomping off? Where are they in the Hindi? A whole reservoir of suggestion and subtle body language is wiped out in such omissions. The exit of Parbatia forms the take-off point for the emergence of the thoughtful, inward looking Sanichari who dominates the action at the end of the scene, and also in the story overall. The English rallies around in the opening line spoken by Sanichari in this section, after Parbatia has left the stage. Sanichari is answering Lachchmi's agitated question just before Parbatia's exit, 'what's the matter, what happened?' 'Nothing. It's my karma that is to blame.'[43] A matching note of fatalism rings in that English rendering of the Hindi's *'Kuchch naheen. Sab merey karmonka dosh hai.'*[44] But after this line a vital stage direction is present in the Hindi, missed out in the English. The stage direction says, *'Harua ko uththaakar Budhua kee charpayee par lita deytee hai'*[45] [Picks up Harua and lays him on Budhua's cot] (Author's translation). That action of Sanichari's is a crucial link in the emergence of her thoughtful, inwardlooking self at the end of the scene. The English omits it. Other omissions follow. Sanichari hands Lachchmi a bag of flour she has ground for payment. Lachchmi asks, *'Tera hissaa?'*[46] ('Your share?') [Author's translation]. On those two words lies balanced the crux of the ensuing portion of the scene. Sanichari calls out to Parbatia to bring out the paraat (kneading dish) for her share to be apportioned. Parbatia does not answer. She will, shortly afterwards, make her stormy entrance to lay down her ultimatum: she will quit the moment Budhua dies.

It is at this juncture a little before Parbatia's entry and ultimatum that the thoughtful, brooding aspect of Sanichari emerges again, inscribing the perennial aspects of her story that transcend its circumstantial aspects. The kneading dish, from which takes off the culminating event of Parbatia's ultimatum, which in turn tapers off to Sanichari's brooding, thus sustains a sequence of events that defines the story in a basic way. The English does not seem alive to this inner sequence. By omitting the two words spoken by Lachchmi—'tera hissaa?'—it dilutes the significance of the kneading dish in Lachchmi's act of keeping aside on its 'floor', Sanichari's portion of the flour she has ground. It conveys the act by means of stage directions that say in a detached, long-winded, third person voice, 'She uses it [the kneading dish] to remove a measure of flour from the bag...'[47] In the Hindi, Lachchmi performs the act of apportioning Sanichari's share in the swing of speaking, without it being detailed by the author. A brief matter-of-fact line of stage direction precedes the act of apportioning: '*Lachchmi rasoi mey jaatee hai, paraat ley aatee hai*,'[48] (Lachchmi goes to the kitchen and brings out the kneading dish) [Author's translation], followed by another brief, fait accompli sentence, '*Ley teraa hissa*,'[49] (here's your share) [Author's translation].

Now comes an interlude of confidential, woman-to-woman exchange that presages the brooding, clear eyed and resigned Sanichari we see at the end of the scene. There is an omission here again in the English. The first line of this section after Lachchmi has portioned out Sanichari's share of the flour is, '*Roti to naheen bana hoga ab tak*,'[50] ('The rotis wouldn't be made yet, would they?') [Author's translation]. This friendly, insider's query which is a statement about the conditions in Sanichari's household, not requiring any answer is followed immediately by the simple yet concerned question, '*budhua kaisaa hai?*'[51] ('How's Budhua?'[52]). Together, the questions lay the foundation of the intimate, confidential character of the exchange between the two women that follows. It is from the lull made by this heart-to-heart that the fresh eruption of hostilities between Sanichari and Parbatia comes as a vivid dramatic contrast. And from the cessation of this uproar rises the portrait of Sanichari in her brooding, unease-laden aspect that remains all through the play as its inner ballast and anchor.

The English, in a rough and ready way, mirrors the moods and mood swings of the original. But can approximations to the original give stature to a translation? In missing out the line, '*roti to naheen bana hoga ab tak?*' it loses a means of establishing the informal/intimate nature of the Sanichari–Lachchmi exchange on the required pitch of unhurriedness, effortlessness and un-self-consciousness. Lachchmi's query—'*How is Budhdhua?*'—which succeeds her statement of fact about the rotis, with its by-the-way air that thinly veils deep concern, further emphasizes the relaxed, mutual compassion of the two women that can make them interact with few words and deep emotion, evoking an abiding quality to their relationship.

This interiority is what gets lost in the omissions of the English translation. A rushed, fleeting quality enters the Sanichari–Lachchmi dialogue, making it unnecessarily, uncharacteristically racy. The use of commonplace English speech modes is no less a cause for this dilution. Here are the two renderings:

> *'Budhua kaisa hai?'* ('How is Budhua?')
>
> *'Haalat theek naahee'* ('Not good.')
>
> *'Davaa daaroo kiya?'* ('Have you given him any medicine?')
>
> *'Ee rahaa dui rupiya, issey noon teyl khareeden yaa'* (Showing her the two rupees) ('Her highness came back with these. A measly two rupees. Do I spend it on medicine or…')
>
> *'Pareyshaan mat ho. Sab ththeek ho jaayegaa. Ee ley bisesar kaa maayee diya hai. Kal subah tak pees dena.'* (aataa deytee hai). *'Ham jaateyn hain.'* ('Don't worry Sanichari…I'm sure everything will work out all right. (Handing over a sack.) Here. Bisesar's mother sent this. Have it ground by tomorrow morning. (Gets up). Okay. I'm off. (Leaves).)

'Not good' has a very English, clipped quality and forward stride to it, at variance with the careworn drawl of the Hindi. But it passes muster and could have set the pace for the succeeding lines. 'Have you given him any medicine?' is the next line. Why not just 'Any medicine?' It could have chimed with 'Not good'. If kept up along with appropriate stage directions, the cumulative terseness could have resiled, and become eloquent with the power of suggestion. Sanichari's response to Lachchmi's question consists of showing her the two rupees Parbatia has given her, and the line: 'Her highness came back with this. A measly two rupees. Do I spend it on medicine or…' Need Parbatia have been referred to at all, when she is not in the Hindi? The focus in the Hindi is purely on the buying power of two rupees, with no explicit remark on its smallness. Sanichari does not *say* 'measly two rupees'. She conveys the measliness through words heavy with irony and a bitter helplessness: *'Ee rahaa dui rupiya. Issey noon teyl khareedeyn yaa…'* The censure of Parbatia is unmistakable in those words, and possibly, the translator felt driven to verbalising the thought, an understandable temptation of translating activity. But 'her highness' is just a run of the mill tart term. It lacks the slow, rumbling foreboding of Sanichari at Parbatia's rebelliousness, felt in the Hindi version. And why the genteel, middle class word 'medicine' in place of the stark, poverty driven term 'noon teyl'—salt and oil? The middle class quality that the English gives to the whole interlude of Sanichari and Lachchmi in their private exchange is particularly strong, particularly jarring, in the concluding lines. This quality, actually, is not absent even in the Hindi. Standard Hindi phrases punctuate the special, rural sounding idiom devised by the playwright, and disrupt the effortless heart-to-heart of the two women, affecting the inner vibrations of the story. Lachchmi's '*Tu pareyshaan na ho*' is as run of the mill as Sanichari's 'Her highness'. But the special idiom otherwise present does neutralise the middle class mundane-ness of this phrase of Lachchmi's, as well as the one '*ham jaateyn hain*'. Considered numerically, this idiom is present only in one line of Lachchmi's four line address to Sanichari at this point. But it does help dilute its middle class 'otherness'. Also, the line just before, '*ee ley bisesar kaa maayee diya hai*,' along with the action of giving Sanichari a bag of wheat for being ground and the friendly order to have it ground by the next morning, restores the climate of intimacy normal between the two women.

The English does not have this natural advantage of idiom. Not that the translator is not alive to this handicap. Far from it. But is a racy, with-it kind of idiom the answer to it? Phrases like 'Okay I'm off', or the term 'here' in 'Here, Bisesar's mother sent this,' or the prissy grammatical correctness of 'Have it ground by tomorrow morning,' or the slangy Americanism of 'Come on out…' only bring in an anglicised flavour worse than the false note and stiffness of standard Hindi that creeps into the idiom of the Hindi rendering.

After these distortions made by anglicisms, comes an alteration in the English quite incomprehensible. Lachchmi leaves. And Sanichari calls out to Parbatia 'angrily', the English says in parenthesis. In the Hindi, there is no such or any other descriptive term for Sanichari's calling out to Parbatia. The anger, the angry mood, build up later, after Parbatia comes on stage in response to Sanichari's yelling for her, and a duel of words sets off between them. The impromptu nature of this battle is affected by the prior naming of it.

This oversight is followed by the one in the line that follows Parbatia's sulky dawdling into view on stage at Sanichari's calling out to her. 'Enough of your tantrums. Come on out,'[53] Sanichari shouts at her. 'Tantrums' is not the word at all for 'nakhra' which is the term in the Hindi: '*Nakhraa na jhaad!*'[54] 'Airs' would be nearer 'nakhra', one would think. 'Enough of your airs' seem closer to the Hindi; it even seems to smooth down the grating Americanism of 'come on out' that follows 'Enough of your tantrums'.

The sound and fury of the altercation between the two women, however, does come out palpably enough in the translation, despite the readymade, unimaginative and unwrought nature of the terms of abuse. This problem with the terms of abuse—the gaalees—is a feature present all through the translation, as pointed out, and as also pointed out, a problem nearly insolvable. But it is in the stage direction with which the scene closes, that an omission occurs in the English that changes the distribution of the dramatic weight noticeably and unaccountably from the Hindi. The English is, 'She (Parbatia) picks up the full kneading dish and stalks off. Sanichari looks after her, then casts a quick glance at Budhua. She resumes grinding the chakki with a vengeance. The light dims slowly.'[55] The Hindi is, '*Parbatia paraat leykar bheetar chali jatee hai. Sanichari usey jaatey huey dekhtee hai. Budhua ko dekhtee hai. Vaapas chakki mein geyhoon daalkar peestee hai.*'[56]

The Sanicharis of the two versions are very different. The one in the Hindi is dialoguing with herself. Her movements are slow, collected. They are as much of the eye, of the gaze of the eyes, as the motor action of the limbs. The intensity of the one and the practised, absent-minded glides of the other complement each other, and recount a saga of adversity which is ceaseless and answerless, and somehow, timeless. It is a deindividualization of Sanichari that is playwright Usha Ganguly's own calculated modification of Mahashweta Devi's severe deindividualization of Sanichari in accordance with the Marxian model. The translator, in her Introduction, questions this emotionalized depiction of Sanichari that results from her adaptation. But what, one wonders, is the rationale in her own, agenda-less shuffling—adla-badli—of the Hindi text?

In the English rendering, Sanichari emerges as an angry woman, visibly and unapologetically angry, with flinging, explosive movements.

Her eye action expresses rage, an aggressive, come-what-may resolve, that speaks of a roused ego, a combativeness avoided in the Hindi. In the Hindi, she just looks, in what seems a drained, wooden look, at the retreating figure of Parbatia striding off the stage. This impression of a spent quietude lying pooled in the eyes is fortified by the very next sentence, 'Budhua ko deykhtee hai' (Looks at Budhua) [Author's translation]. And then, the last sentence, 'Vaapas chakki mein gehun daalkar peestee hai,' reinforces the spent, word-lost state that Parbatia's rebelliousness has put her in. We see a woman with eyes turned down, reading the reality they envision, her hands and trunk swaying to the motions of filling and replenishing the chakki with grain. In the English, there are lines such as 'Sanichari casts a quick glance at Budhua,' then 'resumes grinding the chakki with a vengeance.' And the last line, 'The light dims slowly', apart from not being there in the Hindi at all, underlines the tempestuousness of her motion that the terms 'quick glance' and 'resumes grinding the chakki with a vengeance' evoke, and project a highly extroverted, loud Sanichari.

Another major test for the English translation of the play *Rudali* would be its rendering of the rites that follow Budhua's death. It is a culture specific event. The English, from its given position as a cultural outsider in relation to this event, has to strike a creative outsided-ness with it: a mediatory position that conjoins the vernacular essence with the English mould. What one looks for in the climactic moments of the event we shall consider, should be the pleasure of recognizing and reliving a familiar cultural practice, formulated in the 'other' tongue. Like the pleasure of coming upon and recognizing a close kin in a foreign clime, it is a diasporic experience. Let us see if this electric sensation sweeps us at the climactic points of the death rites dealt with in the scene.

The first such line—'Lower him to the ground'[57]—that is the vaid (doctor) speaking. He says them on the heels of the action he performs, as specified in the text, 'Approaches the charpoy, then stops. He frowns, places his hand under Budhua's nostrils.'[58] Visualize and link that action to the words he speaks, and you are brought up short against the very different ring, very different orientation, of the words; they mean more than what they say. 'Lowering' and 'ground' are more than the simple action cum place. Words they appear, your reflexes tell you. Alerted thus, you read on, till you come to the line in the stage directions, 'Somri breaks into loud wails.'[59] This wailing is special, you see in a rerecognition of fact and experience. One by one other features of the post-death proceedings incurse into the field of your awareness, pattern out, declare themselves. And the whole event emerges recreated in your mind. 'Smash the water pot, brothers,'[60] Bijua cries. 'Budhua re...'[61] Dulan's wife's sharp ritual wail cuts into the melee raised by the villagers. They have the right to make a melee, a right which is more than simple kindness and humanity; you reason and paraphrase the culture of it, the culture of the whole event. They have the right to make common cause with the grief of the dead man's kin, broadcast the death and thereby sublimate the consuming, self-centred pain of personal grief to the assuaging levels of spiritual understanding. 'Cry, cry....it will make you feel better,'[62] Dulan's wife prods Sanichari. Amidst the wailing and the seeming confusion, arrangements for the disposal of the body are going apace:

> 'Make some arrangements, the corpse can't jut lie around,' Bijua says. 'Once the sun goes down there'll be a problem,' Dulan echoes Bijua. 'Bring the firewood. What else is needed,' Dulan becomes brisk. 'Lots. A kriya ceremony comes cheap, you think? Mohanlal Pandit's fee, chivda, dahi, gur—and a goat,' Bijua specifies. A villager gasps, 'All this?' 'More. There's a dahi and gur feast for five Brahmins on the fourth day,' Bijua clarifies, dour but dutiful. 'The bamboo and firewood have come,' Nathua announces. 'Get moving then,' Bijua leads the way. The women break out wailing. 'Cry, Sanichari, cry,' Dulan's wife prods the dazed and dry-eyed Sanichari, 'It will make you feel better.' The men leave with the body. The women wail on.[63]

Yes, the event etches itself on the screen of your mind. But it is your own reflexes and nerve centres of cognition which perform this etching. You, as a cultural insider, can wade into the words and abstract the living fibres of the event they narrate. But you want the narration to do this. You want the words to open under the pressure of your reading, like a screen sliding back under the pressure of your finger and disclose the sinews and joints of the culture on which they have erected their prose. This sense of the language—English—not going home, not touching ground—not giving you the diasporic elation mentioned earlier—makes you examine the English afresh, in a way you are not driven to with the Hindi. And in this reconsideration, you make all due allowances for the language. You accept its 'otherness'. You accept the different pitch and throw of the narrative, the narration, the different dynamics it produces. You accept the untranslatability of the vernacular gestalt: of gestalts in general, realise afresh the standing predicaments of translating into English. But after making full allowance for these factors, you still want to see how the translator has negotiated the predicaments. A lot of translating activity, after all, comprises negotiating the linguistic-cultural rapids.

Yet another test for the negotiating skills of the English translator of 'Rudali' is that of conveying the venomously abusive atmosphere of the Sanichari household. The Hindi enjoys enormous natural advantages here. The sheer variety and hitting power of the terms of abuse available to it gives it a boost of articulation which the English cannot command. '*Kahaan gayee daain?*'[64] Sanichari snarls and curses in one of the scenes, for instance, calling for Parbatia. This sentence is not there in the English. (As said earlier, Katyal's translation, is from a handwritten actors' script, neither available now, nor printed, and is not a verbatim rendering of the published Usha Ganguly text, though it retains most of it.) But the problems it would have raised can be inferred from another sentence in the English where the word 'daain' occurs. 'Arre oh, you daain, will you tell me what's happened?'[65] This too is an off the record rendering. The Ganguly text does not have it, but this need not matter, for it is the general employment and deployment of the English that we are considering, and for this purpose replicated sentences in the two languages are not a strict need.

In the Hindi, 'daain', wherever used, acts as a galvanizing word in the sentence. All the other words gravitate towards it, intensified of impact, giving an added urgency to the feelings of the speakers. Not only 'daain', but all the cuss words that crackle and splutter in the Hindi, give the prose a terse, impatient, tugging-at-the-leash quality. The English rendering could have concentrated on this terseness, on the economy of words the terse style demands. It could, thereby, have made up for its lack of access to the words of abuse. In that sentence present in the English rendering, 'Arre oh, you daain, will you tell me what's happened?' the entire second half of the sentence after 'daain' deadens the franticness of the query. Instead, would not 'What's happened? Arre oh daain, what's *happened*,' have retained and heightened the urgency and franticness? One of the rules of the terse style, after all, is doing away with wordiness, keeping the word load low. All through the English rendering, this avoidable excess load of words occurs, giving the narrative an outward sprawl that robs it of intensity. 'What's the matter…couldn't you hear…'[66] could have been 'What's it? Couldn't hear?' 'Ask your son what the matter is'[67] could have been just 'Ask your son.' 'What's happened to you, beta? Eh, Parbatia, run and fetch the vaidji. This doesn't look good at all,'[68] is almost twice its needed length. 'What's it beta? Parbatia, arri o Parbatia, run bring the vaid!' The line 'This doesn't look good at all' is totally unnecessary, for Budhua's state has been fully described in the stage directions given just before, 'There is blood flowing from his mouth and his eyes are turned up,'[69] the directions explicitly say. To express this in speech, something like 'ai hai, blood!' could have been added to 'What's it beta?' to make it 'What's it beta? Hai hai, blood! Parbatia, arri o Parbatia, run call the vaid!'

A marked casualty of this wordiness of the English is the vaid. He is casteist and he makes no bones about it. It is a bald casteism that bounces off his words. As a character his nastiness is not compelling or vivid as Somri's is. And linguistically, even the Hindi does not come out with flying colours. He speaks a formless, haphazard mix of standard Hindi and the special dialect devised for the play by Usha Ganguly—a recurring feature in the Hindi—that robs him of individuality. The English translation compounds the basic lacklustre of the vaid by its own long-winded prose. 'You people have no respect for time. Such impatience! Can't wait for even a minute! I was looking forward to my afternoon nap after a good meal and you have to drag me here. Where's this son of yours?'[70] The essence of that speech is in the line 'I was looking… nap…me here.'[71] It shows up the guilt-free and sanctioned, indolent way of life the vaid leads and illuminates the social structure and hierarchy under village command. The opening sentences, 'You people have no respect … even a minute' build up to and climax in the sentence referred to earlier. This gradual build up can be said to be the translator's intention too. But word overload, once again, undoes the intention and prevents the cohering and formation of the image latent in that paragraph.

Some simple precautions could have saved the paragraph from this overload and the resulting flattened anti-climactic effect; for instance, the use of pronouns. They could have been either avoided or their placing changed, relocated. Let us try the relocation method first. 'You people' in the beginning of the first line could be placed at the end of it, along with a lighter word for 'respect'. It sounds bombastic and preachy, even for a stick-in-the-mud character like the vaid. Something like 'sense' or 'sense of time,' say. The sentence would then read, 'No sense of time you people have,' It gets a more conversational tone in place of the pedantic, overbearing feel it has now. The vaid most probably is overbearing and pedantic, and the translator meant to create precisely this effect. But it could have been accomplished through a more everyday idiom.

The next two sentences seem dispensable. And the important climactic sentence, 'I was looking forward to my afternoon nap after a good meal,' could, again, do with pronoun relocation. 'Looking forward to a nice long sleep I was, after a good meal, but no, drag me out here, you have to. Where's this son of yours?' The paragraph would then read: 'No sense of time you people have, do you? Nice long sleep I was looking forward to after a nice long meal, but no, drag me out here you have to. All right, where's this son of yours?' That may not be a flawless rendering. But it does become fleeter of foot, runs (hopefully) a little more with the grain of the English of the English-speaking here. And, to recall and restate a premise of this essay, it is to this readership's living of mother tongue and other tongue simultaneously, of translating itself to and back continually in a reflex action, that the English rendering is primarily addressed.

Let us then, follow the vaid right up to the point of his exit. We shall concentrate on the lines where the words misfire. There are quite a few where they do not: where a trimming, even if suggesting itself, would be an alternative form and hence optional, and therefore, not a textual need. 'Lower him to the ground and give me my fee,'[72] makes you halt at the word 'lower'. Is not 'lower' a little stiff? 'Lay him out on the ground,' perhaps? 'Put him on the ground...' alternatives buzz in your head. But you let 'lower' be. It makes a fast connection with the word 'ground', and the whole tableau and complex of ceremony and belief present in the phrase comes alive. Also, could not the line, 'You've dragged me all the way here in the afternoon heat to examine a corpse!'[73] have done without the 'you?' to read, 'Dragged me all the way down here in the midday heat to examine a corpse!' But it can stand, you feel. The stress falls on 'to examine a corpse' and that is a powerful enough imagery and action to detract attention from the earlier portion of the sentence.

But you definitely balk at 'What am I to check? He's as stiff as a log. Come on, hand over my money, let me go home and rest.'[74] Disposable words here create a din and crowd each action and state of being, stifle their dramatic import: the dramatic imports of, namely, checking a corpse as 'stiff as a log', of the crass inhumanity of the vaid. 'Check what? Stiff as a log he's gone. Give me my money quick now, let me go home and rest,' you recast the words, reasonably certain, reasonably hopeful, that your editing has freed the significant latter half of each of the sentences from the smother of standard, everyday phrases preceding them. But your diffidence definitely vanishes when you come to 'Hurry up and give me money. It's getting late. And I'll have to cleanse myself in the river before going home. What're you glaring at me for? Take out the money and pay up.'[75] The ceremony of cleansing oneself in the river catches the attention straightaway. It pushes into the background the vaid's bullying demand for his dues which in any case has already figured in the earlier paragraph. You expect the mystique of the cleansing ceremony to jolt you afresh by the acoustics of English. This can happen only if a close, speaking connection gets established between the words and the action they denote. 'Cleanse' is not a word that forms closeness. On the contrary, it is a divisive, distancing word, marking off the cleansed from the uncleansed. The demarcation is intended: it is meant to be proclaimed. In the Hindi, the vaid says, '*Nahaanaa bhee hai.*'[76] The nondescript word 'Nahaanaa', and the everyday activity it denotes, is galvanised by the context to a level of sanctification. That, of course, is cultural action, organic to the anthropology of the language concerned. It cannot be replicated in the English. But the special meaning and reference have to be evoked by whatever word for which the English translator opts. The English translator has to be alive to the absorptive, connotative capacity expected of the word of his choice. 'Cleanse', as noted above, lacks risibility. It does not have the capacity of 'nahaanaa' to draw us, become expanded with the mystical allusion present in the context in which it is used. It remains indicative, non-risible.

What could be a remedy? A more colloquial, everyday word in tune with 'nahaanaa' perhaps? 'Wash'? 'I'll have to have a wash in the river before going home'? In any case, it eliminates the intrusive, dilatory word, 'myself' present in the text. 'Dip' seems another word worthy of consideration. 'I'll have to take the dip in the river before going home'? *The* dip or *a* dip? 'The', you feel. 'The' refers to the special nature of the dip. 'A' would mean an everyday dip. In any case, both 'dip' and 'wash' share the colloquial-ness of 'nahaanaa', and rub shoulders with the context in which they are placed. The failure of thus rubbing shoulders with the context is what marks the English rendering time and again, undoing the rapport it strikes, not infrequently.

The very next set of lines spoken by the vaid confirms this:

'Did you hear that? Did you hear what this daain said? She's dragged me here by force, and now she's thumbing her nose at me! Arre, till I get my money, I'm not moving an inch! All you low caste people are the same—no knowledge, no religion, no faith, no education!'[77]

That last line there is a monstrosity. It simply goes berserk in its projection of the vaid's casteist taunts. 'You low caste people' is taunt enough. 'You low castes', would have been more hard hitting. The word 'people' is another example of the over-wording to which the English shows itself prone. But you overlook it. Much in the sentence preceding this line comes across despite their painstaking correctitude of language. 'Did you hear that?' could have done with 'Hear that?' Likewise, 'Hear the daain? Drags me here and now thumbs her nose at me! Arre, not an inch am I moving till you've paid up!' would have sufficed. But there is a steady forward movement in those lines as they are in the text, despite the room for curtailment they have. And 'thumbing her nose' stands in well enough for *angootha dikhai rahee hai*,'[78] despite its anglicist flavour. The sustained forward movement of the lines irons out the glitches.

All this gets undone by the thoughtlessness of the words after 'You low caste people': '…are the same, no knowledge of religion, no faith, no education,' These words are not there in the Ganguly text. Possibly, they are or were in the actors' script from which Katyal did her translation. But their source is not the point. They are needless invectives being heaped upon the lower castes, detracting from the main, dramatically relevant charge that the vaid is making against them: non-payment of his fee. Just 'You low castes…' supplemented with some apt-seeming physical action, such as, say, grinding his teeth, would have been enough after 'not an inch…' 'Not an inch am I moving till you've paid up! You low castes!' All the rest about no education, no religion, no knowledge and so on simply holds up the reading, which in turn, slackens the process of visualizing the play that goes on simultaneously with the reading.

Things cheer up again, however, in the last extended speaking by the vaid that occurs a little later. And again it happens quite a bit due to the reprieves we feel compelled to, in all fairness, to make to any English rendering of an ethnocentric play like *Rudali*. Consider this, 'Fifty paise? Do you take me for a beggar! I knew something like this would happen! You low caste people are the all he same! Just you call me again and see…. Daain that you are!'[79] Deletable words swarm this passage and you recast it on the heels of the reading as, 'A beggar you take me for? Something like this *would* happen, I *knew*. You low castes! Just call me again, I'll show you. Daain!' If nothing, even if further modifications are possible, the feel of a packed anger comes through in that rendering, a subdued fury that is the key emotion in the vaid's state of mind there. But as in the lines earlier, a steady fast pace and the sustained interrogative tone lift the attention from the phrasing and the carefully rounded out sentences that take no chances with grammar. Untethered, the attention homes in on the social realities beneath the prose.

The question that, however, remains, is whether this a fulfilling literary experience? A story, play or novel is a blend of social realities and the metaphysic that governs them and is governed by them. The metaphysic is what one misses in the experience afforded by the English rendering. We missed it, as we saw, in the rendering of Budhua's death rituals. Death is a prime causative factor in the development of 'Rudali'.

Sanichari and Bikhni, near-destitute women, meet in the aftermath of the death of Bikhni's husband and the many deaths Sanichari has weathered. The profession of rudali—hired mourners for the dead—which they take to, assures them survival and empowers them with the stamina to hold their own against the maaliks. It is a benefice of death. Death is a liberator in the story. It is this liberating power of death, ringing in the jubilant, carnivalesque abandon of the rudalis that we, the readers, expect to hear through the English articulation.

Let us then come straight to the death scene of Gambhir Singh, arch villain and leading maalik, where the chilling justice and power of death are shown panoramically in speech and action. The rudalis come storming on to the stage. The din and tumult of their entry register on the reader over and above the visual element. The din is graphed in detail in both the texts. In the Hindi as:

> Laash ke charon or chakkar lagaakar khaat pakadkar baithtee hain. Phir roatee hain, phir jodey mein ek dusre ko pakadkar uhthtee hain. Stage left mey jakar baiaththee hain. Phir sir peeththkar rote rote khadd hokar chchaatee peethkar roney lagtee hain.[80]

In the English as:

> They circle the corpse, wailing dramatically. Then they grasp the cot and sit down. Pairing off they sit down stage left, and begin to beat their foreheads and breasts rhythmically in exaggerated, stylized movements. They stand up, beating their breasts and wailing in unison....'[81]

The narrative tone comes across differently in the two renderings. The Hindi is impersonal. The narrating agency is a voice, a reporting voice, no more. No face gets evoked by the voice and nor does the voice make any attempt to discern the faces of the actors whose actions it is detailing. Is this facelessness and the impersonality it signifies a symbol (mask?) of the impersonality of death? Also, a non-verbalism pervades the whole scene. There is din, eloquent weeping, an impassioned, surrealist and frenzied sound and fury, but no words. Facelessness, non-verbalism and swift, flashing movements: don't these suggest the enigmatic, cathartic power of death? It certainly seems not an inapt conclusion to make.

But apt or inapt, there is definitely a mystique to the scene, a sense of deep signification that seems to bare the heart of the play, compelling thoughtful, silent attention. This spell of silence is less pronounced, less forceful, in the English. The lay out is the standard, conventional one of keeping narration and narrative distinct from each other. The narrator is more than a voice. It/he perceives the rudalis in a far less impersonal and rarefied, far more subject-to-object way, than does the narrator in the Hindi. And, by not depersonalizing the narrator and not merging him/her with the narrative, recourse to pronouns is but natural. The undue weightage of pronouns is a feature of the English rendering we have noticed earlier too. In the earlier cases, the damage was to the terseness required in the narrative. In this case, the effect is felt in the decrease of abstraction and a consequent decrease in the heightening of the drama that the abstraction causes. The single pronoun 'they' appended before each of the action of the rudalis—'They circle the corpse,' 'They grasp the cot,' 'They hold each other... They stand up....'—separates them from the action, and separates the narrating voice from the narrative. It creates separate identities, little islets of agency that cut into the formation of the facelessness and non-verbalism from which the deeper significance of the scene rise. The non-verbal aspect is further damaged by the translator's explicit stating of the rudalis' lamentation as:

'Hai re! Hai re!/Hai the master! Hai, father of us all!/Hai, hai smash all your bangles/hai, hai, take off your toe rings!/Hai, hai, wipe off your alta/Hai, hai, wipe off your sindoor!/Hai, hai, Naugad raja, hai, hai!'[82]

Why is this done? That it does not figure in the Hindi is not the point. It is constantly to be kept in mind that Katyal's translation was done from an earlier version of the present published one. The point is that it does not add to the dramatic character or properties of the scene. On the contrary, it is discordant with the suggestive power of the scene.

Fortunately, redeeming features, partly present in the translation, and partly rising from the nature of the words of the lamentation, control the damage caused by the explicit stating of the words. The stress falls on 'hai hai' in all the lines. These two words determine the rhythm and tonal distribution of the paragraph. Read the lines aloud: the flow of reading pools on its own upon the two words. The succeeding words in each line evoke a ritual and a timeworn ceremony, a mood, more than a rationally comprehensible action. Speech and the culture of speaking remain in abeyance. Similarly, the actions described after each use of the pronoun 'they' have such a strong visual and imagistic quality that the pronoun subsides in the reader's scale of awareness. The presence of the narrating voice also, accordingly, loses edge. It unites with the action detailed and settles to non-verbal levels and expressive silence.

It is possible that the English translator has her own view of the scene: a straight, factual view shorn of symbolism or deeper significance. Mahashweta Devi herself is not given to symbolism; in her dictionary it would be equalled with obscurantism. And Usha Ganguly herself, as Katyal argues in her Introduction, has recast the Marxist realism of the Bengali original into a more everyday variety of realism to accord with the temper of a non-Marxist audience.

Such modifications of rendering are understandable. One such understandable change is the direct communication with the audience which Sanichari and the rudalis make. There are two instances of this bold change introduced by the translator. The first is in the description of the rudalis' dance, after their storming in on the stage. It is in the acting directions given in parenthesis. Acting directions, as has been pointed out earlier, are not just verbal exercises but organic parts of the text, waiting to be practically applied. In any case, except for one line of dialogue at the fag end, the whole of this final section is in the form of stage directions. The line in the stage direction is, 'They stand up beating their breasts and wailing in unison, *enjoying the rapt attention they are getting*'[83] (emphasis added). Is this 'rapt attention' from the others on the stage, or from the audience in front of the stage? This is not clear. But whether it is the one or the other, the tongue-in-cheek quality of the rudalis' behaviour is a perfectly credible extension of a trait of theirs shown earlier in the play too, at the funerals of other rogue maaliks. It is a more low key depiction there. The rudalis here catch each other's eyes, covertly giggle at the show of heartbroken grief they are putting up. The translator plays on this private play of the rudalis and makes it public, turns it outward. The effect, of course, would be felt more in the performance of the play than in the reading of it. But it is on the reading that this essay is based; indeed, is made possible at all! And the reading does absorb the change after an initial flinching.

The second similar instance of the translator's initiative occurs at the very last lap of the scene where the stage is near empty, and is on its way to being totally empty. Sanichari is the sole occupant of the stage, a Sanichari become sadder and wiser after the tumultuous display of human emotions that has just got over. Here are the actions she performs in this spent yet alive state of mind she is in. In the Hindi:

> ek dhunkuchi ulta padaa hai, usey uththaakaar seedha kartee hai. Phir neeche padaa ek sikka uththaatee hai. Udaas muskuraaatee hai. Paisa aanchal mey baandhtee hai. Dhirey dhirey aagey badtee hai.[84]

In the English:

> An incense burner is lying overturned. She straightens it. She sees a coin lying beside it. She picks it up. Looks at it. Smiles sadly. Knots it decisively into her clothing. Faces the audience resolutely. (Blackout).[85]

Adjectives vie with pronouns in that rendering, lowering the impersonal tone that marks the Hindi. This is a standing feature of the English, as we have noticed often. But in this instance, the adjectives are not added on to the existing lines in the Hindi. New turns are given to Sanichari's personality by the English, not present in the Hindi at all. The phrase 'knots it decisively' and the next line 'faces the audience resolutely' are the translator's own. They make for a confiding woman, eager for onlookers' sympathy and understanding of the pilferage she has just committed; understanding of the chronic uncertainties of her life that drive her to such acts of pocketing money not her own.

In the Hindi she is not soliciting public sympathy. She does not enter into any direct communication with the audience through gesture or other means. That her conscience does hurt her is shown in the way she walks off the stage: a slow, thoughtful glide forward—'dhire dhire aagey *badtee hai.*'[86] But she is alone with her problems of conscience and existence, content to be so. She is absorbed, cohered within and without. This self-contained figure, her face in profile, becomes frontal in the line, 'faces the audience resolutely.'[87] It is a complete turn around, both in the physical and the mental sense. Do the reader and his reading intelligence absorb it? They do, one feels. It is a freeze action that Sanichari performs. The resolute look is held on the face. If enacted by a good actress backed by appropriate stage effects, the still eyes can steer—as they are expected to—the viewing/reading attention to the history of want and insecurity behind the petty yet ugly theft she has just committed; a history compounded by the crass amorality of the goings on at the funeral ceremony. The entire history of rudalis and the play *Rudali* is encapsulated in that frontal look and the minute dilations and contractions of the eyes emitted by it. It is a valid enough rounding off of the play, and thereby, validation enough of the change to Sanichari's demeanour that the English translation gives.

The English translation of 'Rudali' thus, compels positive response in spite of its handicaps due to its lack of an effortless, para-verbal contact with the play. It calls for 'deep reading', a reading that is alert to inflections in the narrative tone of the writing that evoke or come close to the spirit of the original. It is a reading that requires effort, an effort more than what is ordinarily given to a translation. But it is the right of every translator. The heavy-footed quality of the language, also a feature of the translation as discussed earlier, cannot, however, be made up for by strategies of reading. Sensitive, rigorous editing is the only answer to it. Let us hope editors of the required quality are there in our writing community for future works of translation.

Notes

1. Devi, Mahashweta. 1980. 'Rudali', *Nairitey Megh*. Kolkata: Karuna Prakashini.
2. Ganguly, Usha. 2004. *Rudali*. New Delhi: Radhakrishna Prakashan. Hindi stage adaptation of Devi, op cit.
3. Katyal, Anjum. 1997. *'Rudali': From Fiction to Performance*. Calcutta: Seagull Books. Trans. of. Devi, op cit.
4. Personal communication with Anjum Katyal.
5. Ganguly, p. 9.

6. Katyal, p. 93.
7. Ganguly, p. 10.
8. Katyal, p. 94.
9. Ganguly, p. 10.
10. Katyal, p. 94.
11. Ibid.
12. Ganguly, p. 9.
13. Ibid.
14. Ibid.
15. Katyal, p. 93.
16. Ibid.
17. Ganguly, p. 11.
18. Katyal, p. 95.
19. Ganguly, p. 11.
20. Ibid.
21. Ibid.
22. Ibid.
23. Katyal, p. 96
24. Ganguly, p. 11.
25. Ibid., p. 12.
26. Katyal, p. 96.
27. Ganguly, p. 12.
28. Katyal, p. 96.
29. Ganguly, p.12.
30. Katyal, p. 96.
31. Ganguly, p. 12.
32. Katyal, p. 96.
33. Ganguly, p. 12.
34. Ibid.
35. Katyal, p. 96.
36. Ibid.
37. Ganguly, p. 13.
38. Katyal, p. 97.
39. Ganguly, p. 13.
40. Katyal, p. 97.
41. Ganguly, p. 14.
42. Katyal, p. 98.
43. Ibid.
44. Ganguly, p. 14.
45. Ibid.
46. Ibid.
47. Katyal, p. 98.
48. Ganguly, p. 14.
49. Ibid.

50. Ibid.
51. Ibid.
52. Katyal, p. 98.
53. Ibid.
54. Ganguly, p. 14.
55. Katyal, p. 99.
56. Ganguly, p. 15.
57. Katyal, p. 102.
58. Ibid., p. 101.
59. Ibid., p. 102.
60. Ibid., p. 103.
61. Ganguly, p. 22.
62. Katyal, p. 105.
63. Ibid.
64. Ganguly, p. 20.
65. Katyal, p. 100.
66. Ibid.
67. Ibid.
68. Ibid.
69. Ibid.
70. Ibid., p. 101.
71. Ibid., p. 102.
72. Ibid.
73. Ibid.
74. Ibid.
75. Ibid.
76. Ganguly, p. 21.
77. Katyal, p. 102.
78. Ganguly, p. 21.
79. Katyal, p. 104.
80. Ganguly, p. 103.
81. Katyal, p. 153.
82. Ibid.
83. Ibid.
84. Ganguly, p. 104.
85. Katyal, p. 154.
86. Ganguly, p. 104.
87. Katyal, p. 154.

Chapter 3

A Misleading Simplicity

Nirmal Verma's writing is deceptively simple for rendering into English. Multi-syllables hardly ever occur in his prose. Culture specifics do not hold up the translator. His postmodern sensibility has outgrown the need for cultural esotericisms. Such non-complexities make his writing seem straight, linear, tempting to translate and rerender into another language. But profundities stir below the linearity. If the translator does not feel this stir, hear its breath, and treats the simplicity as the simple, he is only headed for the simplistic, for flatness. This is what has happened with Geeta Kapur's translation[1] of 'Maya Darpan'.[2] It is a story arisen from the flotsam of a way of life fast disappearing. But shoots of hope and a new order are shown springing from the ashes of the dying order. Desolation and promise blend in the chemistry of the story. They murmur in the vocal chords of its narrative in a persistent and languorous drone. And most telling of all, the two moods—desolation and promise—determine the physical aspects of the characters: the still look of eyes and face in contrast with the swift and decisive seeming motions of their hands and bodies that is wrought by projecting segments of time in simultaneous or near simultaneous operation. This layered texture of the narrative is what the translation has to capture. Does it?

Let us analyse the opening paragraphs of the story in the Hindi:

Chchajjey par bhooree, jaltee reyt kee parteyn jum gayeen hain. Havaa chalney par alsaaye sey dhool-kann dhoop mein jhilmil se naachtey rahte hain. Ladaayee ke dinon me jo barrack banaye gaye ththey, vey ab ukhaadey jaa rahen hain. Reyt aur malbey ke dhdhooh aise khadey hain maano kachchee sadak ke maathey par gomdey nikal aayen hon.

Khidkee sey sab kuchch dikhta hai. din aur shaam key beech kitney vichitra rangon kee chchaayaayen teelon par phisaltee rahtee hain!

*Duur sey nirantar sunayee deta hai, paththar todney kee masheen ka
shor, daitya ke ghurraaton kee tarah—ghurr-ghurr-ghurr...
Dopahar kee neend key kachchey kagaaron par yeh avaazen halkee
lahron jaisee ththap-ththap takraatee hain.*[3]

Construction and destruction are shown going on together in
those lines. 'Was', 'is' and the faint outlines of a 'will be' lie astir
in them. The 'is' or the present, as the meeting point of the 'was'
and the 'will be' is in the foreground, vivid and passing like the
currents of a stream. The writing is in the present tense entirely,
balancing on its shoulders the combined weights of 'was' and 'will
be'. In the first sentence, '*chchajjey par bhooree jaltee reyt kee parteyn
jam gayeen hain,*' the oppressive weight of heat and sand press at the
walls of your chest, stoked by the adjectives 'bhooree' and 'jaltee'.
The nouns 'chchajaa', 'reyt kee parteyn' and the verb 'jum gayeen
hain' complement the adjectives, make the sand soaked heat seem
an ever present, gritty factor of the milieu. This ever presentness is
worked upon, projected in various ways in the rest of the extract, till
the timeframe of the narrative stretches away beyond the physical
details of the setting. The din of the stone-breaking machine and
the mounds of rubble 'like warts on the brow of the kutchcha road'
('*maano kachchee sadak ke maathey par gomdey nikal aayen hon*')
[Author's translation] dissolve 'at the frail shores of afternoon sleep'
('*dopahar kee neend ke kachche kagaaron par*') [Author's translation].
The chronic depression and low spirits of the characters of the
story—representing the deeper social malaise of ethical uncertainties
that is the foundation of the story—takes over from the external
clamour which is passing, unlike the standing, internal, unrest of
the characters.

Does Geeta Kapur's translation capture this passage from the
immediate present to the gnawing, larger, ever present present? It is the
defining feature of the story. For the most part, one would say, no.

Here is the translation:

Layers of burning sand had settled on the tin roof. When the wind rose,
a bright curtain of sand flapped around the house. The wartime barracks were being demolished, there were mounds of rubble everywhere
and it looked like the dust road had developed lumpy warts.

One could see everything from the window. Coloured shadows slid across over the hillocks all day long. In the distance one heard, continuously, the sound of the stone-breaking machine. Like a growl-ing giant, grr, grr, grr.

Noises came and swept against the brittle edges of afternoon sleep....[4]

Let us consider this section line by line. We shall deal first with what seems a certain laxness of terminology. '*Chchajjey par bhooree, jaltee reyt kee parteyn jum gayeen hain.*' The term used for 'chchajja' is 'tin roof'. Is not a 'chchaajja' just a roofed projection? 'Balcony', 'a gallery', 'eaves', 'an overhang', 'projection', 'the roof of a porch' are the words in McGregor's Hindi–English Dictionary. Why, then, the particularizing, specifying word 'tin'? It does not blend with the key words of the sentence, such as 'bhooree', 'jaltee', 'reyt kee parteyn'. The heat it denotes is metallic, while the heat suggested by these other words is unaided natural heat. Even overlooking this, why or how have these other heat defining words been either left out or become lost of intensity? 'Jaltee' has been retained. But 'bhooree' has been left out. Let us say, not without reason. For 'jaltee reyt kee parteyn'—minus 'bhoorie'—is vivid enough, conveys the same intensity of heat. But 'layers', used for 'parteyn' does not evoke the latter's image of a thing packed yet sharply segregated. It is not easy to translate, simple though it looks. Further, it receives and absorbs the feel of searing heat generated by the words 'jaltee reyt' (with or without 'bhoorie'), as if molten by the proximity of the words, and become almost one with them.

Such a fusion of chemistries does not take place between 'layers' and 'burning sand'. The Hindi phrase, 'bhoorie, jaltee reyt kee partein', in fact, overrides the other words of the sentence, 'chchajja' and 'jum gayeen hain', and stays as the dominant image in the line. When this hellfire heat forms the heart of the narrative, could not—should not—the translator have ensured for it a matching importance in her rendering, whatever sorting out of words she adopts? In addition to 'layers' and 'tin roof', '(had) settled' is the other offender. The Hindi is in the present tense—'jam gayeen hai'—the tense used in the story for the most part. It has a close bearing on the theme of play of time, which is a major propeller of the story. The translator has been inattentive to this special, defining feature of the story all along in her rendering.

Let us come to the second line now. The Hindi runs, '*havaa chalney par alsaaye se dhool kan dhoop meyn jhil-mil se naachtey rahtey hain.*' The lilt of that sentence washes into the ear. The chain of heavy consonants—'dhool kan', 'dhoop meyn', 'jhil-mil se'—which sound like the bols of a kathak recital are irreproducible in English. 'Alsaaye se', in conjunction with 'jhil-mil se', weaves an aura of languor and iridescence that makes 'dhool-kan' and 'dhoop' come even more alive. The verb phrase 'naachtey rahtey hain' is an inevitable climax into which this construct of nouns and adjectives terminates. We want to see the translator grapple with this put-together of sound and suggestion, lyricism and logic, choose words that mirror it. Here is what she says, 'When the wind rose, a bright curtain of sand flapped around the house.' You look for the lambency of 'jhil-mil', the word in the Hindi that twinkles into your attention. You look for the wonder of the minute and microscopic that the word 'dhool-kan' wakes you to, and you look for the pleasurable feel of rhythmic motion that the phrase 'naachtey rahtey hain' bring you. For 'jhil-mil', you find 'a bright curtain of sand'. The carrying word here is 'bright', lacking the tremulous transparency of 'jhil-mil'. It is static and does not wake the silvery quality of sand and sun as 'jhil-mil' does. 'Dhool-kan' has been drained of its sense of puckish play and straitjacketed into the one syllabic word 'sand'. And most inexplicable and incomprehensible of all, 'naachtey rahtey hain' has been mutated into 'flapped around the house'. From 'dancing' ('naachtey rahtey hain'), to 'flapping around', from 'house' (nowhere mentioned in the original), to 'chchajja' (terrace), you strive in vain to see links of some kind, even far fetched, metaphysical ones.

The third sentence is, '*ladaayee ke dinon meyn jo barrack banaye gaye ththey vey ab ukhaadey jaa rahey hain.*' The English runs, 'The wartime barracks were being demolished…' Is 'demolished' the right word for 'ukhaadey jaa raheey hain'? 'Ukhaadnaa' has a cyclical feel to it, a sense of continuity. Its reverse 'lagaanaa' or 'banaanaa' is not far from it. 'Demolished' is a cut-and-dried, once-and-for-all act, with a finality to it. And finalities, as we marked, do not have a place in Verma's writing. In the fourth sentence, again, two segments of time—a 'then' and a 'now'—are in simultaneous action. The sentence runs, '*Reyt aur malbey ke dhdhooh aise khadey hain maano kachchee sadak key maathey par gomdey nikal aaye hon*.' Taking off on the heels of the earlier sentence, it foregrounds the destruction more as, 'reyt aur malbey ke dhdhooh' (mounds of sand and litter), makes more immediate and alive that which is being destroyed. The 'kachchee sadak' (unpaved road) dying minute by minute seems more alive as it lies supine, bearing the indignities being visited on it. The simile '*maano kachchee sadak ke maaththey par gomdey nikal aayen hon*'—as if boils had broken out on its forehead—makes it more alive lying on the brink of death.

This concurrence, this sense of forked time, is what one expects to see reflected in the translation. The translation runs as, 'There were mounds of rubble everywhere and it looked like the dust road had developed lumpy warts.' The word 'everywhere' is not there at all in the Hindi, not even by implication. The locale is specific, clearly defined: the road. Why dilute this specificity? And just 'rubble' for 'reyt aur malbey ke dhdhooh' (piles of sand and rubble) further dilutes the specificity. Sand is the central motif of the narrative here. It cannot be dropped at whim. To sum up, then, the locale is diluted, and the visible, physical signs of destruction are diluted. As a result of these, the image of the road blurs. This, in turn, makes the imagery of bumps broken out on the brow of the road stand loose, not tethered enough to the parent image of the road. Furthermore, the word 'maathaa'— 'brow' or 'forehead'—is left out, emphasizing the blurring of the road, with the result that the English statement lacks the feel of completion it gets in the Hindi.

The acts of omission are compound by acts of commission too; 'it looked like', for instance. A brashness incurs into the narrative from the Americanism, a lanky, slapdash kind of informality out of keeping with the temper of polite yet firm dissent that characterizes Verma's writing. Why not, simply, 'seemed as if?' Then, 'dust road' for 'kachchee sadak'. Again, a populist Americanese going ill with the well-rounded, fully articulated prose style of Nirmal Verma. Would not 'unpaved road' or 'untarred road' or 'unmetalled road' keep the meaning and retain the prose spirit of the original? And 'developed lumpy warts' is just uncouth. 'Gomdey nikal aaye hon' is the Hindi. The speculative tone is marked. In the other two relevant words of the full sentence—'aise' and 'maano'—the speculative line climaxes and terminates with the phrase 'gomdey nikal aye hon', (as though blisters had broken out) [Author's translation]. The 'gomdey' or blisters become the active, causative element in that sentence despite the speculative phrase 'as though', wresting the initiative from the 'mounds of rubble and the road on which they are standing' ('*reyt aur malbey ke dhdhooh aise khadey hain*'). The road, in particular, becomes the passive object at this point. The shift has not been marked by the translator. In her rendering the road seems to have developed the 'lumpy warts' by choice, because it wanted to! The slow, explorative tone of the Hindi, powered by a nimble pitting of shadow against substance and vice versa, and the open ended quality of the narrative this makes for, gets buried by the translator's lack of patience or bent for such shuffling of shadow and substance, for an easy, relaxed accommodation of the shadow into her narrative and leaving it open ended.

And 'lumpy warts' is ugly, plain ugly. Firstly, why the adjective when there is none in the original? And second, 'warts' does not assonate with 'gomdey'. It has a clipped, hard edged texture produced by the letter, 't', and the vowel-less ending, while 'gomdey', the Hindi word, has a liquid sound produced by the letter 'da', the corresponding letter for 'd', and its multi-vowelled build. But both words mean the same, or, practically the same; one might say, both words denote ugly eruptions of the skin. But beyond meaning lies the realm of association, suggestion and sound—all the para-physical joys of literature. Should not the translator be sensitive to these nerve centres of special joy present in the original and strive to reproduce them or help recall them by his/her rendering? This extended feel into the body of the original to capture its pulse and mien does not seem to be part of the efforts of Geeta Kapur.

And now the remaining four sentences of that section, from '*khidkee sey sab kuchch dikhta hai*', to '*dopahar kee neend ke kachchey kagaaron par yeh aavaazen halkee lahron jaisee takraatee hain.*' Again, the 'is' or the present, made visible with its din of machines flows vivid in the foreground, till its collision with the bigger present of chronic inner turmoil caused by invisible forces. The visible, outer present is impersonal. There is no agency in the first two sentences and in most of the last sentence. In the third, the agency of the stone-breaking machine is briefly noted but it is a distant sound, made surreal by its being likened to a demon's growls: '*daitya ke ghurraton kee tarahh – ghurr... ghurr..ghurr...*' This feature of impersonality, of agencyless-ness, has gone totally unnoticed by the translator. 'One could see everything from the window,' she says. The word 'one' demolishes any sense of agencyless-ness. It establishes a doer, an active onlooker's presence playing the mouthpiece of the narrator. It filters into the sentence that follows, making its presence felt strongly, in 'coloured shadows lid across over the hillocks all day long.' It is the voice of the onlooking presence that we hear in those words. But above all, how stolid, staid those words are set against the Hindi! '*Din aur shaam ke beech kitney vichitr rangon kee chchaayaayen teelon par phisalti rahtee hain!*' The first ten words in which are encompassed a childlike wonder and joy at the play of colours down the hill face have been drained and packed thoughtlessly into the two words, 'coloured shadows'. And for the full-fledged, photographic phrase 'din aur raat ke beech', the rendering is a harsh, matter-of-fact, 'all day long'. The sap of the original has been wiped clear.

Anyway, let us forget the verbal shortcomings, and get back to the translator's skimpy reading of the original. Let us get back to the short sighted insertion of the word 'one' into the prose and its far reaching effects. The word occurs again in the next sentence after the one about the play of colours considered above. 'In the distance, *one* heard continuously the sound of the stone breaking machine' (emphasis added). Here was a chance to undo the effect of the word in the preceding sentence. Some slight modifications would have done it. For instance, 'From far away came continuously the din of the stone-breaking machine.' In the Hindi, the sentence joins up with the phrase 'like the growls of a demon, ghurr ... ghurr ... ghurr....' (Author's translation). In the English, the concluding trope-phrase forms a separate sentence and this break emphasizes the erasure of the Hindi's impersonality we noted earlier. The voice of the 'one' stays alive, fortified by the break.

A second reading of the lines confirms this. It runs as, 'In the distance, one heard, continuously, the sound of the stone breaking machine. Like a growling giant, grr ... grr ... grr....' The pitch of voice does not change from one sentence to the other. 'Like a growling giant…' the sentence echoes the manner and voice of the 'one' as the agent of the narrating voice in the preceding sentence. The sentence retains the onomatopoeia used in the Hindi. But how stripped of resonance the English onomatopoeia becomes without the heavy tone of the Hindi, produced by the joint consonant 'g' and 'h'! Of course, this heavy tone is not there in the acoustics of English. But the translator does not seem aware of the difference made by the omission of the 'gh' sound, settling cheerfully for the 'g' sound. 'Like a growling giant, grr…grr…grrr…' her translation goes. It is a buzzing compared to the deep-bellied bass of 'ghurr…ghurr…ghurr…' The 'r's rumble here. They roll, whipped by the rapid bounces of the tongue off the roof of the mouth. If only she had been alive to this inherent difference of tone, of 'svar', she might have incorporated without change, the Hindi onomatopoeia. This kind of transliteration, of free exchange, is particularly possible in non-verbal, onomatopoeic writing. Geeta Kapur has just not made use of the facilities available to her.

From this point, as said before, the physically definable present recedes, and the present of social–psychological–emotional tensions takes over. The shift is subtly but clearly indicated in the succeeding sentence, '*Dopahar kee neend key kachchey kagaaron par yeh avaazen halkee lahron jaisee ththap-ththap takraatee hain.*' (at the low shorelines of midday sleep, these sounds knock lightly like playful waves) [Author's translation]. These sounds, '*yeh avaazen*', the narrative makes clear, level-headed amidst its lyrical sweep. And this small word of everyday import anchors the sentence firmly to the larger present implied in the follwing sentence, '*Taran akbakaakar jag gayee,*'[5] (Taran woke up with a start) [Author's translation]. This key word that gives form and shape to the narrative has been dropped in the English translation. 'Noises came and swept against the brittle edges of afternoon sleep.' The noises seem a general commotion, lost of their individual tones so keenly detailed in the preceding lines. Even the bare addition of the definitive article 'the' would have kept the sentence in place, firmed the context and consolidated the narrative. Then 'swept against the brittle edges of afternoon sleep.' There is a muscular force felt in that line, not there at all in the Hindi. 'Swept' is very different from 'ththap ththap takraanaa' [lightly knocking at] and 'halkee lahron jaisey' (like fleeting waves) [Author's translation]. This telling simile of the waves has been left out in the English. The noises seem more like grating sounds fighting the air than the smooth, gliding things they are in the Hindi. And it is not the 'crumbly edges of an afternoon nap that they knock at like small waves,' (Author's translation) but 'against the brittle edges of afternoon sleep.' 'Brittle'—hardly anything, anyone, is 'brittle', 'breakable' in Verma's fiction. Enduring, long-suffering, yes, as is Taran in 'Maya Darpan'. But nobody, nothing, is in danger of breaking down. The times that oppress and overwhelm, transit to other times. Transition is a keynote in the movement of his fiction. Taran's sleep too, thus, glides over to a collected wakefulness, despite the jerky awakening. In '*Taran akbakaakar jaag gayee*'—'Taran woke up in a flurry'—Geeta Kapur's translation of 'akbakaakar' is 'start'. Does 'start' evoke the same sensation as 'akbakaakar'? Is it not a word too sharp of outline, suggesting a state quickly aroused and quickly over? The two 't's in the word, separated by a single syllable emphasize its short-lived feel. 'Akbakaakar', in contrast, is a roomier word, spacious, suggesting a more lingering state. The sound of a word, one cannot help repeating even at the risk of rousing boredom, has its own story to tell, its own realities of being! And a translator, one repeats, once again risking boredom, has to play it by the ear, has to listen to the voice of the text he is handling, evoke it in his language and prose.

This dearth of hearing becomes a graver fault at those levels of the story where the present operates as the larger present, and bears down on the characters with the weight of history. The events that signify these cumulative aspects of the present are the propellers of the story. The translation, thus, has to capture the essence of these events. Let us, then, consider some climactic moments in the story where this sense of history speaks from within the events being related.

One such moment is centred round the problem of finding a boy for Taran. Her father is fixated on things like status, standing, class and so forth, all of which he has lost, but which still define for him the life of worth or the worth of life. 'Who goes by the family's name these days? It's more than enough if one can find a decent fellow,'[6] Taran's aunt—Bua, as she is referred to all along in the story—protests to the father, in Geeta Kapur's translation. The corresponding Hindi is, '*Oonchey khaandaan ko laykar aajkal kaun baitha rahtaa hai? Achchaa ladkaa milay to sub kuchch hai.*[7] A song of sheer fatigue sings behind those words. Anger and helplessness jostle. And they make the occasion pictorial. We can see the speaker's face, eyes wide, mute with knowledge about the ways of life. We can see her gestures, see the backward sway of hands into the void as she says, 'kaun baiththaa rahtaa hai…?' We see her hand sway back into position with the concluding words, 'to sab kuchch hai'. 'Sab kuchch'—everything worth anything—are loaded words, packed with a lifetime's knowledge of the ways of the society she lives in, and which define her world. We see her form, clothed in faded garments, a wet, pungent odour of cooking and slogging in the kitchen clinging to her person.

Where is this pictorial power in 'who goes by….' and 'more than enough?', you wonder. Where is the trapped, dumb desperation produced by a past dead but still haunting? Can the reader not read the conflict of moods by his own involuntary responses, by his own recalls of cultural references, it may be asked. But is this justification enough for the exercise of translation? The translator has to create the tensions of a bleak, stagnant present and the glimmer of a promising future. It is a skill expected of the translator. 'Oonchey khaandaan' is the other central phrase here, encompassing a time span of 'then' and 'now', of 'those days' and 'these days'. The two lines spoken by Bua constitute, in effect, a panorama of the changes wrought by time. Does the English capture this story of time inscribed into the bone work of the story? Let us see.

'Family name' is the term used for 'oonchey khaandaan'. The latter invokes stateliness, a pride of lineage which is more than money, though money is an important part of it. A sense of history enters the sense of identity of the members of a khaandaan. This in-depth psycho-historical connection with time is not suggested by 'family's name'. The arena seems shrunk, fenced. Why not remove the apostrophe, separate the words with an 'and' between 'family' and 'name' to read 'family and name'? Does it not free the word 'family' of the sense of the here and now, of the particularity that the apostrophe gives it? Then 'who cares?' for 'kaun baiththa rahtaa hai?' Are not the nuances different in the Hindi? The sense of futility, crushing though it is, has not come to the defiant 'to hell with it' state of mind that speaks in 'who cares?' It is an important distinction that a translator should note and re-reflect in his translation, for it makes the sense of a watershed in time, a duality, more felt in the fabric of the story. A nearer rendering, perhaps, would be 'Who sits around day-dreaming of family, name, and so forth?' The pace is closer to the original, for one thing, less hurried, echoes to some extent at least, the heavy drag in the voice of the speaker in the Hindi. Then, 'decent fellow' for 'achchaa ladkaa'. Does not the slangy word 'fellow' jar? It is faceless, the adjective 'decent' does not en-face it. It generalizes it more, makes it taper away into 'any decent guy...' 'Achchaa ladkaa', in contrast, evokes a definite bearing, a certain cast of face, for the phrase carries cultural overtones. Why not just 'a good boy'? The overtones define the term, make it explicit. And finally, 'it's more than enough' for 'sab kuchch hai'. 'Sab kuchch hai' has a sense of thankfulness about it, a sense of gratitude overflowing. The speaker seems to be sending up prayers to the gods. 'Bhagwan ki daya', his speech cords seem to vibrate without words. This play of sound and imagery is very curtailed and clipped in '...it's more than enough'. It smacks of satisfaction, images a brief nod of relief by the speaker at a job over and done with, thank you.

The translator's task, then, to sum up this exercise in deconstruction, is to recreate the measured pace resulting from the recapitulative temper of the narrative. Suppose those two sentences had been rendered thus: 'Who sits around pipe-dreaming of birth and prize genes? Just getting a good boy is prize enough...' It could seem limp, lacking the smart, crisp and off-hand turns of phrase associated with English. 'Who goes by?', 'more than enough', 'decent fellow' might well be liked precisely because of their trendy, racy flavour. But trendiness vogue, e tcetera are no part of Nirmal Verma's prose substance. The word 'fellow', for example, that Geeta Kapur uses, cheapens the fibre of Nirmal Verma's prose. Likewise, in 'who goes by...' and 'more than enough', there is a certain prefabricated quality, a utilitarian approach to the craft of writing that goes ill with the calm, observant, inside–outsider tone that stays in Verma's narrative even in his recounting of extreme situations. The glibness and packaged phrasing that English can supply is among the traps that a translator into that language has to be on guard against. It is one test of his or her own creativity.

Let us now get back to the standing, defining feature of 'Maya Darpan'—its view of time—to which the translator is expected to be alive. A particularly vivid image of multi-limbed time occurs in this early passage of the story:

Itnee umar mey bhee buaa ko sab kuchch yaad rahtaa hai. Lagtaa hai jaise uththte-baiththte, sotey-jaagtey unkee cheytna kee dore baaboo kee dincharya sey judee rahtee hai. Apnee kothree kee dehree par oonghtee rahteen hain bua, aas-paas key kaarya-kalaap sey nirlipt. Is par bhee unhey baaboo kee har zaroorat kaa aabhaas kaisey ho jataa hai, taran kay liye yehee sabsey badaa aashcharya hai.

The pivotal line of that passage is of Bua in a snooze, seated at the threshold of her lean-to. 'Oonghtee rahteen hain', the Hindi says. 'Oonghnaa', meaning a sleep just off the periphery of wakefulness is a recurring motif in the story. In the very early sections of the story, let us recall, the droopy, midday sleep of Taran with its crisscross of reality and fantasy is used as a trope for the crisscross of what is and what is presaged, that forms the plinth of the story. It is a driven, involuntary state, and the language conveys it through vivid phrases that leap out of the text and spin their own imageries, giving added strength to the narrative.

The phrase 'chetna kee dor', for instance, means the nerve cord of awareness. It yanks the reader from the narrative and sets off its own visual frames within him. 'Chetna kee dor', the phrase echoes as images of a cord with live, quivery ends like antennae stream though the reader's mind. Bua's state gets defined and explicated more sharply by this incursion of a sub-stream in the narrative. Similarly, the term 'nirlipt', meaning 'unaffected', 'untouched', 'detached'. Again, images flood the mind, images of a yogic insulation from the outer, physical panorama, which the eyes and postures of the women of the myths invoke. Bua seems a strong, committed woman by this application of the word 'nirlipt' to her. And then, the word 'aabhaas', meaning tremors of knowing, or apprehending. Through these terms of description, not only is the make up of Bua's inner state unfolded, but the span of awareness stretched taut between memories and now, stays in focus.

Does the English contain into itself these thrusts of the Hindi and present a transparent yet composite image of the character, and secondly, the time span and setting that is the keynote of the story? Here is the translation, 'Even at her age Bua remembered everything. It seemed that while she did her chores, or even sat dozing by her door, her attention was tugged about by Babu's every need.'

It is a drastic curtailment. But we do not want to dwell on it, for a clipped, tailored expression does remain a trait of English, even if it is ill used by translators. Nonetheless, we scan the words for suggestions—for 'aabhaas'—of soft endings that open inward into the body of the narrative and map it from within. The phrase 'her attention was tugged about' catches the eye. There is movement in it. It recalls the parent image 'chetna kee dor'. The action of tugging about suggests halts, breaks, during which the imagination can slip into the interiors of the narrative and read a larger design into it. But the concluding phrase '...(by) Babu's every need' rules out the possibility. It is just too finite, and cause and effect are just too closely related to allow speculation. The pity is that this stiff, impenetrable feel of the narrative could have been dispelled by retaining the final phrase of the Hindi, '...taran ke liye yehee sabsey bada aashcharya hai.' It need not have been retained as the final phrase. The rhythm and construction of the English translation allows options. It could have been, 'It seemed, to Taran's unceasing surprise, that whether at her chores, or even just seated and dozing at the doorstep of her kothree, Bua's attention was alive to and tugged at by every need of Babu's.' 'Chetna kee dor" does get accommodated in that rendering, which is the translator's own rendering for the most part. So does the word 'aabhaas', even if in a muted way. The term 'attention' contains it, even if in a distant way. But 'nirlipt', sensuous and pictorial, stays unaccommodated. However, the narrative tone expands and gathers into its range the perspectives of others besides its own. And this gives the narrative some of the spaciousness that characterises the Hindi, invokes its time range.

The discretion to omit words and phrases that translators claim and are allowed, are to be availed of with care, but more than ordinary care is needed in decisions to scissor the crafted prose of Nirmal Verma. One wonders if Geeta Kapur has been alive enough to the inner wirings of 'Maya Darpan', to the functionality of the words that she drops in her translation. In the very early, opening sections of the story, for instance, are these lines, '*sookhee reyt ke kann titeeree dhoop mein motiyon sey jhilmilaa uthtey they. Taran ko lagaa maano uskey daanton ke bheetar bhee reyt charmaraa rahey hon.*'[8] The translation is, 'The sand was ablaze. Taran could feel it crackling between her teeth.'[9] Where is the musical word 'titeeree', describing the sun? Where is 'kann', the word that brings alive the fine-ness of the sand? And where, above all, is 'motiyon sey jhilmilaa uthtey they', the phrase that makes the sun and the sand precious phenomena? Obviously, they seemed dispensable to the translator, ornate insertions made by the writer in a fit of self-indulgence. A few minutes' sober study would have woken Geeta Kapur to the empowerment of the harsh, punishing environment that they effect, which in turn, heightens and makes heavier the standing, gnawing unhappiness of the characters. The gritty effect made by these elite seeming words is a dramatic device, a conscious recourse to anthropomorphism that brings into focus the particular axis of time that is the pivot of the story and on which it stands.

One can argue that the time factor does come across in the narrative. It is encapsulated, one could say, in the line that speaks of Taran looking 'out over the fields where they were pulling down the barracks. Half demolished, they stood around like broken down skeletons.'[10] In the erasure of familiar features of the landscape, and its reemergence in a different form implicit in those lines, the storyline is expressed, one could say. But does one read a translation merely for the story? Do not the aesthetics of the writing being translated matter? Do these aesthetics—the finer points that make a writing literature—not have to be reflected in the translation? A translation is read for reading pleasure as much as for the catalogue information that a particular book in a particular language exists. Geeta Kapur's translation does not set at rest these still contested issues, however reduced in importance word is made in relation to essence. Repeatedly, in one paragraph after another, we read the translated story stripped to the bare essentials, to an everyday level, in marked contrast to the Hindi, where the everyday is infused with the extraordinary, where the elements of nature and the thwacks of machinery are given the human faculties of will and intent. This humanizing of inanimate forces, as we noted earlier, in its turn expands into a more empowered sway of Here and Now. And this immediate and enveloping Now drives the writing mode to the present continuous form.

In not registering, in skipping, this strand of anthropomorphism embedded in the Hindi, the English translation becomes bereft of soul. We see this strongly even in an innocuous seeming line, 'Even as a child she had kept her head bowed before him.'[11] The context is of Bua's undying timidity in the presence of Babuji, her brother. In the Hindi, the timidity is projected as a force overcoming her in the way the wind overcomes a tree. The Hindi is, '*Chchote thee tho bhee bhaiyya key samney sir jhukaa rahtaa thaa*'[12] (As a child too her head stayed bowed in Babu's presence) [Author's translation]. The bowing was a reflex action, the Hindi implies. It came unbidden, called forth by untaught, undismissable forces resident within her. It is the active agent, while she, Taran, is the passive agent, the acted upon. The two are separate. Taran's bowed head seems a factor in itself, distinct from Taran, the girl.

This separation of action from the person acted upon has been wiped out in the English. Action and actor seem logically linked. The hint of compulsion in the bowed head seems a normal degree of compulsion. The play of suggestion that gives the Hindi its rich texture has been expunged.

Similarly, consider this passage where the anthropomorphism has come in for more explicit articulation, Taran '*baraandey kee aavaazon ko nahee suntee, suntee hai to nirbhedya maun ko, jo saarey ghar mein chhaayaa hai, jiskey bheetar yeh aavzen paraayee, aparichit, bhayaavah see jaan padtee hain.*' (Taran does not hear the voices in the verandah, hears the impenetrable silence that lies over the house, swathed in the folds of which, the sounds seem alien, unfamiliar, fear-rousing) [author's translation]. The English runs as, 'The thick silence of the house pressed against her, the voices from the verandah were left floating out there, detached, unfamiliar, a little fearful.'[13] Does the silence in the Hindi at all seem to make this direct, demanding and boorish contact with her, which is there in the 'pressed against her' of the English? It remains a presence, spread over the house like a mantle. 'Chhaayaa rahtaa hai' is the Hindi. 'Chhaayaa' is the operative word

here, meaning 'overspread', immobile but tactile, and never pushy like
the silence of the English that presses against you in a crass physical
pressure. And 'thick silence'? The Hindi silence, 'maun', is 'nirbhedya',
impenetrable. The word gets its force from its negative prefix. Should
not the translator have noted this and selected a negative, prefixed word
for assonance, for camaraderie with the spirit of the original? And then,
in the English, 'the voices from the verandah' are 'left floating out
there, detached, unfamiliar, a little fearful'. In the Hindi, the voices
are presented as existent within the body of the silence, from where—
'jiskey bheetar sey'—they seem alien, unfamiliar and fearsome. The
voices are not left floating out there. 'Paraayee' does not translate well
as 'detached'. 'Bhayaavah see' is more positive than 'a little fearful';
'fearful-seeming' seems nearer. Such disturbances of balance at the
verbal level of word and phrase—at the lexical level—seem fallouts of
the initial shortfalls of the translator noted before. Firstly, her failure
to perceive the invasive power—the anthropomorphism—that the
writer of the original gives the sights and sounds of the environment;
secondly, the intensification of personal memory and personal loss
that this invasion by the environment causes; and thirdly, the resolu-
tion of this tension of Then and Now, of Past and Present, by the
advent of the future. By not perceiving the structural cohesiveness
that this interaction of these facets of time give to the story, and the
way particular words are geared to the highlighting of this structural
feature, the verbal alterations by the translator have good chances of
blunting the drama of time written into the story.

This incomplete—even impaired—vision of the story carries on
to the end. In the original, Taran's breakout from the prison, the
clutches of her past and present, are faintly but unarguably outlined.
She is shown on the threshold of the future, which is far in terms of
physical distance or time, but a certainty because it is there within her
as an embryo. And like an embryo it will attain shape, presence. We
see the varied dimensions of time holding the story, and amalgamate
and give it a flat, unbroken expanse. We also see the motif of sleep
coming in for a round up reiteration. Here is the passage in Hindi,
which we shall consider in instalments for easier reference: '*Khidkee
sey hatkar Taran apney palang par leyt gayee. Thakaan sey palkeyn
bhaaree ho gayee ththeen. Phir bhee dayr tak sona naheen ho sakaa.*'[14]

The English runs as, 'She came away from the window and lay on the bed. Her eyes were heavy but she could not sleep for a long time.'[15] In the Hindi, Taran remains a recipient of sensations she is not able to regulate, and the absence of sleep seems like the action upon her of forces with a will of their own. Sleep finally obliges, as we shall see, and as it does all through the story, by a fitful slumber which is like an epiphany again, in keeping with the pattern established in the story. In the English, Taran's position as a recipient is not dramatized as in the Hindi. The narrative tone is not objective, is not observant of her from the outside as in the Hindi. The narrator/translator is proprietorial about her, speaks in strong, assured tones about her thoughts and feelings, like a parent for her ward.

One feature of the disciplined yet involved objectivity of the Hindi is the absence in it of the pronoun 'she'. Taran is mentioned by name only twice, in the first and third lines of that paragraph. 'Khidkee sey hutkar Taran palang par leyt gayee' (Moving away from the window Taran lay on her bed) [Author's translation]. Thereafter, except for the second reference to her by name a line or two later, all her thoughts and actions are without the motor power of a pronoun. Yet Taran's presence remains felt and is in no way diminished. It stays in close link with the narrator's voice, connected but distinct. This insulation is the springboard for the eventual levelling up of the segments of time portrayed in the story, a levelling up we shall see augured in the passage.

Before coming to it, let us make note of the free usage in the English of the pronoun 'she' for Taran, for gauging the diminishing effect of this upon the narrative. The frontal narratorial emphasis on Taran made by the translator's liberal employment of the pronoun 'she' third persons Taran in a way that is more than a turn of grammar. It affects, as we said, the process of levelling out the segments of time that brings the story to its climax. The Hindi of the climax runs as, 'Ek baar beech mai kachchee neend kaa halkaa saa jhonkaa aayaa ththaa to lagaa thaa jaisey saamney bhaaee khadey hon … vaisee hee shakl thee, vohee udaas see aankheyn….'[16] The autonomous working of the nervous, bodily functions continues in the phrase 'ek baar beech mein kachchee … aayaa ththaa…' The light brush of slumber seems to be indulging in sport with her. It comes to a dramatic heightening in the brief sketch of the brother's face risen from the vapours of daytime slumber, as 'vaisee hee shakl thee… vohee udaas see aankheyn…' The narrative voice changes here and focuses on Taran directly in just the one line, 'Aur Taran deyr tak bhaaee ke baarey mein sochtee rahee thee.' Immediately after, the narrative reverts to the method of telling the story of Taran by viewing it through the operation of a three-headed foregrounded time that unifies into a single vision.

Before coming to these concluding lines, let us consider the English of the lines discussed above:

> Once she was swept by a light save of sleep and dreamt her brother stood before her. That dear familiar face with its lonely eyes…It was so long ago that she had seen him, would she know him now if she ever chanced upon him, all of a sudden?[17]

Once again, the wilfulness of bodily functions and their decisive effect on the workings of mind and intelligence, so defining a feature of the Hindi, is blurred in the English. Look at the difference of stress in the two versions. In the Hindi, 'Ek baar beech mein kachchee neend kaa jhonkaa aayaa thhaa…,' the spotlight is squarely on the 'kachchee neend' (light slumber) and its sweep ('jhonkaa'), which makes it a causative factor. In the English, the spotlight is on 'she', Taran. 'She' was swept by a light wave of sleep…' The whole sentence is passive in construction, 'swept by…' which further diminishes the action of the wave of sleep. The 'neend kaa jhonkaa' is self-propelled, whereas the 'wave of sleep' is activated by the narrator's voice.

Then, the conclusion of the sentence: '(she) dreamt her brother stood before her.' The word 'dream' is a simplification and an over-concretization of Taran's state of mind portrayed in the Hindi. 'Lagaa thaa…' is the phrase in the Hindi. 'She thought' or 'It seemed to her…' are nearer it. This nebulous state condenses step by step along the succeeding lines to a picture of an impending reality, agleam with streaks of certainty. The translator does not seem to have been alive enough to the play of probability and certainty contained in the parent narrative. Continuing from '…(she) dreamt her brother stood before her', she says, 'That dear familiar face, with its lonely eyes…' Again 'familiar face' is too stated a phrase, needlessly paraphrasing the

Hindi, articulating what is best left unarticulated, rich with conjecture. The phrase, 'Vaisee hee shakl' dances with speculations set off in the reader's mind—'Kaisee?' (like what?)—and the speculations buzz, provide a clue in the succeeding phrase 'vohee udaas see aankhen'. The two phrases combine and reiterate the slow tempo and the explorative quality of the narrative.

This rich, satisfying conjunction does not really take place in the English, once again, because of the translator's under-reading of the original text, the lack of vigilance to the bent of mind powering the narrative, and the subtle implications this gives to the words. How does one explain the utter mismatch of 'that dear, familiar face' with 'vaisee hee shakl?' Why, how, the open, loud, positive statement of feelings in the one as against the impersonal, careful understatement of the other? And where above all, is even a hint of the word 'dear' in the Hindi? And then, crowning it all, is the word 'lonely' for 'udaas see'. The speculative spirit and temper of the Hindi suffers a particularly heavy blow here. 'Sad seeming' or 'sad looking' is what is meant here by 'udaas see', not loneliness, and the set, condensed, inward state it denotes as against the fluid, seeking, outward quality of 'sad seeming' eyes.

As said earlier in this analysis, the narrative voice in the Hindi changes focus here. It speaks about Taran directly, stepping out of the wings from where, for the most part, it observes and interprets her. This change of form comprises just one sentence. But this one sentence is important for the added impact it gives to the finale to the story of Taran and the story of time contained in the lines that follow it. It is a spacing, strategic line, a watershed line. The line is, 'Aur Taran deyr tak bhaaee ke baaraey mein sochtee rahee thee.'[18] After this, the narrative reverts to its basic style of telling Taran's story in a closely involved yet objective way. The English has missed out this line. In a way, this can be overlooked. For, on a second reading of the line in the Hindi, it does seem dispensable. The change of narrative manner it introduces need not have been there, you feel. From the sentence preceding it to the one coming after it, it continues as a smooth, sustained depiction of the sway of time and space over the human condition that is the core of the story. Let us read the preceding and succeeding lines without the intervening sentence, deleted in the

English: '...*vaisee hee shakl thee, vohee udaas see aankhen*' (preceding line) '*kitney barson sey unhey naheen dekha hai! Abtak to shaayad voh bilkul hee badal gaye hongey...*' (succeeding line). The flow is maintained. The thematic fulcrum is not affected.

But the English translation, as has been pointed out all along in this essay, has not been particularly attentive to this thematic feature of the story. Throughout, the English has kept Taran in the foreground, tuned its own narrative voice to voice her directly in the conventional way, ignored the sparkle to character and theme that the Hindi's offbeat, indirect approach imparts to the narrative.

In keeping with her own manner of narration, the translator could have retained the line in question. It would have fitted with the rhythm of her prose. This is how it would have read, 'That dear, familiar face with its lonely eyes... Taran stayed awake long, thinking about her brother...It was so long ago that she had seen him, would she know him now if she ever chanced upon him all, of a sudden?' '*Kitney barson sey unhey naheen dekhaa hai...*' is the Hindi for 'It was so long ago that she had seen him...' Are the tones of the two at all in any kind of assonance with each other? The Hindi is negative in construction. '...*naheen dekhaa hai...*' Taran is in a lamenting state, which is negative. The non-seeing of him is the force of the line. '*Kitney barson se...*' remains audible in the ear, brings home the weight of years fruitless and gone. But '*naheen dekhnaa*' (not seeing) is the reigning truth highlighted in the sentence. It is the bigger truth of the two truths of time gone and the non-presence of the brother that make the sentence. And this juxtaposing of phenomena—truths of human being and truths of environment—is the defining feature of the weave of the story.

Should not the translator be alive to such links and networks present in the material he is translating? Does he have the right to dismiss such fusions and lacework, and bludgeon the material into a standard form, a stereotype?

These questions come up again and again in Geeta Kapur's translation. The plaintive tone of '*Kitney barson se...*', with the music and fullness of the Hindi is not there in 'It was so long ago that she had seen him.' The rich tone of the Hindi is struck from the compassion ridden yet judicious manner of the narrative tone, a compound never noticed and hence not even attempted in the English. Could it not have been, say, 'For so many long years he'd been away, out of sight...'? The pause—or break—between 'away' and 'out of sight' that the reader makes without a conscious attempt echoes the same sort of pause between 'kitney barson sey' and 'naheen dekhnaa' that the Hindi too produces involuntarily in the reading.

The suggested rendering may not be acceptable to all, or in fact, may be unacceptable to most. But it is not its acceptability that is the point at issue. The point is the translator's effort, and the perceptions into his material that the effort signifies. The second part of the sentence runs, '...would she know him now if she ever chanced upon him, all of a sudden?' The Hindi is 'ab tak to shaayad voh bilkul badal gaye hon gey...' Where, one wonders, is there any parallel between the two? Why has the English taken the trouble to prise out the suppressed premonition of failure to recognize her brother that can be said to be stirring deep down in the depths of Taran's thoughts? And then, 'if she ever chanced upon him, all of a sudden'! Forget the fact that the premonition in this phrase is felt in the Hindi at a level even deeper than the one about failure to recognize the brother. Even if it had been pronounced, a translator *should* skip it: it is that bald a statement.

The English of those two lines could have been, 'For so many (for all these many?) years he had been out of sight...must have become beyond recognition...' or 'All these many years...out of sight he's been, totally changed...he would be of face...' Of course, there can be more variations. But the point is that the attempt to echo the speech–prose rhythm of the Hindi is palpable in those samples. And this effort, irrespective of its success or otherwise, is what defines a translation, makes it reckonable. The speculative strain of those lines is carried forward into the last three lines of the story. It is tinged with certitude; just tinged. But it is on this certitude that the thrust of the narrative is centred. The tenacious hold of past and present seems set to give way to the future. And a robust, expectant tone of voice rings in the bare recounting of the landmarks of this future. The story of Taran becomes a continuing, evolving story.

Here, the Hindi is, '*Ek dhundhlee see tasveer aankhon ke saamney ubhar aatee hai, kaheen bahut duur chai ke baagon ke jhurmut mey unkaa banglaa chhipaa hogaa. Kahtey hain vahaan steemar par jaanaa padtaa hai. Na jaaney steemar mein baithkar kaisaa lagtaa hogaa.*[19] Phrase by phrase, sentence by sentence, a process of the growth of will and a sense of achievability, a concretization, is seen in this paragraph. Dream is turning into likelihood, and possibly, reality. A foggy picture—'ek dhundhlee see tasveer'—the sentence begins. From 'dhundhlee' (foggy) to 'tasveer' (picture) is the first leg in the process of dream becoming reality. The phrase 'Ubhar aatee hai' (rises into view) which follows 'tasveer' reinforces the sense of the abstract becoming concrete. 'Ubhar Aanaa' (to rise up) is a firm statement of a firm act. The concretization is more open and stated in the next sentence, *'chaai ke baaghon kay jhurmut mein unkaa banglaa chhipaa hogaa'* (among the dense plantations of tea, his bungalow would be lying hidden) [Author's translation]. 'Chaai kay baag', 'banglaa' are all solid objects, set in a clear, recognizable habitat. And most importantly, in the phrase 'unkaa banglaa chhipaa hogaa', the narrative voice merges conclusively with, lends muscle to, and thereby externalizes Taran's interior monologue, and gives it the stamp of imminent actualization. This sense of near certainty deepens and a near-firm map of the future sketches itself out in the concluding two lines of the story, *'kahtein hain vahaan steemar par jaanaa padtaa haik. Naa jaaney steemar mein baithkar kaisaa lagtaa hogaa'* (You have to go in a steamer to go there, they say. Wonder what it feels like to go in a steamer) [Author's translation].

The decisive word in those two lines is 'steemar'. It breathes movement, a motion ahead, onward and charted. It symbolizes time and character shaken out of their stupor, become mobile again. And Taran's muted, monologueing voice, leavened by the acclaiming tones of the narrative voice, wings out with the hope filled momentum of the steamer. Time becomes a continuum, ironed of seams. On its waves, human aspirations ride with faith despite heavy odds.

Does the English unfold into a matching mood of this liberating yet thoughtful exultation? Here's the relevant paragraph:

> And then it all came floating before her eyes.... Somewhere very far away, hidden in the shades of a plantation, her brother's house. They say you have to go aboard a steamer to get there ... wonder how it feels to travel on a steamer![20]

The last line, with its two sections, does reflect the mood of elation risen above forebodings that marks the Hindi. The way this has been accomplished is so different from the Hindi that it calls for examination. In the Hindi, the romance of 'dhundhlee see tasveer' (faint picture) of the brother's bungalow nestling among tea plantations glides smoothly to the other romance of travelling by steamer. The two romances mingle and help silhouette the landscape of the future forming in Taran's mind, as *'Naa jaaney steemar may baithkar kaisa lagtaa hogaa.'* A decisiveness rings in the voice despite its speculative streak. The journey seems a certainty. In the opening words, 'naa jaaney', the speculative streak lingers. But in the concluding words 'steemar may baiathkar kaisaa lagtaa hogaa', the feel of the enclosed, defined space of the steamer is so strong that it overrides the speculative strain of 'naa jaaney…' The image of the steamer coursing over turbulent waters stays solid and meaningful before the eye. It becomes a metaphor for the statement contained in the story, that time moves, moves on, and halts are illusory. Character and events are illumined, redefined by the metaphor. Taran too emerges redefined.

This close weave of mood, character, happening and underlying meaning is not felt in the English. The effectiveness of its last line, referred to earlier, comes from the abrupt, and unplanned seeming, shift in the tone of the narrative voice. The sleepy, day-dreaming tone of the lines before—'And then it all came floating before her eyes… Somewhere very far away, hidden in the shades of a plantation, her brother's house'—makes a sudden jump to directly voicing Taran, 'They say you have to go a road a steamer to get there…Wonder how it feels to travel on a steamer!' The jump pays off. The volume of Taran's voice, the open, exteriorized quality to it, come about by the usage of the solid, third person plural 'they', accords with the animation of voice in the Hindi text. There is more body to her animation in the Hindi. Part of the reason could be the straight flow of the last but one sentence to the last, the two sentences where Taran's surge of buoyancy is felt strongly and conclusively. There are no dots between the sentences that would suggest uncertainty or doubt. 'Kahtey hain', the first line begins, rising clear and firm of voice, saddled on the consonant rich words, leaving behind the romantic haziness of the imagery of 'swarming tea plantations and the brother's house nestled amidst them' ('*chaai ke baagon ke jhurmut mein unkaa banglaa chhipaa hogaa*'), which comprises the preceding line. The firm tone of voice carries over to the solid, concrete image of the steamer, and then gets infused with the anticipatory joys of the steamer journey materializing that stir in Taran's musings: '…steemar mai baithkar kaisa lagtaa hogaa'.

This smooth establishment of the optimistic state of mind is breached by the dots between the two sentences inserted in the English. The breach is restored, granted. The last sentence does emerge astir with a sense of imminence, with a feeling that a steamer voyage is in the offing. But there is a scattering of mood, that cannot but evoke comparison with the Hindi where the pitch is sustained, unbroken, and thereby of more impact. Why have the dots at all? The mood comes across smooth and unimpeded without them, as 'They say you have to go aboard a steamer to get there…wonder how it feels to travel on a steamer!' Dots such as these are stylistic devices that affect the overall impact, if not the meaning, and the Hindi has them in plenty. The translator, therefore, has to be vigilant about using them on his own, thinking that they are a general facility open to him as much as to the prior writer.

Let us, however, forget the dots. The mood does get established in those two sentences, even if thinned somewhat. We *can* put it down as a plus point for the translation. But can the success of individual sentences make up for the non-emergence in the final count, of a collective, cohering statement? That whole paragraph in the Hindi is, as we saw, a rich junctioning of character, mood and circumstance that levers out and redefines the founding statement of the story that time is ever-moving, and timeless. Doubts about the junctioning taking place set in, in fact, from the very first sentence of the paragraph. The Hindi of that line is, '*ek dhundlee see tasveer ubhar aatee hai,*' And the English is, 'And then it all came floating before her eyes…' What is the concord between 'ubhar aanaa' and 'floating'? The motions evoked by the two terms are different. 'Ubhar aanaa' suggests an emergence from spaces unseen, from the depths of the mind. 'Floating' suggests a materialization from somewhere just off the screen of vision.

Further, the speculative mode is not completely eliminated from the sentence. It says, 'unkaa banglaa chchipaa *hogaa*' meaning '*would* be

lying hidden' (emphases added). The speculative tone is reined in by
the realistic image of tea plantations evoked by 'chaai ke baagh'. The
abstract and the material make a satisfying chiaroscuro of the now and
the near-at-hand. The English dispenses with the speculative strand
altogether and presents a living, reigning reality. 'And then *it all* came
floating before her eyes' (emphasis added). The term 'it all' makes
the picture of the house amongst tea gardens a concrete, experienced
reality recovered by the normal tug and pull of memory. No further
development of mood or sense is possible after that definite picture.

This makes us redefine the sense of appropriateness that we said
earlier, the last sentence gives us. It parallels the Hindi, we said. But
when considered in context with the previous sentence(s), it is more
a carryover of the sense of the definite already established in them.
There it seems a flaw. But here, in the last sentence, it finds proper
anchorage—to use a nautical simile—in keeping with the image of
the steamer prominent in that line. We admit the effectiveness of
that line. But it only makes us repeat our central question voiced
earlier: can the success of individual lines cancel out the thinness of
the English text, resulting from the thinness of the translator's reading of the Hindi?

Nirmal Verma's writing calls for even greater aliveness from the
translator to the nerve centres beating below the word in his prose. The
simplicity of Verma's prose is translucent. It has to be deciphered, read
and worked into the rerendering. Otherwise the simplicity becomes
superficiality.

▌ Notes

1. Kapur, Geeta. 1986. 'Maya Darpan', *Maya Darpan and Other Stories*. Three
   Crown Series. New Delhi: Oxford University Press. Trans. of. Nirmal Verma.
   1965. 'Maya Darpan', *Jalti Jhadi*. New Delhi: Rajkamal Prakashan.
2. Verma, Nirmal. 1965. 'Maya Darpan', *Jalti Jhadi*. New Delhi: Rajkamal
   Prakashan.
3. Ibid., p. 24.
4. Kapur, p. 113.
5. Verma, p. 24.
6. Kapur, p. 124.
7. Verma, p. 36.

8. Ibid., p. 25.
9. Kapur, p. 114.
10. Ibid., p. 113.
11. Ibid., p. 114.
12. Verma, p. 25.
13. Kapur, p. 116.
14. Verma, p. 45.
15. Kapur, p. 132.
16. Verma, p. 45.
17. Kapur, p. 132.
18. Verma, p. 45.
19. Ibid., p. 45.
20. Kapur, p. 132.

Chapter 4

The Implications of Bilingualism

The proposition being put forward in this study of the English translation[1] of Vijay Tendulkar's widely acclaimed play in Marathi, *Shantata! Court Chaaloo Aahey!*[2] is based broadly along the following considerations. Firstly, that English has acquired a coopted status with Indian languages. We see this at an obvious, everyday level in the free use of English terms in Indian language writings and speech habits. Purists would see this as a hangover of the subaltern make up. Maybe it is that. But it can also be seen as the ex-colonized's rising sense of equanimity with the ex-colonizer's language, as a process of decolonizing through a state of reciprocity, free of coercion or capitulation. The Hindi version of the play[3]—which I have taken as my source text since I am not Marathi speaking (an allowable option in our multilingual milieu)—abounds with English terms, speech phrases and even popular English jingles and ditties. With one or two exceptions, the characters are English-speaking Indians, moving easily into and out of the language. Here are a few samples:

> 'Humbug! *Tabiyat ko meri kya huaa hai?* I'm fine, perfectly fine!'
> —Benare (Act One, *Khaamosh! Adaalat Jaaaree Hai!*
> [hereafter K!AJH]).

Immediately after, she hums and claps to a song:

> 'O I have a sweet heart/who carries all my books/he plays in my doll's house/and says he likes my looks....'

> 'Here it is! *Mil hee gaya aakhir!*'
> —Sukhaatmey (Act One, K!AJH)

> 'O, gosh! *Dekhoon kahan hai!*'
> —Ponkshe (Act One, K!AJH)

'Right! *Tum to khaasey budhdhimaan maaloom padtey ho!*'[4]
                                          —Benare (Act One, K!AJH)

This free employment of English terms in Hindi speech situations is seen operating at a subtler level too. Benare recasts into Hindi the English saying 'the hand that rocks the cradle ...' in free play with the word 'hand'. She substitutes for it the term 'string'. 'Mrs Paalney Ki Dor', she calls Mrs Kashikar, one of the few characters in the play untouched by English. The Hindi-izing of the phrase adds to the irony and banter of that passage, and enriches it linguistically, it can be said safely. This coopted status of English in our overall language sensibility has implications for English translations of Indian language texts, or in official terminology, bhasha texts. This is the second statement that this study of *Silence! The Court is in Session* makes, and elaborates upon, hopefully in a convincing way.

Before going deeper into these two aspects of the operation of English in our processes of self-definition and cognition, let us take the English translation at a more primary translatorial level. At the level, say, of the way it tackles the culturalism cum mannerism, 'jee', that Mrs Kashikar uses to address her husband. '*Hai ki nahi, jee?*'[5] she asks him, seeking corroboration for something she has just said. The English is, 'Didn't I, dear?'[6] This is just too English a decorousness for a dyed-in-the-wool desi brand of domesticity. The 'jee' word trips up the translator again soon after, when Mrs Kashikar says, apropos train timings, '*Suno jee, yeh Balu kah raha hai...*'[7] The English is again, 'Dear, Balu here says...'[8] The cultural dissonance between 'jee' and 'dear' is far too strong, far too pronounced, to make the reader desist from examining the rendering a little more. 'Jee' has to it a tone of prescriptive, seemly, wifely tentativeness of speech, a proper, halting manner. 'Suno jee!' Mrs Kashikar begins, and seems to be collecting herself before proceeding farther. The tentativeness lingers yet. '*Yeh Balu kah raha hai...*' she procrastinates, bringing a third party into the picture before saying what she really has to say. This hedging, further, is an essential feature in the portraiture of her personality as the play progresses. She flings it aside when she makes her fierce attacks on Leela Benare and on the culture of the strong, single woman. The ferocity of these attacks stands out in the straight, bitchy figure she cuts. Even before she launches on her heavy, hammer and tongs

attacks on the girl, her interactions with her are insulting and belittling. 'Kyon ree, Benare...'⁹ or 'Ai, Benare!'¹⁰ are her usual opening
words in all her dialoguing with her. She addresses her in the second
person singular form 'tu', untranslatable into English. The real Mrs
Kashikar is seen only in her treatment of Benare. And the venom of
this self and behaviour of her comes as a dramatic contrast to her
sweet acquiescent behaviour vis-à-vis her husband. The acquiescence,
therefore, is important for reasons of dramatic impact. The relevant
words have to echo in the reader's ears with retrospective ironic force
in counterpoint to the tart manner of Mrs Kashikar with Benare.

But the English translations—'Didn't I, dear?' for 'Hai ki nahee, jee?',
or 'Dear, Balu jeer says...' for 'Suno jee, yeh Balukeh raha hai...'—as
pointed out earlier, do not strike the right note. They cannot, for they
do not get the right sustenance from their language. The language *is*
their cultural alien. How is the translation to get round this built in
alienness?

One way out could lie in giving directions for voice modulation
or some behavioural gesture to the speaker. 'Dear, Balu here says...'
could then be written as 'Listen! (attuning voice to respectful mode)
Balu here says...' and 'Didn't I, dear?' could be 'Didn't I, tell me,
didn't I? (Glancing coyly at Kashikar)'. This could seem inappropri-
ate, unsatisfying. Other ways of dealing with the problem may also be
devised. But the translation has to suggest that effort has been made to
deal with the problem, that the translator is alive to the problem. Part
of the pleasure of reading a translation lies in sensing the efforts made
by the translator to get round the problems of transference and relocation. Adarkar, one feels, has not ventured too far beyond the verbal
levels of the terms concerned. She has not, for the most part, deep-read
their role in the inner dramatic web of the play. The same thing can
be said about the translator's handling of the terms of address used
by Mrs Kashikar for Benare; for the most part it is not imaginative.
The exceptions which we shall deal with, in addition to giving reading
pleasure, affirm the viability of the method proposed earlier: of doing
away with the translation-resistant words, isolating their implications
and incorporating them into the body of the translation.

Mrs Kashikar says at one point, *'Mai bataatee hoon, jee! pandrah second huey hain.'*¹¹ The English is, 'I'll tell you. It was fifteen seconds.'¹²
The 'jee' is omitted, or elided. This omission or elision is a form of

negotiating the culturalism of the word. Yet, the tartness of Mrs Kashikar's reply comes across. The tartness is unmistakable in the Hindi. The English, let us say, is acid or dour. But these differences spell a continuum, and not a break of basic spirit as in the earlier instances cited. The omission is a strategy, a tactic, a device—what you will—adopted by the translator. And this kind of close oarsmanship in the waters of the original text, this reconnoitering, is expected of the translator.

Another instance of imaginative and apt rendering is seen in the following lines of dialogue between Mrs Kashikar and Benare:

> Mrs K: *'Achchaa-achchaa! School kaisa chal raha hai tera?.'*
> Benare *(Chaunk-kar)*: *'chal kahaan rahaa hai? Vaheen kaa vaheen hai.'*[13]

The English is:

> Mrs K: 'Well, what does your school have to say for itself?'
> Benare (Carefully): 'My school says nothing.'[14]

The word 'tera' is untranslatable into English, even more than 'jee'. The translator recognizes this, does not attempt approximations or substitutions, but foregrounds the snickering insolence of the question through a different way of querying, such as '...have to say for itself?' It is a very English way of conveying lack of respect, of making it clear to the other person, 'I'm the one that counts here, so there!' All the contempt in the word 'tera' gets pumped into the query, depersonalizing Benare in a chilly, English way. And exactly as in the Hindi, Benare lampoons the quizzing by word play, and drags it to a literal level. '*Chal kahaan rahaa hai, vaheen ka vaheen hai,*' for '*kaisa chal raha hai?*' is matched in the English by 'My school says nothing,' for 'what does your school have to say...?' Of course, subtler implications are present, as indicated in the respective Hindi and English terms inserted as acting directions in the two texts: 'Benare (chaunkkar): ...' in the Hindi, and 'Benare (carefully): ...' in the English. But these subtleties need not concern us here. The point is that by a more-than-the-word reading of the bhasha text, whether Hindi or Marathi, the English translation has got round the problem of the untranslatability of the pronoun 'tera'.

The translator's handling of the other untranslatable terms present in the Hindi, alas, is not as ingenious; in fact, far from it. *'Kyon ree, Benare...'*[15] Mrs Kashikar calls out to Benare in the heckling tone she reserves for her. The English is, 'I say, Benare....'[16] It is a grating dissonance which we feel between the two. The slangy incivility of the Hindi stays defiant and unaffected by the urbanely off-hand tones of the English. It might be argued that the slangy, provocative tone of the Hindi can be injected into the English by throw of voice, by the tonal inflexions of the actor calling out 'I say...' But the translation has to be read too, in addition to being enacted, being seen. And many readers may never get to see it enacted. A translation operates and engages the attention at the reading level primarily, alerting the comparative, critical faculties of the reader. The reading of a translation is a double-aspected job: firstly, reading it as a product of the target language, and secondly, as a refraction of the parent text, both interacting closely with each other. Into this intense and fine tuned exercise, to bring in parameters like acting skill or dramatic improvisation is to make it more complex. The written translation comes to the reader, in effect, as an artefact on its own. To perfect this artefact, nullify its shortfalls, only written means can be had recourse to. And this is where the method of writing down acting directions within parentheses, discussed earlier, before or after the dialogue line, commends itself again for consideration. To recapitulate the lines, then, the Hindi is, *'Kyon ree, Benare! (joodey mey lagey gajrey ko tatolkar).'* The translation is, 'I say Benare... (stroking the garland in her hair).' The word 'stroking' is not quite the word for 'tatolkar'. But that is by the way. Our real purpose here is to seek a word or exclamation as near the needling tone of *'kyon ree, Benare!'* as possible, and then supplement it, in parenthesis, with directions for a body language that evokes this mix of amusement and malice present in the Hindi. One option could be as:

Mrs Kashikar: E, Benare! (Twirling round her finger the garland in her hair. Voice swift and supercilious). Very nearly got a garland for you too, I swear! (Tossing her head, shaking out the garland, rewinding it into her hair) No? (Turning to her husband with a coy air, eyes fluttery) No?

The off-hand, couldn't-care-less tone demanded of the actress playing the role and the airy, dressing table gestures prescribed for her *could* add up to the ingrained rudeness of '*kyon ree, Benare!*' A variation of this approach, somewhat radical, suggests itself for another stubbornly vernacular interjection employed by Mrs Kashikar for Benare, as 'A ("a" as in "happy", "apple") Benare....' She calls out to the girl in peremptory tones, detaining her without second thoughts or as much as a by-your-leave while she is making her way elsewhere across the stage. The line could run, '*A Benare, yeh chautha gavaah kaise lag rahaa hai tujhey? Kyon!*' Apart from the belittling pronoun 'tujhey' that is untranslatable into English, the word 'kyon', as used here is another stumbling block. 'Go on, answer the question, and no airs now!' Mrs Kashikar is saying in effect, with that one word. We can picture her, eyes thrust masterfully at the girl, body held stiff in her usual confronting way with the girl. The as yet restrained taunt in 'A Benare...' rings more openly in her voice with her query, 'kyon?'

In the translation, thus, the taunting tone and the masterful manner have to sound, set in, with the very opening words, 'A Benare...' to climax with force with the single word 'kyon', occurring after the sentence, 'yeh chautha gavaah...' The English is, 'Look here, Benare, (she comes over) what do you think of this gentleman as the fourth witness?'[17] 'Look here...' is not bad, not dismissible, as a form of address curt and bullying, provided one reads the translation as an original composition in the language. But as has been implied all along in this essay, a translation cannot claim this kind of independence. It has to invoke the original either through echo of sound, assonance of tone, or through calculated deviations that highlight the original. More specifically, as has been held in this essay, the bitchiness of Mrs Kashikar vis-à-vis Benare is dramatically important in the final statement of stark misogyny that emerges from the play. We set the bitchiness against the honeyed tones adopted by the speaker—Mrs Kashikar—in her parleys with all the others. And we perceive it as a build up to the venomous and womanist attacks that she makes on Benare in her depositions at the trial. 'A Benare', 'Kyon ree Benare...' and so forth, thus, call for translating that hits the bull's eye, highlights the dramatically important feature of mala fide contrasts that mark Mrs Kashikar's character. English equivalents of terms such as these, we can safely assume, are not available. The method of elision, considered earlier, calls for ingenuities not easily commanded.

A solution seems possible by straight and bare incorporation of the resistant words into the English, again, with acting directions. 'A Benare…!' could be brought in verbatim into the English with directions of voice usage to the actor, to neutralize the very un-English throaty quality of the phrase. The actor could be directed to say the words fast, pause a fraction of a minute, lean towards Benare with a taut, emphatic set of the body, and fire her question, 'How 'bout him (gesturing at him with an upward tilt of face) as the fourth witness? Eh? What d'you think?' The words, the manner of speaking them and the body language *could* unite to convey the sense of the dismissive behaviour of Mrs Kashikar with Benare.

Such attempts at interlingual renderings, either by incorporating Hindi terms in an English text, or vice versa, examined in the beginning of this essay, point to larger implications about our lingua franca. One of these implications, of relevance to this essay, and again, dealt with in the beginning, is the coopted status of English in the Indian languages, from the osmosis of their thinking. To get an idea of the privileging of English and western ways of apprehending our social realities that we have come to accept, let us study our reactions as we watch or read the drama of Benare. This drama, like all powerful dramas, etches itself down to a stark mimetic, imageric level of evocation. The distraught face of Benare, and the supplicating gestures of her hand, body and eyes that are thrown off by her declamatory, impassioned voice, stay foregrounded in the reader/viewer's field of awareness. This image that reiterates the powerful, still living, social realities of Benare's plight surmounts language, and it ensures strong reader/audience engagement with the play. Not only do we feel a nearness and alterity with Benare, we feel urged to articulate her state, voice her and express her in words that complement the realities conveyed by the two texts of the play.

It is this duologue we are driven to with the written texts and the archetypal image of Benare that best illustrates our equidistance between English and our bhashas. Let us take this extract from the long, very long, monologue by Benare that comes towards the end of the play that begins with the stage direction '*bhai sey mooh chchipaakar*

vyaakul svar mein' to *'tan sey naheen to man se to mar hee gayee hoon.'*
Some twenty lines:

*'kabool kartee hoon mainey paap kiya hai. Mainey maa ke bhai se prem
kiya hai. Magar ghar ke bandhdhanon ke beech—meri khiltee gadraatee
huyee deh kee bahaar mein akela vohee to mere kareeb aayaa ththaa—usee
ney to us bahaar kaa din-raat bakhaan kiya thaa…laad kiya, dulrayaa..
mujhey kya pataa thaa ki hriday se jiske saath ekroop honey kee teevr
ichchaa hoti ho…jiske keval sampark se sampoorn jeevan saarthak-saa
lagtaa hoo voh agar maa kaa bhaayee hai to sab kuch paap mey badal
jeeyega. Arey kul chaudah saal ke to ththee main, paap kiya hota hai yeh
jaantee bhee nahee ththee mai—maa ki saugandh. (chchotee bachchee
kee taarah bilakhkar rote huyee) mainey vivah ke liye zid kee thee to sirf
isliye ki auron kee tarah ek sukhee grihasti kee kalpana merey man mey
bhee thee. Magar sabke saath meri ma ne bhee uska virodh hee kiya. Mere
purush eum dabaakar bhaag gaya. Itna krodh aayaa us par ki jee chaahaa
sarey bazaar khadaa karey uska munh tod doon. Thook doon uskey mooh
par. Par us samay mai bahuat chhotee thee, kamzor thee, anjaan thee.
Apney ko mrityu ke havaaley karney ke liye ghar ke chhajjey pr se kood
padi. Magar maar naheen sake. Sochaa tan se naheen sake to man se to
maar hee gayee hoon.'*[18]

The English of that section is:

'(Terrified, she hides her face and trembles) It's true, I did commit a
sin. I was in love with my mother's brother. But in our strict house,
in the prime of my unfolding youth, he was the one who came close
to me. He praised my bloom every day. He gave me love…How was
I to know that if you felt like breaking yourself into bits and melting
into one with someone—if you felt that just being with him gave a
whole meaning to life—and if he was your uncle, it was a sin! Why, I
was hardly fourteen! I didn't even know what sin was—I swear by my
mother, I didn't! (she sobs loudly like a little girl.) I insisted on marriage. So I could live my beautiful lovely dream openly. Like everyone
else! But all of them—my mother too—were against it. And my brave
man turned tail and ran. Such a rage—I felt such a rage against him
then—I felt like smashing his face in public and spitting on it! But I
was ignorant. Instead, I threw myself off a parapet of our house—to
embrace death. But I didn't die. My body didn't die! I felt as if feelings were dead.'[19]

The language is stage-y, in both the Hindi and the English. Of course, the play is meant for the stage, and what seems stage-y in print might well get neutralized by visual/cultural factors. But it is the translation that is the take-off point for this essay, and as has been pointed out also, a translation is primarily considered at the lingual level, even for saying that the lingual level by itself is not enough. Furthermore, the subsided, and hence, more complex, role that language comes to have in our interactions with Benare and the continuing topicality of the social realities she projects, makes the language-level consideration of the play as, if not more, important as a consideration of its stage worthiness.

Let us take the lines in that section quoted above, where Benare's aggressive defence of herself rises to a pitch so much melodramatic that the reader cannot absorb it, even keeping in mind the moderation it might undergo from stage delivery. The lines meant are the seven lines from the stage direction *'bhai sey mooh chchipaakar'* to *'jiskey keval sampark sey sampoorn jeevan saarththaksaa lagtaa ho voh agar maa kaa bhai hai to sab kuchch paap mey badal jaayega,'* or 'Terrified, she hides her face and trembles' to 'how was I to know...that if you felt that just being with him gave a whole meaning to life—and if he was your uncle it was a sin!' in the Hindi and English, respectively. Would she not know? A counter interrogation sets off within you on the heels of those declamatory pronouncements. Would not the secrecy of the meetings and their raptures rouse guilt, the sense of sin, of wrongdoing in the girl? Benare's pleadings leave you unmoved. You go deaf to their din. You stay cool to her cry *'Arey, kul chaudhah saal kee to thee mein!'* ('Only fourteen I was, no more, only fourteen!') [Author's translation]. You continue cool, unmoved, at *'Paap kya hota hai yeh jaantee bhee naheen ththee mein,'* till 'maa kee saugandh', at the end of the line, at which you halt. It is a powerful oath, so laden, saturated with collective ideation that it defies melodrama, persuades a naiveté not put on, however unbelievable. But a phrase, even a potent one such as this, cannot undo the bombast of the lines gone earlier, cannot galvanize them in any true sense. You remain cool to the clamour of the language, but not to the story of Benare, or to the reality of Benare independent of the hyperboles of language and narrative. You trim and pare the language, pluck at the deposits of raw truth below its thick folds, and plead for Benare, interpret her in the light of this truth.

Yes, you reason, the line between sin and virtue *can* get blurred in the harshness of these realities, in the special rigour with which they are applied to women. And once this happens, Benare seems a type, no longer an individual of distinct physique or feature. The words come clear of their tonal wraps, stand stripped to the down-to-earth realities that give them their inner veracity and physiognomy. The concrete, immediate reality of the play-on-stage gives way to a wider, graver and immanent reality. The sob stuff coating Benare's speech evaporates, and we engage with her at a conceptual and existential level. Yes, these disclosures of hers are not dismissible; a parallel line of reasoning raps itself out on the anvil of your mind. A taboo can seem less of a taboo, this reasoning goes; the breaking of it can seem justifiable when weighed against the mental torture that the breach can help end. Benare's protestations that she had no inkling that the blood link between her and the man made her act a particularly heinous sin lose their hard-to-believe strain, which becomes inconsequential in the face of this all-pervading, oppressive reality.

The run-of-the-mill feel of the monologue lifts, and lifts explosively, towards the end when she groans—'veydnaa sey vyaakul hokar' (beside herself with anguish) is the script direction—that she wants her body. Despite the situations it leads her into, she wants it for the sake of the life growing in it. That life needs a mother, has the right to a father. It needs a home, needs care and legitimacy. In this open and pragmatic upholding of the body that Benare makes, she is echoing a major proposition of the women's empowerment struggle, that the stern ideals of service laid down for women, amounting to abrogation by her of her own body should give way to the concept of her proprietorship over her body. Benare now seems like a representative figure posited in feminist discourses.

The language of the original (the Hindi in this case) is powerful here. Short sentences with refrains –'usey ghar *chaahiyay,* prathishththaa *chaahiyay...*'[20] ('He must have a mother...a father to call his own'[21]) strike up with telling force, set off by the emotional density packed in the lines just preceding '*yeh shaareer mujhey chaahiye...sachmuch chaahiyey...*'[22] ('I want my body now for him—for him alone'[23]) Sheer acting skill can add to the effect. Not that specific stage directions are given to regulate the voice to dramatic pitches, thereby charting the overall emotional orchestration of the passage. No specific directions are there in the printed versions. At one place, the monologueing first person voice turns upon itself, becomes its own you, reverting to a consolidated first person voice a little later. No specific stage directions for voice modulation are given in the printed version, as said. But the voice dynamics undergoes alterations on its own in these places, audible even in print.

The spell cast by the frenzy of the prose, the reverberating passion wrung by sheer writing acumen and sound theatre instinct, is not the deciding factor in the grip of the drama of Benare upon our mind. The deciding factor, as has been reiterated in this essay, is the savage and grim factuality of the circumstances being dramatized on the stage. The play, with all its force of language, subsides in the reader/viewer's spectrum of awareness, in the presence of this stark, ground reality. It is with this breathing, envoiced presence which we too, Benares in the mass, have internalized, that we interact and treat as touchstone, as we hear the dramatic outpourings of Benare on the stage.

In what language do we carry on this interaction? Some form of communication through speech has to be there in such interactions, however much of a construct the interactee is. The language is both mother tongue and English. For the construct is a product of articulations in all the languages of this country, in a pedagogic equation vis-à-vis English equivalents and words of summing up flash into the mind from the imagery thrown up by the Hindi declamatories. Take these lines, '*yehee hai voh sharer jisney tapkar tujhko ek atishay sukhdayee svaargik tripti diya tha…yehee hai voh jisney tujhey shareer sey parey—bahot oonchey divyalok menh us kshann pahunchaa diyaa thaa*'[24] ('It was your body that once burnt and gave you a moment so beautiful, so blissful, so near to heaven!'[25]). 'Atishay', 'Sukhdaayee', 'Svaargik'—the high-powered words explode and blossom in the mind like fireworks, and configure as the body ('shareer') rocked and stilled in a swoon by the transporting, ecstatic state denoted by the words. English co-words or co-phrases streak out from the beds of the Hindi and stand unfurled as subtitles. 'Ultimate Satisfaction', the term write-speaks in your mind. 'Given by the body': '(The) Ultimate satisfaction given by the body.' It completes itself, and you read the many faces of the reality lying below the drama on the stage in alternating flashes of Hindi and English. Or, take these lines, '*maaatrutva nishkalank aur pavitra hona chahiyey. Us pavitrataa mey daag lagaakar tumney paramparaon kee neev mein jo baarood lagaayee hai…*'[26] ('Motherhood should be spotless and pure. By sullying that purity, the explosive that you have planted in the foundations of tradition…') [Author's translation]. The sheer bombast of these lines takes your breath away. 'Matrutva', 'Nishkalank', 'Pavitr'—the heavy, morality-laden words boom in your head and shying away from their stentorian harangue, you reach for their simpler, less culture-crossed English equivalents, such as 'Motherhood', 'Spotless', and 'Pure', respectively. All are not free, to the same degree, of the religious–cultural baggage you wish jettisoned, and the terms secularized. 'Motherhood' comes closest to it; uncomplex, denoting a state of simple fulfilment. 'Spotless' and 'Pure' have undertones—if not overtones—of chastity and body-linked scruples that feminist discourses want redefined. But their injunctional element, the scare-quotient of all the three words, is still much less than that of their Hindi counterparts. You set these friendlier terms and terminology vis-à-vis the Hindi, and acquire the polemical sinews to question and make answerable, even if not vanquish, the face of gender-based absolutism that stares from the Hindi terms. A fast alternating sequence of Hindi–English is set off within you as you read or hear those lines.

English is thus an enabling and buttressing factor in our full apprehending and absorption of the stern reality below the drama of Benare. And it is with this prior endorsement and empowerment that the English rendering of the play done by Priya Adarkar comes to us. It makes the tart note—rising to defiance—that the translator inserts into the passage just considered where Benare holds forth at length, not at odds at all with the Hindi in which the tone is defensive with a strong hint of tears: a tone free of jibes, a tone and timbre come to be associated in our collective imagination with the woman pleading not guilty to charges of immoral conduct brought against her. The defensive tone often rises to defiance, as *'meri ichchaa meri hai, usey koi kuchal naheen saktaa—koi bhee nahee. Mai apna yaa apnee zindagee mein jo jee mein aayaa karoongee. Apna bhavishya mai svayam nirthdhaarit karoongee'*[27] ('My wishes are my own. No one can kill those—no one! I'll do what I like with myself and my life! I'll decide…'[28]) But it is far too desperate and out of breath sounding, its emergence contingent on the high, tragedienne's voice of a woman at bay, speaking for herself.

Here is the passage in English in which the above line occurs:

> I'm used to standing while teaching. In class, I never sit when teaching. That's how I keep my eye on the whole class. No one has a chance to play up. My class is scared stiff of me! And they adore me too. My children will do anything for me. For I'd give the last drop of my blood to teach them. (In a different tone) That's why people are jealous. Specially the other teachers and the management. But what can they do to me? However hard they try, what *can* they do? They're holding an enquiry, if you please! But my teaching's perfect. I've put my whole life into it—I've worn myself to a shadow in this job! Just because of one bit of slander, what can they do to me? Throw me out? Let them! I haven't hurt anyone. Anyone at all! If I've hurt anybody, it's been myself. But is that any kind of reason for throwing me out? Who are these people to say what I can or can't do? My life is my own—I haven't sold it to anyone for a job! My will is my own. My wishes are my own. No one can kill those—no one! I'll do what I like with myself and my life! I'll decide.[29]

The desperate tone is just audible, a vibration under the surface. The speech and speaking are I-driven, I-centred, firmly and unambiguously tethered to the 'I' in a way the Hindi is just not. The 'I' there is scattered, made contingent upon the other factors listed there, viz., not doing her teaching seated and thereby getting an overview of her class, the sheer sweat work she has put in for her students, and her faultless service record. The strength she derives from these accomplishments, in keeping with the values and more of society, gives the 'I' a protective padding, a wary quality. The padding gets shed as the speech progresses. The wariness is dispelled. If they sack her from her job, they are welcome, she shrugs. But in the very next sentences the voice of the beleaguered 'I', the hunted, victim 'I', breaks out from the covering, as '*Kisi aur kaa ahit nahee kiya hai mainey! Kiyaa hai to apnaa hee. Magar yeh bhee kya aisa gunah hai ki mujhey naukree sey nijaal diyaa jai?*' Courage and dare make a comeback in the last seven lines of that passage, as '*Apnee zindagee kaise bitaun....svayam nirdhaarit karoongee.*' Courage bids for ascendancy again. But feelings of injustice, of being wronged—the primal feelings of victimhood—still quaver behind the bravery. The whole passage becomes tremulous, multi-voiced and polyphonic.

The English rendering is devoid of this multi-tonality. The 'I' is a firmer, unified force here. The 'I'-word, as a rule, seems and sounds more entrenched in English, more organically connected to it, running with the grain. It comes out and stays a decisive, active force in almost every sentence of that passage where Benare narrates the facts of her situation, and the ways she is facing them. 'I'm used to standing while teaching. In class, I never sit when teaching. That's how I keep my eye on the whole class. No one has a chance to play up. My class is scared stiff of me! And they adore me too! My children will any thing for me...' The 'I' is the supreme agency here, the agency that defines and articulates the objective situation, and asserts its own status and standing in it, which is one of more than equality. It is a confident, action-oriented 'I' that speaks in those lines; an 'I' not unduly worried about keeping its head above the swirling waters of tradition it has let loose.

The colloquialisms of the language help it along. 'That's how I *keep my eye* on the whole class! No one has a chance to *play up*! My class is *scared stiff* of me...' The 'I' rings out loud and clear in each of these sentences, its sway intact and reasserted at the end of each. The words demand and dictate a sharp, assertive tone of voice from the reader/actor. The culture and politics that have gone into the words contour their acoustics, and the reader/actor picks up the wavelength instinctively. The Hindi, as we said, does not have this heightened effect. The 'I' staggers in those sentences, holds on for support and exoneration to the beneficial effects it claims for its classroom and professional behaviour, seeks exoneration on the grounds of these effects. The difference in the impacts of the two language can be, perhaps, explained on the basis of the differences between 'aham', meaning ego, and 'swayam', meaning the self. The Hindi Benare is not egoistic. She does not have the ego to decontextualize herself that the egoistic position demands. The exonerations she seeks and the backgrounds she presents as justification for her demand for exoneration, furnish her with the context she needs. She is still at the level of the self ('swayam') in her process of growth. And the self is an animal more social than the ego, with more of give-and-take to its make up than the finite ways of the ego, as is clear from, '*Meyri ichchaa meyri hai. Usey koi kuchal naheen saktaa—koi bhee nahee. Mai apna yah apanee zindagee mein jo jee may aayaa karoongee. Apnaa bhavishya mai svayam nirdhaaarit karoongee.*'

The finiteness and the absolutist voice are very much muted here. The thrust of the words is inward, towards her self. Benare seems to be giving herself a pep talk, bucking herself up, keeping her morale up. In contrast, the thrust of the words in the English is outward, to the asserting, interrogating 'I', which is thrown into focus explosively, and on which the rhetoric of the words stays centred.

But this difference does not distort our perception of the Benare story, nor disturb our interaction with it or her. The fleet, onward-flowing and externalized tone of the English, the rhetoric implicit in it, seem a desired, wished for evolution by us in our strivings for feminine empowerment, in our articulations of it. We apprehend the Benare story—as we have been maintaining all along—we recount it to ourselves in the self-addressing, self-communicating mood in which all powerful stories put us in a bilingual medium. This has implications for an English translation. It has the liberty to go to Hindi, render in Hindi without italics or transliteration, passages of strong dramatic import not quite filterable in English. One place where this bilingual potential of the English could have been, but has not been, put to use, is in Act One where the wounded yet puckish and leg pulling Benare decides to recite a poem. It is a Marathi poem by Mrs Shirish Pai, and in a footnote (in the English edition), Tendulkar is quoted as having implied in his preface to the play that he found close links between Benare and the mood of the poem. The poem is an ode to futility, an ode to the philosophy of futility. The poet persona's voice enacts the philosophy. We feel the ache and the crucifying ordeal of pain to which man is condemned for life, condemned to strive in the face of ordained failure. Written in the first person voice, it is a sustained lament, strongly etched, linear.

All these centripetal currents are dissipated in the English translation, careful though it is. The first person voice is missed. It should have been caught in the very opening line. 'Yeh merey paon'[30] is the Hindi. The English is 'Our feet'.[31] The pluralizing kills the clearly stated 'me' of the opening voice, the 'I'. And on this opening declaration of I-ness, the ensuing first person quiver and immediacy of the whole poem rests, stays tethered to it. This underlying linkage flashes into arresting, open articulation in the line '*mithee key yeh mere haath/ baar baar jalten hain, bujhtey hain/phir phir jal uththten hain.*'[32] The fierce, almost masochistic glee of pain in those lines is wiped out in the English rendering. 'Our earthern hands burn out, and then/again in flames they are alight.'[33] The pluralizing of 'mere' (my) to 'our', once again does the maximum harm, not only clouding the I-ness and bringing in a we-ness and anonymity, but also making the burning bereft of fire, the singeing bereft of scar.

The off-key quality of the English shows up again badly, this time in an inverted form, from the singularizing of the plural. The Hindi is '*yudh hotein hi hain kuchh aise/jinkee pariniti sirf parajay/vyarthth jaaney deney ko hee/leney hoten hain/kuchch anubhav.*'[34] The defeat underwritten in war, even if it is won, the fatal attraction this game holds for man, and the devastation it wreaks, are bitter truths learnt at a close, personal level by the reciting voice, you feel, reading those lines in Hindi. Macro truths are being conveyed through economic, micro means. The stoic impersonality of grand tragedy and the harrowing tones of personal experience combine in the Hindi in a poetic texture totally lacking in the English. The English rendering is, 'There is a battle some times, where/Defeat is destined as the end.'[35] The stoic note sounds in the imagery of defeat as destiny, in the cause and effect yoking of the two. But where is the harrowing tone of personal experience? It is such tapering off into the personal from the impersonal, from the immediate to the immanent that gives its strength to the Hindi poem, and that, in turn, connects tellingly with the true, undying story of Benare.

The singularizing of 'yudh' (war) dispels this to and fro movement between the present and the ever present, and this, in turn, thwarts the connection with the true story of Benare which it has to make. But it is in the last two lines of the English that its shortcomings go beyond misapplications of the singular and the plural, to just bad poetry. 'Some experiences are meant/To taste, then just to waste and spend.'[36] The debacle starts with the facile rhyming of 'taste' and 'waste'. The two words jump out of the lines and assault the ears even before you are through with the lines. Reaching for balance, you read the lines again, but this brings to fresh notice the looseness of the first line, 'Some experiences are meant...,' unleavened or untautened by any feel of a more-than-the-word sense stirring them. You stumble along to the second line, hearing the 'taste'/'waste' jingle go up in the ears anew, and showing up the sheer vacuity of the phrase 'waste and spend'. The Hindi is *'vyarthth jaaney deney ko hee/leney hotein hain kuchh anubhav.'* Now, this is not without its own jingle—'jaaney', 'leney', 'deney'—bordering on triteness. But the border is not breached. The personal tone is too inbuilt in the Hindi to be knocked down by hasty or indifferent poetic diction. This personal tone, as pointed out earlier, is not a feature of the English at any stage. And the poem, also pointed out, is integral to the inner structure of the play.

Could not the poem, then, in view of its importance and the space for bilingualism present in the story of Benare, have been retained in the Hindi in the English rendering? In a small but marked way, English incurses into the Hindi version in those sections of the play where Benare recites English nursery rhymes and popular verse in her own tongue, passing smoothly from Hindi to English, assimilating both into each other. 'O I have a sweetheart/who carries all my books/he plays in my dolls' house/And says he likes my looks....'[37] Or, 'The grass is green/the rose is red/this books is mine...till I am dead. Till I am dead...'[38] Benare is bilingual like so many of us are. We incorporate mother tongue and English into our systems without strain. The English version, then, could well have been kept in the Hindi verbatim. A few stage directions—a short burst of tabla beats, perhaps, or a strain of a classical or neo-classical Hindustani music— could have set the mood and Benare could have sung or chanted the poem to a simple taal, or just recited it in Hindi.

This lack of vision by the translator tells badly at the end of the translation, where, again, the finale is effected by means of a song/ poem. The linguistic disharmony and disconnectedness implicit in this shortfall of vision is presaged in the translation of the stage direction given in the Hindi. Samant, the sensitive and helplessly pushed member of the lynch group around Benare, is shown trying to wake her from the swoon into which she falls after the court verdict. He calls out to her, 'Miss...' That prefix is a jolting, jarring Anglicism which could easily have been circumvented by retaining the Hindi word 'bai'. But the translated poem that follows wreaks havoc. The Hindi is a construct of sheer onomatopoeia: the open-ended vowel terminations natural to Hindi help no little in producing the sound-over-word quality of the composition—'Sugana', 'Sunana', 'Daataa', 'Bitaaoon', 'Basera', 'Bahnaa', ... An aftermath of tonal play and lambent crisscrossing lingers in the ears when the poem finishes. The story of Benare ends as a dirge. It dissolves in a stream of timeless-ness and ever present-ness. The poem is sung, yes. And it is possible that by the artistry of voice and musicianship, the sharply outlined, finite sound quality of the English words could lift and the strand of lament in the Benare story that the Hindi song brings up filters into the ear.

But a translation is meant to be read too, as much and just as the original is. It is a literary exercise as much as theatre craft. And at the reading level, a lot more about the translation seems open to question. The line 'Kyon geeley terey nain?'[39] (why are your eyes wet?) is rendered as 'Why, oh why, are your eyes so red?'[40] 'Why, oh why' seems understandable. The repetition is a way of conveying the acute helplessness and pathos that sing in the Hindi like the keynotes of a raga of sorrow, say, Todi. Such a compound of word and tone spring-ing from cultural usages would be impossible to reproduce in English. The repetition, buttressed by the tiny exclamation 'oh', does suggest if not evoke, the intensity of the Hindi. Also, one can say that the beat of the three words and the whole line is a satisfying read: why/oh why/are your/eyes so red—1/2–3/4–5/6–7–8. But 'red'? It seems more a device to rhyme with 'said' occurring in the preceding line: 'The parrot to the sparrow said...'[41] Red eyes and wet eyes do not evoke the same image, the same kind of misery. Red eyes spell a bout of weeping, whereas wet eyes spell a standing, stoically borne grief.

One other modification that does go home despite seeming extreme is the refrain 'Sparrow, sparrow, poor, little sparrow.'[42] It is for '*chiv chiv chiv/chiv chiv chiv rey/chiv chiv chiv*,'[43] which is a vocalizing of the sparrow's call. More, it is an incorporation of the musical style of bhajans in which single words are flung in an interjectory mode, making for an explosive heightening of religious ecstasy. It has, in other words, some formal features of music. Reading it, tone and beat rise on their own into the reading or speaking voice. The image of a robed bhikshuni swaying to the clacks of the karataal in her hands rises without effort. Benare's anguish acquires religious overtones. It is an enhancement which is not only dramatic, not only philosophical, but thoroughly colloquial. We experience the Benare story in a climactic, renewed burst of familiarity and perenniality. The play ends with the song, bathing us with a sense of aesthetic fulfilment despite the tragedy because it spells a structural completion. The English rendering of it cannot, and does not, attain this total, near-cathartic sweep. Yet it does, to quite an extent, engage the mind at the reading level. The alterations and modifications introduced serve to coax the understanding of the task of translation, and win acceptance.

But the grand fusion of voice and person that the Hindi brings about remains out of ken for it. The poem stays just that, a poem. It does not become song. It does not morph into the face and figure of a singer. This amalgamation is necessary, as we said earlier, for it makes for a total art experience. Could not the English have achieved, at least come nearer to it, if the poem had been retained in the Hindi? The question asks itself again, demands consideration. Hindi, or any other language of the country we call our mother tongue, and English are not separate areas of language employment for us; all colonized and ex-colonized people, live this bilingual condition.

Other reasons too for retaining the Hindi original in the English rendering present themselves. The poem is to be sung. The stage directions clearly say so. '*Kaheen se usee ke svar may geet ke bol sunaayee deteyn hain*,'[44] and 'From somewhere unseen, her own voice is heard singing softly'[45] are the directions in the respective languages. Here we come to another aspect of the Hindi–English tie up, or any other Indian language and English. Our voices are of a heavier cast. Their take-offs are different. They do not make contact with the English words with the lightness and fleecy quality of Anglo-European voices. This difference between voice timbre and language is felt even in speaking. But meaning and rhetoric cancel out the physical differences, and the language comes to be possessed by us. But singing is a form distinct from speaking, not as much word-based, and it does not provide the latter's leeway for possessing the language.

How, then, is Benare—that her singing is off stage does not matter—to sing and make the total evocation detailed before, in a language that becomes distant and estranging at this crucial point in the play? The translator does not seem to have paid attention enough to this practical problem, and made the stage direction meaningful. It might be contended here that earlier in the play, Benare sings English nursery rhymes and jingles that do not jar, that run with the grain. But nursery rhymes are friendlier, outgoing, and more adaptive to differences of voice and tone, to otherness. Adult poems, with their concentrated inner-ness and a core existentialist essence, are not so. Also, Benare sings the nursery rhymes amidst a lot of flurry and bustle on the stage, while the play is unfolding amidst much crosstalk and chatter from the participants. The physical stir and the suspense of events in the offing can be trusted to iron out incompatibilities of tone and musical diction that may arise in the singing. The Song of the Sparrow that comes at the absolute end of the play has no such facilitating factors. It is a point of climax. It carries the full weight of the dramatic impact of the play in which the story of Benare gets retold in the reader/viewer's mind in a dance idiom of voice, word and echo.

When so much is at stake, the poem could have been subjected to more scrutiny than the translator has done. She could have taken fresh stock of the methodology of translation, of the usual options exercised by her. She could have been more alive to the Indian fibre of the English of India. She could have kept the Hindi original and let the monotonal laments of the sparrow invoke the impassioned yet patterned interrogations of society that Benare makes in her mono-logue. It could have made for the depersonalized enhancement of her story to the dimensions of a saga that the Hindi effects. The English could have done this too. By a little more insight into the language it employs, by a little more awareness of the bilingual, bicultural permissiveness the language has today, it could have accomplished much, much more.

▌ Notes

1. Adarkar, Priya. 1978. *Silence! The Court is in Session.* Kolkata: Oxford University Press.
2. Tendulkar, Vijay. 1968. *Shantata! Court Chaaloo Aahey!* Mumbai: Mauj Prakashan.

3. Verma, Sarojini. 1994. *Khaamosh! Adaalat Jaaaree Hai!* New Delhi: Vidya Prakashan Mandir. Trans. of. Tendulkar, op cit.
4. Ibid., p. 15.
5. Ibid., p. 27.
6. Adarkar, p. 14.
7. Verma, p. 30.
8. Adarkar, p. 16.
9. Verma, p. 27.
10. Ibid., p. 32.
11. Ibid., p. 44.
12. Adarkar, p. 28.
13. Verma, p. 28.
14. Adarkar,. p. 15.
15. Verma, p. 27.
16. Adarkar, p. 14.
17. Ibid., p. 18.
18. Verma, p. 107.
19. Adarkar, p. 74.
20. Verma, p. 108.
21. Adarkar, p. 75.
22. Verma, p. 108.
23. Adarkar, p. 75.
24. Verma, p. 108.
25. Adarkar, p. 75.
26. Verma, p. 109.
27. Ibid., p. 14.
28. Adarkar, p. 5.
29. Ibid., p. 4.
30. Verma, p. 21.
31. Adarkar, p. 10.
32. Verma, p. 21.
33. Adarkar, p. 10.
34. Verma, p. 21.
35. Adarkar, p. 10.
36. Ibid.
37. Ibid., p. 5.
38. Ibid., p. 9.
39. Ibid., p. 39.
40. Ibid., p. 23.
41. Ibid., p. 23.
42. Ibid., p. 23.
43. Verma, p. 39.
44. Ibid., p. 112.
45. Adarkar, p. 78.

Chapter 5

The Road to Rebirth

▌ Rules of Nearness

If a novel has been translated into many languages, some of which you know, but is originally written in a language you do not know, how do you assess the translations? I would say, treat the language nearest the original as your touchstone and proceed, assuming, of course, that you know such a close ally. If the original is in, say, Bangla, and you do not know Bangla but do know Assamese, the chances of your getting the flavour of the original from the Assamese are higher than, say, a Gujarati or a Marathi translation. This is the basis on which I have dealt with U.R. Anantha Murthy's celebrated novel *Samskara*[1] in Kannada. I do not speak or read Kannada. But I do read and speak Tamil, a language arisen from common Dravidian roots. Moreover, the Tamil translation, done by T.S. Sadasivan,[2] shows an intimacy with the main character, Praneshacharya, and his dilemma, which is the central feature of *Samskara*. So strong is this total merging of the narrating persona with the main character—a main character—a merging which is more than the normal empathy of fiction writing, original or translation, that we feel justified in looking for it in the other translations, in the hope that a viable critical principle of the discipline of translation will result thereby. We could, perhaps, therefore go deeper into the dilemma of Praneshacharya as a first step towards examining the translations in Hindi and English, the two other languages I am more or less versed in.

▌ Concretizing the Abstract

Praneshacharya is experiencing the tremors and trepidations of rebirth. A.K. Ramanujan, the English translator, in his Afterword, calls it succinctly and accurately enough 'a rite of passage'.[3] But the high emotional scale of his experience makes it more an ordeal by fire, an *agni pareeksha*, than a choreographed rite. Briefly stated, Praneshacharya transits to the universe and culture of touch from a stern code of anti-touch. Waking to the power and idiom of touch is on par with slipping into infanthood, where the registrations of touch are felt acutely, minutely. Furthermore, infanthood signifies a birth anew, a new beginning. The whole trope of birth anew and a new beginning is projected through the terminology of motherhood and maternalism that strengthens the stark physical feel of Praneshacharya's transformation that the reader gets. This solid materiality of the abstract, metaphysical strivings of Praneshacharya, the feature that keeps the reader connected to the novel, is what he/she looks for in the translations.

| Tamil's Headstart

Before coming to that part of this essay, perhaps we could consider the means adopted by the Tamil translator, T.S. Sadasivam, to achieve, firstly, the intense physical feel of Praneshacharya's strivings, and secondly, achieve the total identification of the narrative voice with Praneshacharya, which results from the means adopted. The quality of the language seems a key determining factor here. There is a virtuosity in Sadasivam's usage, and a class-wise adaptation of it, which gives a firm, realistic footing to the story, and brings nearer the poignancy of Praneshacharya's situation. There are three variants to the language. There is, firstly, the straight, point-by-point narration where the prose is brisk with long sentences that are nevertheless not long-winded. They make a maze of images through a multiplicity of nouns, adjectives and strategically placed verbs which bind the whole mass of images, nouns and adjectives into a dominant, governing image and mood.

As an illustration, take the first sentence of paragraph five in Chapter Two of the Tamil version. Here are the main events and circumstances described: the Brahmins are trudging up to the nearby village, Paarijatapauram. The heat is so fierce that grain can roast in it. The Brahmins cover their heads with their shoulder cloths to ward off the heat. They are limp with hunger. On the way, they cross the

Tungabhadra river which is flowing in three branches. They enter the cool forest. They trudge for one full hour. They reach Paarijatapuram. This whole table of events and circumstances has been knit into a single continuous line of action in the Tamil. The flow, rhythm and narrative specifics in this sentence evoke an aspect of the basic spirit of the story, which the reader expects to see similarly evoked in the other translations. It may, therefore, be of interest to see the structure of this marathon sentence.

There are six sections to it. Each section wends its way through a row of adjectives and nouns, culminates briefly in an inclusive verb, and without terminating goes on to join with the next section, where the process starts again, and so on, to the final section. The verbs heighten the impact of the nouns and adjectives that precede them. 'Down the agrahara road, become hot to the point of corn roasting if it chanced to fall on it...' [Author's translation from Tamil] begins the sentence. This is not Ramanujan's translation. It is a word for word prosaic translation for explaining the argument being made here. In the Tamil, that beginning has a bounce and a steady forward momentum all its own. But let us forget that. The point is that the fierce intensity of the heat registers strongly in the reader's mind. And it gets added strength by the verb that follows: '*covering* their heads with their shoulder cloths' [Author's translation from Tamil]. This is the pattern all down the long sentence; a strong image, strengthened by a sharp verb. The second image— 'Limp with hunger' [Author's translation from Tamil]—is reinforced by the common but well-timed verb 'walking'. The 'river Tungabhadra forking out in three streams' [Author's translation from Tamil], is consolidated by the Brahmins' act of crossing it. 'The cool forest' [Author's translation from Tamil] becomes cooler and greener by the hot, dusty, hungry Brahmins' 'entering' it and soothing their hot, dusty, hungry bodies. And finally comes the image of the Brahmins reaching their destination, complemented by their hour-long 'trekking' through the forest.

Let us attempt now to put together these adjectives and verbs into one unbroken sentence, and try to approximate the Tamil:

On this side, the brahmins walked along the agrahara road that was heated to roasting point, covering their heads with their shoulder-cloths, and, limp with hunger, they forded the three-pronged flow of the Tungabhadra river, plunging into the cool forest, and then, after an hour-long trek through it, reached Paarijatapuram village.

That is unsatisfying, to put it mildly. There are usages of grammar in Tamil which facilitate the linking of sentences. Secondly, each linking verb in the Tamil produces the impression of an ongoing action. And this, continuing-ness, in turn, emphasizes the crisis situation confronting the Brahmins, which forms the take-off point of the story. Consider the word 'nadandu' (walking) in Tamil. To denote the continuing, ongoing quality it has in the sentence, the English version will have to be 'kept walking' or 'walking on'; the Hindi will have to be 'chalte huey' or 'chalte rahey'. These additions to the verb tell on the sense of urgency that is the underlying feature of *Samskara*.

Keeping in mind these inherent problems of language, then, let us see how the English and the Hindi translations render this sentence. The Hindi divides it into two. The first sentence packs in all the similes and imagery about the heat figuring in the Tamil, and halts at the point where the Brahmin walk on, covering their heads with their shoulder-cloths. In the second sentence are assembled the images of the river, forking out in three streams, the Brahmins' hunger-filled frames crossing the river, and their passage into the cool forest after another hour long trudge. That amounts to quite an impressive chain of images per sentence. It might be argued that the whole thing could have been one sentence with just an 'aur' (and) between the two sentences. It would perhaps not have the fluid onward motion of the Tamil. But it would have been feasible in structural terms, despite the greater facilities in the Tamil language, pointed out earlier.

But would it have highlighted the inner urgency of Praneshacharya and the practical urgencies of the Brahmins a whole? The Tamil rendering does this, as pointed out in the beginning. The language is, of course, an aid in this, but even the most accommodating language needs craftsmanship to reflect the thought, attitude and intent of the writer.

Before coming to this question in detail, let us first consider the English translation done by A.K. Ramanujan:

The agrahara street was hot, so hot you could pop corn on it. The Brahmins walked through it. Weak with hunger, their heads covered with their upper cloths, they crossed the three pronged river. And they entered the cool forest to reach Paarijatapuram after an hour's trudging.[4]

There are four sentences here. But they form a unity brought about by the sharp and sustained critical alertness of the narrative voice to the issue at stake, and the consequent need to shape the language, make it reflect the insight gained by this awareness. Impelled thus, the language acquires a timbre that is on par with the dramatic core of *Samskara*. It is this critical awareness that the Hindi appears to lack, and hence seems bogged down in a narrative of semblances. It is a narrative that recalls the original—the original here standing for the Tamil rendering, it should be kept in mind—in faint, far-off echoes. Therefore, even if it had replicated the one-sentence structure of the Tamil, the dramatic urgency of the Tamil may not have been captured.

The second of the three linguistic variants that I said are present in the Tamil translation has to do with the speech modes and usage among the Brahmins. It is the everyday, spoken Tamil of the Brahmin community. And again, the homely shortening and shading-off of words creates an intimacy with the issue at stake that alerts the reader afresh, all over again, to the emergency confronting the Brahmins. There is the Brahmin Dasacharya, for instance, pleading with Praneshacharya to decide soon about the disposal of Narannappa's body festering in the agrahara. Dasacharya is on the verge of collapsing with hunger because of the injunction against eating as long as the dead body of a Brahmin lay untended. In a tone and logic bathed in the style of humility bred by unquestioning adherence to scriptural tenets, shaking with the fear of death from hunger, he implores Praneshacharya to find a way out of the impasse.

It is not possible to convey to those not familiar with the inflections of Tamil, the emotive strength of this appeal by Dasacharya. 'Just say the word, Acharya!' he beseeches Praneshacharya, 'Your word is the word of the vedas ('vedavaakyam') Just say the word! Four of us, this very minute, will carry the corpse, and cremate it' [author's translation from Tamil]. In the Tamil, the phrase 'Just say the word, Acharya!', has a brevity plus an impassioned yet clipped tone of deep supplication. This is enhanced by a near-confluence of first and second person pronouns that seems peculiar to Tamil. 'Neengal', which is the Tamil for 'aap' of Hindi is shortened to 'Neenga' (the last vowel short) in accordance with speech informalities. And its complement 'Naangal', for 'hum' Hindi or 'us' of English seems to chime somewhere close by. Both the pronouns become elastic and limber by everyday speech modes seem to be uttered together in Dasacharya's entreaty. The sharp immediacy of the novel's theme that this combination of idiom and emotion makes for is not hard to imagine.

| The Placid Tone of the Hindi

What is the equivalent or alternative in the Hindi and English of this everyday speech style that makes for such far-reaching effects? The Hindi[5] appears unaware of the advantages of colloquializing the language and thereby making the story immediate, palpable. The translator, Chandrakant Kusnoor, has adopted a formal Hindi with a Sanskritic leaning in the speech interludes. 'I do not enjoy good health. I may die if I do not eat,' [Author's translation] Dasacharya wails to Praneshacharya in pedantic tones, 'I request you to proffer me a solution. Or tell us what we should best do in this emergency…' The Hindi runs as, '*Mera swasthya theek naheen hai. Bhojan na karoon to meri jaan ko khatra hai. Aap koi na koi raah sujhaayen. Yaa yeh bataaiye ki is vipada mey karna kya chahiye.*'[6]

There is none of the agitated, tumbling forward motion of the Tamil in these words. And nothing else has been substituted either for keeping alive in the reader's awareness the abstract and complex issue that is the triggering point of the novel. Efforts to keep the reader's mind at the right receptive pitch have to be made in the writing of a difficult novel like *Samskara*, whether original or translation. Idiomatic variation is one strategy in the task. If it does not figure in the translator' approach, what other means has he adopted for the purpose?

This is an important consideration in studying the translations. The Hindi translation shows no awareness of this basic problem and challenge from *Samskara*. The language does not deviate from the formal Hindi that the translator has apparently seen as the right lingua franca for a community considered educated. Tethered thus to an unvarying atonality of pitch, the narrative seldom, if ever, soars to the emotional height and vividness that, as in the Tamil, connects the reader to the core problems portrayed in the novel. This absence of a sharp enough, deep enough, critical reading of the novel is felt most acutely in the interaction between Praneshacharya and the cartman, Putta. Putta is not of the twice born caste and is rustic of speech. This factor of Putta's rusticity is important because he is a threshold figure, the figure at the portals of the boldly lusty, freely sensuous, extrovert world which Praneshacharya seems about to pass into. His experience with Chandri, let us recall, has catapulted him into the world of grassroots physical realities and basic animal pleasures which make a mockery of his ardent Brahmanical pieties. Putta is his liaison for domiciling him in this world of sensuality. His interaction with him has a meaning and significance going down to the basics of the story. And Putta's rough hewn speech invokes this central purpose.

And yet, despite this crucial importance of Putta's speech style, Chandrakant Kusnoor, the Hindi translator, has kept to his uniform prose style of decorous, middle class Hindi. It is discordant, to say the least. (And why, one wonders, has Putta's name been shortened to 'Putt', 'Hindustani-ized'? Another irritant!)

Look at this passage, for instance. Putta and Praneshacharya are in the thick of a village fair, drowned in the primal, visceral excitements that its sights set off. Set floundering by this onslaught of savage, unfamiliar yet inciting sights, Praneshacharya tries to deal with them by quizzing himself: should he decide to give up a quarter century of discipline and become a man of the world? No, no, Naranappa's funeral comes before all else. After that come other decisions. But if the Supreme Acharya of Kanchi disallows it—his problems are upon him again, he is his old, harassed self again. What is right, what is wrong—he wrestles with himself, battles amidst the metaphysical strengths of the fair; a blind beggar singing in wild abandon, beating his drone box: 'how shall I praise you, how shall I worship you, Lord?' [Author's translation from Tamil]. A swarm of leprous beggars materialize from the vortex of the crowd, waving their maimed limbs, showing the stumps of rotted fingers. 'No hands, no leg, limb-less I am, master...' 'Let us go. Let's be off,' he plucks Putta by the sleeve [Author's translation from Tamil]. The rotted, rotting bodies violently jerk him back to the image of the festering corpse of Naranappa. 'No, you should have your food first. There's a Brahmin congregation in the temple,' Putta says [Author's translation from Tamil]. 'You come with me too…' [Author's translation from Tamil] Praneshacharya is unhinged by his confusions. He is inviting an ineligible cart man to share a meal with twice born, doubly eligible Brahmins.

And this is where Putta's unpolished speech gains a sparkle which cannot but catch the attention of the reader, cannot but set problems for the translator. Again, it should be borne in mind that it is the Tamil translation that has been taken as the base. But again, as we have been emphasizing, this need not be a limiting factor. No translation gets its highlights unless the basic substance of these highlights is present in the original, in latent or overt forms. Therefore, even if the Hindi and English translations that we are considering here have been done from the Kannada original, the sparkle of Putta's speech in the Tamil referred to above, would be at least suggested in the other two translations.

Let us now attempt a paraphrase-cum-translation of Putta's reply to Praneshacharya's invitation. Consider the following speech:

'Are you joking? (pulling my leg? playing the fool with me?) Everyone knows me here, sir! I'd have sneaked in all right if it weren't for this! But hey, listen! Think I haven't done all this? I've tucked in well and good into a brahmins' feast in Udipi! Who'd know me in Udipi, eh? Hey, you've heard of that spawn of a goldsmith that lied his way to a job in the temple? Look, we people can flaunt the sacred thread no less than you lot! Of course that's neither here nor there! Just telling you, that's all! Haven't gone so swell-headed as to eat with you. You go in, take your time, sir! I'll wait here, right here.' [Author's translation from Tamil]

The operative word in that rough and ready translation of the Tamil is 'Oi' or 'Oye' for 'hey'. It is not the Punjabi 'oye', with its heckling irreverence. This Tamil 'oi' is basically a respectful term of address used for the elderly, with a tinge—sometimes more than a tinge—of familiarity. Try to imagine the incident of the cheeky prank being narrated by Putta, interspersed with these explosive/respectable 'ois', and you will have a rough idea of the speech characteristics of the man. This barrage of dialect, moreover, that is conveying a mass of confidential information, is being flung at a deeply troubled and shaken man, contemplating a flight from his own world of standing and privilege to the faceless, disenfranchized world of the lowly cart-man. The strategic importance and dramatic significance of Putta's outpouring is thus, evident.

The Hindi translation hardly performs the task of re-evoking the basic dramatic issue that Putta's speech forms do in the Tamil text. '*Yeh jagah merey parichiton sey bharee huee hai...*,'[7] he says for 'everyone knows me hereabouts' [Author's translation from Hindi]. The word 'parichiton' is just too staid, too flat, lacking the sense of long-standing familiarity conveyed by the Tamil word 'terinjavanga'. Again, for 'I haven't gone so swollen-headed as to sit down and eat with you' [Author's translation from Hindi], the Hindi is, '*Aap ke sang baithkar bhojan karney kaa naa mujhmey sahas hai, na aisi udhvat-tata kaa bhaav hai.*'[8] The high Hindi not only jars, but worse, bogs the speech in flowery courteousness and does not make the dramatic epicentre of the book flash into view.

The Vivacity of the English Translation

The English translation, in contrast, has its hand sure and firm on this pulse of the novel's drama, and makes it throb anew from time to time. No substitute for dialect has been attempted. It is an impossible job. But the language has been kept at a racy, give-and-take level that allows for the throw and play of tone. This, in turn, keeps the central dramatic problem alive, thereby keeping the whole story in motion. Even so, the deletion of the ear-catching word 'oi' in the Tamil jars somewhere. Could not a word like 'hey' or 'eh?' have been worked in? However, such absences and deletions do get made good by the one sentence, 'I really don't have the gall, the guts, to sit and eat a meal with you.'[9] That is for the Tamil, which we roughly translated as 'Haven't gone so swell-headed as to eat with you.' In place of the replication that the rough translation attempts, Ramanujan's is the interpretative approach. And one cannot but acknowledge its efficacy. 'Don't have the gall, the guts...' has an outward fling, sweep and carrying power that shakes up the prosaic rendering of the preceding and succeeding lines, infuses the whole paragraph with the heat and secret glee of Putta's confidings.

Ramanujan's prose does not have the genetic links of language and culture that the Tamil version has. At times, it is even stolid and bereft of movement. Yet it repeatedly makes the story, theme and action surge anew into the reader's mind, no less than the Tamil does. What could this be due to? An answer could perhaps be found in the later sections of the novel where the scenes of the fair at Meligey town are described in rich, sensuous, almost larger-than-life detail. The fair ground is of tremendous symbolic significance in the book, as we said earlier. It is the borderland between the ritual-ridden, touch-shunning Brahmanical world of Praneshacharya, and the riotously hedonistic, free-touching world of others. If he, Praneshacharya, is able to plunge into the orgies of violent and raw sensory titillation that he sees going on before him, if he can be one with the revellers, it would mean a baptism for him to launch on starting life with Chandri that he is contemplating. Standing on the brink, he can look back and ahead, at past and future. He is seeing the bacchanalian scenes in front of him, and he is also seeing himself see them. This double vision is a very important, key element in the whole interlude of the fair. It brings into retrospect the full drama and metaphysics of the rebirth of Praneshacharya which has been set in motion by the death of Naranappa.

A translation has to be alive to this doubling in Praneshacharya's vision to give the narrative a supple enough texture, thereby drawing into view the main activating elements of the story. Ramanujan provides this suppleness by adopting a disciplined observer's stance. From his total understanding of Praneshacharya and the refracted state he is in, he expresses the varied emotions evoked in the fairground setting. There's humour, for instance, in the sketch of peasant women 'shyly drinking soda-pop from the sweet-smelling bottles...Their heads oiled and combed sleek. Knots of flower in their hair.'[10] It is the light, teasing humour of noticing details of get up and attire on special occasions. The humour tapers off to simple observer's pleasure, as:

> The squeak and gurgle of the soda water as they push down the glass marbles in the soda bottle ... the belch that comes up the throat after a drink of the sweet-coloured aerated waters ... a matter of expectation, experience, contentment. Of the many pleasures of a temple festival, this too was one. Everyone thinks of it early and earmarks enough money for it.[11]

Eventually, the light heartedness subsides, to clear the stage for the return of the dominant mood of the novel, that is, a tense, empirical inquiry into a metaphysical problem. Consider this:

> Purposeful eyes everywhere, engaged in things. His eyes, the only dis-engaged ones, incapable of involvement in anything. Putta was right. Even my meeting him here must have been destined. To fulfill my resolution I should be capable of his involvement in living. Chandri's too is the same world. But I am neither here, nor there. I am caught in this play of opposites.[12]

This swing between the outer area of vision and the deeper perceptions of the inner eye is among the defining features of the novel. It follows, then, that the more vividly a translation reflects this swing the more of a realized text it becomes.

Imagery

A consideration of some more aspects of the metaphysical issue of *Samskara* because of its heavy bearing on the resulting prose style—original or translation—seems called for at this point. Praneshacharya's is the ancient battle of instinct versus reason, sensual pleasure versus abstinence, an age-old tension of human culture. He decides in favour of reason, of the non-sensual, but he admits the reality and force of the sensual, of the instinctual. He will bring all his doings into the open, will tell all to the Brahmins waiting for his decision on the last rites of Naranappa:

> 'I slept with Chandri. I felt disgust for my wife. I drank coffee in a com-mon shop in a fair. I went to see a cock fight. I lusted after Padmavati. Even at a time of mourning and pollution, I sat in a temple-line with Brahmins and ate a holy feast. I even invited a Malera boy to come into the temple and join me....'[13]

But it will not be a confession. There will be no remorse, no begging for forgiveness. He will tell because as a priest he has no private life. He has to be transparent. And with this transparency, this clear display of the inner and the outer, he will 'turn into a new man,'[14] will be born again. But to truly arrive at this decisive point of rebirth, he has to wage a bitter battle with himself. He has to engage in tortuous debates with himself, strip himself bare. He conducts his own inquisition of himself, probes himself to the very limits of his consciousness.

Another point to keep in mind is that this intense, obsessive self-searching takes place mostly in isolation, either in the forest away from human habitation, or within the four walls of his home, each site a vacuum like the vacuum of the womb. And in this womb, the conception of the Praneshacharya that is to emerge seems to be taking place. We see him wander away to the spot in the forest where he and Chandri had laid together, see him plucking out the grasses and herbs still flattened by the weight of their bodies on it. He smells their deep, grassy green, taking in the smells; smells compounded of sky, sun and the cool of the earth. Having become essence and kin of the earth, the smells enter the depths of his senses. With redoubled greed and hunger he smells them once more, and yet again. This frenzied embracing of the earth which seems like a physical union with it, and also like the first push against the mother's body of the child striving to emerge, is a powerful imagery of birth and renewal, which is the theme of the book. How has this imagery been handled in the English and Hindi translations?

▎ Run Up

A few more words about the theme before we come to the translations. The theme does not move in a straight line to its climax. Praneshacharya's wife dies. In her bedridden state, his wife facilitated the abstinences he had adopted. By attending upon her, his aura of saintliness increased. She was the anvil upon which he forged the raw ore of his virtue and set it gleaming. Her death is his virtual death. This inner death sets him off on the wandering phase of his quest for rebirth. On this odyssey he attempts meticulously to divest himself of his Brahmanical modes of thought and behaviour. He wants to clear away the cobwebs of dead habit clinging to him. Invoking God is dead habit, he thinks. God is not necessary to him any more. 'Once you snap links with god,' his thoughts run, 'you have to snap links with your parents, snap links with the concern for links with god' [Author's paraphrase of the English] which means pitching camp outside the society he knows and lives in. But he is not cut out for fringe living. He needs interaction with fellow Brahmins to give his dissent and thereby his life, form and meaning. No, this world of bold, boisterous grabbing of pleasure which is Putta's world and the world of Chandri too, cannot be his. He is afraid of being seen and recognized here, being spotted in these unholy fair grounds, by a chance acquaintance. He is afraid of being recognized by the Brahmins of the temple, where the pest Putta is insisting he goes for refreshments. And he will be afraid all his life, of being caught living with Chandri.

Maddened by fear he rushes out headlong from the fair grounds. He must rid himself of his fear. How? Firstly, by acknowledging in a public gesture that he is first and last a Brahmin, that he cannot belong to Putta's and Chandri's world. But he will formulate his own view of the Brahmin way of life. It will admit the validity of the body. He will place his formulation to the Brahmins back in the village he has fled from. He will narrate to them his own experiences of the sway of the body, without apology. Truthful, untainted by guilt, he will be born a new man.

Extreme, Edged Imminence

With this clear reiteration of his course of action, the stage of wandering and inquiry in his trek for rebirth ceases. He moves up to the very threshold of birth, in an atmosphere of extreme, edged imminence. The birth is about to take place. And Praneshacharya is hurrying to the site where it is to occur. The novel seems about to have a new beginning. Which of the two translations that we are comparing with the Tamil, best captures this imminence? The reader will feel the full force and impact of this imminence in proportion to the degree to which the translator perceives, understands and projects the stages towards it. These stages, as we might gather from the precis given above, can be divided, firstly, into the intense awareness of his body that comes to Praneshacharya after his sexual union with Chandri. As stated, he wakes to the myriad pleasurable sensations that a woman's body can let loose upon him, overpower him with novelty and familiarity, with the known and the unknown. The deep draughts that he drinks of herb and grass, with the earth clinging to them, exhilarate him with novelty and familiarity, with the known and the unknown. The deep draughts that he drinks of herb and grass, with the earth clinging to them, exhilarate him, transport him to memories, recall an association beyond the specifics of what, when or where. The aromas tumefy and evoke the sensations of touch, the nourishing goodness of generous, downy flesh: Chandri's, woman's, all mothers', mother earth's.

Physical sensations and inner awakenings surge together in these sections. They do not combine but interact with each other as distinct and strong presences. The narrating tone has to echo this interaction, and proclaim the aspirations of Praneshacharya with the right dramatic heightening. The English translation achieves this balance by an assured manipulation of language. The high-pitched outpouring of words that comes with the culture that rears and nourishes them has been replaced by the calm and deliberate employment of words not belonging to the culture they seek to mirror. Most importantly, this is achieved by recourse to poetic prose. Consider these lines as example:

> To be, just to be. To be keen, in the heat, in the cool, to the grass, the green, the flower, the pang, the heat, the shade. Putting aside both desire and value. Not leaping, when the invisible says, 'Here!' To receive it gratefully. Not climbing, not reaching out, not scrambling.[15]

The objects listed in those lines sing out their secret restorative power. Their singing complements the agonized desire of Praneshacharya to be with them in their condition of pure, strive-less being. The state of mind reflected in those lines, a state of attachment born of the purest detachment, forms a running vein to the grand climax of rebirth that is to follow. The ballet of inner speech and outer stance of body for steering towards a contemplated end that we feel all through the novel under its crust of words comes to one of its many high-water marks at this point.

How fine tuned are the translations we are considering, to this play of sound, to the sight and meaning of sound, in this representative segment?

▌Tamil Again

In Tamil, the language is a facilitator. After each object in the list referred to earlier, the possessive pronoun word-byte 'kku' is attached. 'Pullukku', meaning 'for the sake of the grass' ('pul', 'grass'); 'pasumai-kku' meaning 'for the sake of the green'; 'malarukku' meaning 'for the sake of the flower', and so on. The effect of this is that the noun and the qualifying word-byte attached to it come as one unit. The object and the quality ascribed to it register in the reader's mind in a cinematic, kinetic way. A whole group of objects impacting thus collectively in the reader's mind keep him sharply and steadily alerted to the major wish/sentiment contained in those phrases 'irundu viduvom', 'irundu viduvadu', 'to be', 'just be'.

This direct and full-blooded connection with the activating thought of the lines under consideration becomes somewhat remote in the English. The noun-adjectives 'heat', 'cool', 'grass', 'green', 'flower', 'pang', 'heat' and 'shade' stay individual and static, become distant from the stir and ferment of the causative phrases 'to be' or 'just to be'. The translation prefixes the phrase 'to be' at the beginning of the body of nouns. 'To be keen, in the heat, the cool, to the grass, the green…' The prefixed phrase has to vibrate in the entire assemblage of nouns. It does not do this in the instantaneous way that the Tamil suffix 'kku' does, not having the linguistic aid mentioned above. But each noun rings out sharp and individual, as each single hailstone does in a hailstorm. In the flurry that this barrage raises in the reader's mind, in his urge to locate the eye of the storm, he is led to the hold-ing phrases, 'to be', 'just to be'.

This slow motion from the word to the narrative essence behind the word is as beautiful as the explosive motion from word to essence that takes place in the Tamil. And this beauty would not have come about if the translator was not tuned in so consistently and so unwav-eringly to the pulse of the novel, compelling him to mould the tone of his prose to the cadences of the original. (In this case, the original of course, is the Kannada, his own language. But the assumption in this essay, as we have been saying, and may well say once again, is that between the Kannada original and the Tamil translation the affinities would be strong enough to warrant taking the latter as the touchstone of our analysis.) The clipped, staccato effect of the English—'the grass, the green, the flower, the pang, the heat, the shade. Putting aside both desire and value... Not climbing, not reaching out, not scrambling...'—differs evocatively enough from the chain-reactive, garland effect of the Tamil where each word glides to the next on the wings of articulation, to justify compare and contrast studies.

In the Hindi this aliveness to the pulse of the novel is much less intense, less consistent. The inapt word in this sample paragraph we are considering is 'chahiye', meaning 'should', 'ought to'. Till its advent, the lines run smoothly enough. Maybe there is a touch more than necessary of literary-ness in phrases like 'pran-pan se hona'[16] for 'to be, just to be'. In the Tamil, that phrase is only two words packed close with the wish and the thing wished for. But the approach of the Hindi is still within the limits of the flexibility allowed to the translator. Even a phrase like 'virah ki anayaas peeda men,'[17] for the one word 'novu', in Tamil, meaning 'ailment' or 'affliction', free-translated in the English as 'pang', does not cause problems. Nor does the phrase 'asumprukt hokar'[18] for 'putting aside' which is a near-equivalent of the Tamil 'talli vithuvittu', trouble the reader with its heavy Sanskritic idiom.

A case for this markedly Sanskrit-tinged Hindi can be made by recourse to the Kannada introduction by T.R. Nagarajan. The Introduction has been rendered into Tamil by the Tamil translator, T.S. Sadasivam. 'The creative fibre of the language resulting from the union of Sanskrit and Kannada, cannot be realized in an English translation. For today's English (speakers and writers) what are Kannada and Sanskrit worth? Both are the same.'[19] Sanskritized Kannada is an important factor in any consideration of *Samskara*, runs Nagarajan's argument.

What makes the reader balk in this paragraph of the Hindi translation being considered, as mentioned earlier, is the word 'chahiye' in the sentence. 'Not leaping, when the invisible says "Here!". To receive it gratefully. Not climbing, not reaching out, not scrambling' is rendered as *'jab kaheen adrishya se awaaz aatee hai, "yahaan!", to bahut dhanyavaad purvak uska swaagat karnaa chaahiye, utaavali mein haath naheen phailanaa, oopar naheen chadhna, chcheena jhaptee me naheen padnaa chahiye.'*[20]

The ambiguity and self-questioning that form the essence of not just that paragraph but of the whole novel, are badly mauled by that word 'chaahiye' and the didactic tone which it brings in. And this seems a shortcoming in the translator's feel of the pulse of the novel, which, we have maintained, is essential for eloquence in a translation.

▌The Onslaught of Sound

Let us now go to another stage in the evolution and transformation of Praneshacharya. This is the stage seen in the section showing him in the fairground. A sea of sounds engulfs him here. If his sprawling in the forest and close hugging of grass and earth wake him to the sensory capacities of body and skin, the tornado of sounds in the fairground rouse him in a different way. They whip him into deep engagement with the meanings and associations wrapped around the sounds. The sounds are of toy whistles: a myriad toy whistles beeping from the mouths of a myriad boys who had wrested from unwilling parents the one paisa per whistle. The sounds are of the lusty call of the peepshow man to 'come see the Mysore Maharaja, aha, the splendour of the Maharaja's court; the Madras prostitute, the god of Tirupati, aha-ha, all for one paisa, just one paisa' [author's translation from Hindi, Tamil and English]. And the sounds are of the drumbeats going on for the acrobat pivoting on her bare belly atop a bamboo pole. The sounds are of the flinty cluck-cluck of fighting cocks lunging at each other, and the growling commands of the owners to their birds; of the zing and pop of soda bottles being opened; of the nose-ripping burps afterward.

Praneshacharya is dumb with fear. These raw, earthy joys are too raw and earthy for him. He cannot live them, even for the sake of Chandri, a natural denizen of this world of hot-blooded sensuality, the woman who made him man from an automated Brahmin. He cannot set up home with her as he had intended to. He does not have either the guts or the temperament for that kind of life. Fear grips him. He must get away from here fast, before some fellow Brahmin recognizes him, and this utterly private conflict he is going through becomes public talk. He dashes out of the fairground. The third and final stage of his evolution will set in now.

Let us see how well the translations we are considering capture this penultimate stage in Praneshacharya's eventual emergence in a reincarnated state. For the sounds we listed above, the Tamil revels in a natural, effortless onomatopoeia. 'Kuing', 'Koing', went the soda water bottles when their glass marbles were pressed down. And then, after a gulp of the sweet, coloured, gaseous water, 'karak' came the burp—expectation ('vetkai'), experience ('anubhavam'), fulfilment ('tripti'). The last section of the sentence—'vetkai', 'anubavam', 'tripti'—rises on the wings of the thought contained in it, and reaches a crescendo on the sound-speak of the language. Praneshacharya stands outside this world where the full power of everyday pleasures reign, looking round at the faces.

That could be taken as a fairly representative sample of Praneshacharya's state of mind at this stage. He stands wavering at the edge of this world that he sees spread about him. The Tamil, as we said, is able to evoke fact, wish and doubt, on the sweep of the language and its acoustic fibre. The English, we see this again, acquires its effect by steering the language to the theme of vacillation contained in Praneshacharya's state of mind. The English rendering runs as:

> The squeak and gurgle of the soda water as they push down the glass marbles in the soda bottles: the belch that comes up the throat after a drink of the sweet-coloured aerated waters—the whole thing was a matter of expectation, experience, contentment.... Praneshacharya stood outside this world of ordinary pleasures and looked at the gathered crowd.[21]

The intensity of the Tamil is replaced by the sane, perceptive voice of the translator, reaching out to the core of Praneshacharya's dilemma with creative detachment. (And here we might, in passing, take note of an unchanging, unchangeable feature of Indian writing in English, to which translations into English from Indian language have a blood tie, namely, its distanced, 'non-resident' quality. The English writer has to clip and whittle his language to make it echo the reality he is trying to portray, with much more conscious craft than does, usually, the Indian language writer. I think this remains an axiom in Indian English writing, original or translated.) The outcome of this necessarily virtuoso performance is seen in the sense and timbre of the passage quoted above. 'Squeak' and 'gurgle' are the words used by Ramanujan for 'Kuying' and 'Koying'. They are not onomatopoeic, as are the latter. They are proper, grammatical words. But they are sound related, and gain space in the context and allusions of the full sentence. We wake to the role that sound is playing in Praneshacharya's rebirth. We wake to his passage from the mute, however intense, stimuli of touch to the more eloquent stirrings from the stimuli of sound that he is exposed to. 'The whole thing was a matter of "expectation, experience, contentment",'[22] the sentence goes on. The translating voice is strong here, proxying for Praneshacharya, paraphrasing his feelings. Driven by this strong inner contact with the main character and the need to pick words that contain and communicate this insight into his condition, the writing emerges with taut adequacy. And because of this total balance of word, substance and implication, the translation acquires a kind of immediacy. Praneshacharya's vacillation gets evoked strongly, and gives sufficient dramatic momentum for the unfolding of his subsequent behaviour.

Now let us turn to the Hindi rendering of this section. Onomatopoeia has also been resorted to here. 'Kal-kal' is the equivalent for the 'kuying'and 'koying' of soda water bottles opening. It lacks force, lacks the thwack and explosive quality of the latter. And it does not have the searching quality of the English. 'Kal-kal' is the word usually used to describe the sound of running water, a running stream. The gentleness, the soft undulating motion associated with rivers—despite their furies of flood—does not fit in with the strident quality of the sounds assailing Praneshacharya. Nor does the translator's usage make it virile.

An interesting variation occurs in the Hindi. 'The sounds of the belches that broke out after just a few sips of the coloured soda water,' it says [author's paraphrasing]. Neither the English nor the Tamil translation talks of 'just a few sips of the coloured soda water' and the 'funny sounds of the belches afterwards.' The Hindi runs as, *'us rangeen sodey ke do chaar ghoont hee peekar dakaaron kee kaisee avazen nikalti ththeen.'*[23] Both the languages—English and Tamil—talk, respectively, of *the* belch that comes up after a drink of the soda water, and the belch that comes out 'karrkh' after drinking the soda. The belch is one special belch, and the soda is the whole bottle, not jut a few sips. But this difference in the Hindi does not become a fault. It simply draws attention to the interesting fact of variations in translations that do not basically change the text but do tease the reader about how and why they occur.

Here is another instance of a harmless yet intriguing variation. The Brahmins trudging to the neighbouring village Parijatapuram in the hot sun, enter a betel nut grove on the way. This is how the three translations we are considering here describe the moist air of the grove. The Tamil talks of the verdant green fronds of the betel nut orchard which hugged close and preserved the moisture of the earth. The English rendering is, 'The green of the betel nut grove lifted the earth's coolness to the heat of the sky.' The Hindi says the betel nut trees spread the coolness of the earth. Thus, the earth's coolness is hugged close and preserved in one case, is lifted to the sky in the other, and spread in the third! The reader can take his pick! Unfortunately, all the variations are not benign like these. To get back to the sounds of the soda water bottles being opened at the fair, the Hindi term 'kal-kal', as we said earlier, does not approximate to the timbre, spirit and significance of the sound being described. This shortfall gets marked in the subsequent section of that line. To transliterate it, '*yeh sab drishya aur shravya men swayam ek sambhaavnaa, ek anubhav, ek trupti ka sanchaar karta thaa.*'[24] Let us here recall the Tamil and the English of that sentence for quick and easy comparison. The English translation by Ramanujan is, as observed earlier, 'the whole thing was a matter of expectation, experience, contentment.' The Hindi sounds long-winded. 'Sambhaavna' which means 'possibility', dilutes the sense of definiteness present in the English and Tamil equivalents, 'expectation' and 'veytkai'. The idea of hope in these two words inclines markedly towards the sense of an assurance of occurrence.

Two words not present in the other two translations are also a feature of Hindi: 'shravya aur drishya' (sound and sight). Despite what we said earlier about variations and liberties in translations, this particular insertion, along with its heavy Sanskritic flavour becomes an overloading. '*Shravya aur drishya mey swayam ek sambhaavnaa, ek anubhav, ek trupti ka anchaar kartaa thaa.*'[25] There is a slowing down now and the pace drags. And inevitably, the intensity of the experience being sought to be conveyed, its tie-up with the high-pressure tumult raging in Praneshacharya's mind, gets softened, remote. I think a general rule can be drawn from the Hindi rendering. For communicating tense, emotional moment, short words with a cutting edge in a currently used idiom are more effective than loose-jointed, multi-syllabic words in a literary idiom. The idea contained in the full phrase '...*kaa sanchaar kartaa thaa*'[26] has been made implicit in the English rendering by the low profile phrase/sentence, '*the whole thing was a matter of...*,'[27] and it has been almost encompassed in one word 'adu' (that) in the Tamil.

| The Fear of Being Recognized

The third and final stage in the rebirth of Praneshacharya sets in when his inner turmoil has risen to fever pitch. His gut feeling that the gaudy world of the fairground, which is Chandri's habitat cannot be his, has strengthened. But he is caught in the fear that he might be recognized, for Putta has steered him into the temple, where he will eat the feast along with the other Brahmins. He is not yet free of the ritual pollution clinging to him after the death of his wife, and he is polluting the other Brahmins, the temple, the feast, in other words, the entire setting. What if he is recognized? He is. One of the Brahmins serving the guests, does recognize him and is all set for a chat. Beside himself with fear, he rushes out of the hall, shaking off the fellow Brahmins' attempt to stop him and do justice to the gourmet fare laid out for them. This fear of Praneshacharya is the dynamizing emotion in this entire section of the novel. And it is seen in one of its fullest, dialectically most intense form in the passages that follow.

A brief resume of these sections seems in order here. Praneshacharya's fear now is not merely that of being recognized. It is compounded by feelings of guilt. For, by sitting down to eat with the Brahamins in his polluted condition he is spreading pollution, 'infecting' them. What right did he have to do this? Was he any different basically from Naranappa, the crude exhibitionist who caught the sacred fish from the temple pond, fed them to Muslims, and guffawed at the outraged Brahmins? If his polluted state became public knowledge, all hell would break loose! The temple chariot would not move, the chariot race would stop and thousands of eyes would devour him. With this sequential thinking, his fears leap sky high, exploding into a passionate self-interrogation:

> 'God mine, what is the origin of this fear? Is it the first pang of rebirth? Is it only the fear of being found out? How shall I pluck out this fear by the root? Is it the kind of fear that will go if I bed with Padmavati tonight? Is it the kind that will be exorcised if I live with Chandri? What is the worth of any decision of mine? Where does it stand? Is mine a mindless state of indecisiveness, to become permanent in my life…?' [Author's translation]

Yes! All his reasoning power tells him that a neither-here-nor there state is indeed, what he has reaped from his flight after cohabitation with Chandri, following his wife's death. He cannot get liberation from his fear by a facile exercise of confession. By explaining himself and the true nature of his Brahmanism to those who have seen it grow and develop, the lives of those too would be sullied. Did he have the right to play with the lives of others in his decision? His thoughts stampede about him.

The agony of deciding whether to confess or not, and the fear of being recognized, drive him to calling out to god in a frenzy, to free him from the onus of making a decision. Let a course of action happen without his volition, as it happened without his volition with Chandri in the dark forest, he calls out. Let a new being be born now, *now*! But painfully, slowly, the decision to speak out to the Brahmins back home takes root in the churned, churning soil of his mind. At midnight, he will stand naked, far away from the fairground, naked before the eye of the Brahmins. And in that hour of night, he, the old familiar one who had lived among them and then left them, will become a new man. When he relates his story to them there is to be no trace of regret at having turned sinful. Else his two-ness will not go from him. His conflicts will not cease:

> On the night sky now are the stars, the crescent moon, the constellation of the seven rishis. A roll of drums from the temple sweeps down. Torches flare and dot the hillside. The oxen pant as they climb. Their bells tinkle. Some four or five hours more left now of journeying. And then? [Author's translation]

Let us now see how the above passages have been dealt with in the translations, passages where Praneshacharya's feelings rise to a dramatic height and throw the burden of the novel into sharp relief.

In the passage where Praneshacharya cries out to god above, beseeching him for explanation of where the root of his fear lies, the dramatic impact results from his sustained questioning. Where? What? How? Is it to be so? Is it not to be so? Why? Speak, O you god up there! Can you not speak? In the Tamil, as pointed out in our analysis of other watershed stages in the story, the questioning tone and the question-shaping words dart out as one composite unit. At the end of each sentence, the question, the questioning tone, and the import of the question ring out together in a flood of sound and meaning. The sense of crisis, of restlessness, gets etched deeper in the next passage, in which the special brahmanical ritual of serving food is highlighted. Fast, non-stop motor action is the dominant feature of this ritual. One Brahmin, says the Tamil rendering, quick-stepped along the row of diners, spooning ghee on the thin end of each plantain leaf. Close on his heels follows another, ladling payasam on the broader end of each leaf. After him come two hefty Brahmins serving rice, calling out 'gangway, gangway' as they walk down the line. And then follow a new, different face for each subsequent item: salad, cucumber, lentils. Each new face stokes afresh Praneshacharya's fear: what if this one, or that one behind, or that other, knows him, recognizes him...?

Praneshacharya is going to be recognized within the next half hour or so. His fears are going to coil around him like snakes. This half hour of premonition, during which he reiterates to himself his reasons for confessing his deeds to the Brahmins back home, and listens mechanically to the chatter of the Brahmin sitting next to him, is thus of strategic importance in the final act about to take place.

To what extent, then, have the other two translations we are considering registered in their renderings this quickening of pulse?

The English dredges into itself an assonance with the Tamil. The rise and fall of voice and words in it echo the 'original', that is, the Tamil. The pitch is higher in the Tamil; a passionate, declamatory pitch like that of a bhakta locked in confrontation with his god, demanding answers. Let us see where the stress falls in each sentence of this questioning. We shall give the gist of each sentence of the Tamil.

In the Tamil rendering of the sentence, 'God above! Where is the root of this fear? Is it the first pang of rebirth?' [Author's translation from Tamil] the stress falls in a natural way on the word 'root' ('moolam'). In the next sentence, it falls on 'first pang' ('mudal vedanai'). The stress is more or less even in the third sentence, 'Is it the dread of being found out?' [Author's translation from Tamil]. The Tamil here is only four complex, suffixed words that raise in level tones the three notions of 'someone': (*i*) 'yaaravadu' (recognizes me?), (*ii*) 'kandupidittuvittaal?' (is this the fear?), (*iii*) 'yennum achchamaa?'

In the fifth sentence, the last three words, '*vilagakkudiya bayamaa idu?*'[28] (is it the kind of fear that can be removed by...), wrest and bear the full weight of the sentence which begins with a slow, even distribution of import and supposition, '*inru iravu padmaavatiyun paduttaal...*'[29] ('If I sleep with Padmavati tonight'[30]). It is the same pattern with the sixth sentence where the latter half speculates upon the nature of the fear ('*theerakkoodiya bayama idu?*'[31]) and wrests the attention from the cure contemplated for it, that of casting his lot with Chandri. Then, '*Ennudaya teermaanathhin vilai enna?*'[32] (What is the value of my decision?) Again, the stress in the Tamil here falls on the word 'vilai' (value) which occurs in the latter half of the sentence.

After the full reading of the passage, after the assumptions and anxieties constituting it have fallen in place and the dust settled, the basic metaphysical problem of the indecisiveness and vacillation that have overtaken Praneshacharya stands out sharply. The whole book comes alive yet again, with yet another shake of its body, like an animal shaking itself back into form.

Let us now resume our consideration of the English translation of that passage. As we have observed, the English version draws into itself the sound-weave of the Tamil. The fall of stress on the sentences is almost matching, as:

'O God, what's the root of this dread? Are these the first pains of rebirth? Is it the kind of fear that will be quenched if I sleep with Padmavati tonight? Will it be quenched if I go live with Chandri? What's my decision worth? Am I forever to be a ghost of a man, hovering in indecision?'[33]

The frenzy is lower than in the Tamil. But there is an edged quality to the questioning, which gets muffled in the Tamil by the passion of the questioning. In the English, a sustained, intellectual–analytical probing reins in the passion. And yet, the same motifs that are stressed in the Tamil get stressed in the English too. What is 'the root of this dread?' we read, supplying the stress on the word 'root' just as we did in Tamil. 'Are these the first pains of a *rebirth*? Is it the kind of fear that will be *quenched* if I *go live with Chandri*? What's my decision *worth*? Am I forever to be *a ghost of a man, hovering* in indecision?'

The probing, analytical drive generates it own heat. And the passage becomes a compound of intellect and passion, like the Tamil, even though the distribution of the two qualities is different in the English. The English, we conclude then, lights up the inner spring of the novel in its own way. We get a clear impression of Praneshacharya caught in his indecisiveness.

Let us turn to the Hindi version now. A radical difference in the motion and behaviour of language is noticeable almost straightaway. The words are heavy-footed, the voice dragging. Consider this:

> '*Parmaatmaa! Is saarey bhay, aatank, kaa mool kaaran kya hai? Kya kisi naye janam se purv kee yeh prasav peeda hai? Yah ye bhai us praakaarka hai jo aaj raat yadi main padmavati ke saath so jaaun to lupt ho jaayegaa? Yadi main jakar chandri ke saathth rahney lagunga, to kya yeh nirmool ho jayega? Merey nirnay ka koi moolya bhi hai kya? Merey praarabdh mein kahin aisa to naheen hai ki manushya ke roop mein hi prêt bunkar sadev sanshay-asanshay ke beech dolta rahoongaa?*'[34]

The words are simply too literary. Take the first sentence, '*Paramaatmaa! Is saarey bhay, aatank, kaa mool kaaran kyaa hai?*' As in Tamil and English, the attention alights on the term for root and moolam—'mool kaaran'. The exact meaning of 'mool kaaran' would be 'main reason' but it evokes the sense of 'beginning', of 'origin', as well as do 'root' and 'moolam'. However, the true effectiveness of the sentence comes from the quick glide of the reading from 'fear' to 'root', or from 'root' to 'fear' in the syntax of the English rendering, and the conjugation of the two terms into one complex state. In the Hindi, this glide between the equivalent words 'bhay' and 'mool kaaran' is relatively low, ponderous of gait. This heaviness is felt all through the passage. Assumption and query do not come to a head on collision as in the other two renderings. The line, '*Kya yeh bhai us prakaar kaa hai jo ki aaj raat yadi main padmaavati ke saath so jaaun to lupt ho jaayega?*' is too sedate! '*Yadi main padmaavatee ke sath so jaaun*' is just too much loaded with supposition, too iffy. 'If', of course, figures in or is contained in the English and Tamil too. 'If I sleep with Padmaavati tonight...' and the succinct Tamil in which the 'if' comes as part of the term 'paduttaal'. But 'yadi' is not absorptive in the way its Tamil equivalent is, not fleet in the way 'if' is. Between the word 'yadi' and the event supposed—sleeping with Padmavati—the time lag is just too marked, too pronounced, the take-off too slow. Throughout, the supposition and the query never collide with each other forcefully enough to make the basic feeling of dread seem conquerable by the supposition. In the English and the Tamil, the dread, the supposition and the query unite in a loose yet perceptible confederation. In the Hindi, such a drawing together is not felt at all. The elements stay separate, only faintly veering towards each other. The underlying idea cementing that monologue of Praneshacharya, that his fear is indeed unconquerable, that his fear is indeed fearful, is projected by the reader's own prompting. In the English and Tamil, the idea springs out full-throated with the words and their oral force. The Hindi, as we said, is hampered by its over-literary idiom and by the diffident, puritanical flavour that this gives to the writing.

The Fear of Being Recognized

Let us now consider another passage where Praneshacharya's fear of being recognized is seen risen to fever pitch, imparting maximum momentum to the climax that is soon to follow: his headlong, precipitate rush from the dining hall. As we said earlier, his strong desire to lay bare his transgressions before the Brahmins back home is being undermined by equally strong fears about the shock effects of his disclosures upon the other Brahmins, which drive him to his helpless cry to God to rid him of the onus of deciding. This helpless, impassioned pleading is important. In the next few minutes, he will be recognized. And he will make a wild rush out of the hall, his hands unwashed, smeared with food. And at this point the tide will turn: the resolve to lay himself bare before his people takes firm, firmer shape within him. Let us now see how this feverish pitch of his self-dialoguing is tackled in the three renderings. On the effectiveness of the rendering here will depend the impact of the final act of return that Praneshacharya is to perform.

Degrees of Intimacy

Here too, as in the other instances, the Tamil is able to combine brevity and passion, infuse them with each other. Praneshacharya's cry to God is an intimate cry of agony and appeal, the cry of a son to his father, a father who is both pal and parent, a figure the son can both appeal to and demand of. Love and the sense of proprietorship fortify each other in this relationship. The son is calling upon his powerful father, is staking a son's claim to his father's omniscience to work a miracle for him. And here again, in what seems a hallmark of the Tamil, the speaker and the thing he is speaking about merge into a third reality that penetrates and packs the sentence, giving it a new dimension. He cries, 'God mine above, strip me of the onus of deciding' [Author's translation]. It is a piercing cry; its waves burst through the boundary of words and etch the tormented figure of Praneshacharya. It articulates the metaphysical ethical problem haunting Praneshacharya, and electrifies the entire sentence with the thrum of polemics. The English translation captures the tonal drama of that sentence, 'O God, take from me the burden of decision.'[35] The intimate cry heard in the Tamil version is not so strong. But it remains a fervent, personal call, a clear, individual voice that illuminates the core of the story, and gives the scene the necessary weight to make the final section's impact on the reader's mind with the required force.

The intimate tone is markedly absent in the Hindi rendering. Here is how it goes, '*Hay parmaatmaa, nirnay karney kay is daayitva ko tum mujhsay ley lo.*'[36] The language is formal, bookish. Between the God and the man calling to him, there is no emotional bond, no attachment of the genes of spirit that give him the guts to demand special indulgence from his maker. His is a formal petition to a higher up that happens to be God. Yes, he does address him in the second person singular 'tum', but the tone remains so correct and formal that 'tum' virtually sounds like 'aap'. Could not 'tu' have been used in place of 'aap'? Would it not have made for the clamour of feelings that produces the sense of impending tragedy, of doom apprehended, as in the Tamil and English? Would it not have brought God nearer, within the sphere of the sentence, made him immediate? And would not this nearness and immediacy have brought about the fast-forward motion so marked in the other two renderings, but lacking here?

An acute and clearly formulated agitation of Praneshacharya at this point is the springboard for the further development of the story. The next important halt in the course of the story occurs when Praneshacharya collects his breath after his headlong rush from the dining hall, and looks at the landscape around him. By looking at it, noting its features and registering its evocation of vignettes in the agrahara of his own village, he is proclaiming who and what he is, will always be. It is an insight into his essential self, and the image of this essential undying self is what is projected in the end. And for this finale to break in with the necessary force and impact, the steps preceding it have to provide the necessary momentum. Here are the salient features of this watershed moment: Praneshacharya looks up. The long, summer evening hours lie gathered. In the west russet lights lie spattered. White herons fly in formation westwards. A stork stands in semi-sleep on the pond's edge. It's lighting up time... And his thoughts fly agrahara-wards: how long is it since lights were lit there: how long since the cows were milked, tethered, the evening rituals observed? The shapes of the western range are fading from this instant to the next, like the fading of a dream world. The sky is denuded. It is the phase past the new moon. The evening prayers are ending. The tumult of the fair is lessening. 'If I set out now I shall be in the agra-hara by midnight, far away from this world' [Author's paraphrasing from English] his thoughts gallop, the refrain from Jayadeva's song breaks out within him, and swaying to its lilt he reaches forward and places his hand on Putta's shoulder, draws him close. Touching the untouchable, he frees himself from his old self, tethers himself to his new, evolving self. This evolving self will be made public at the assembly of the Brahmins tonight.

Praneshacharya, thus, is standing on the hair's breadth line dividing the past, present and the future. And, as in the fairground where also he had stood, aware, on the brink between the ferociously sensuous world spread out before him and the discreet, genteel world he knew, he is aware now too of the simultaneity of vision come to him.

To what extent have the renderings we are considering touched this pulse of tranquil and rounded self-awareness in this section? The Tamil, as we have been noticing throughout, winds smoothly, effortlessly, between the objective, narrative tone and the foregrounded monologuic tone of Praneshacharya's reflections. The result is that both spill into each other, and evolve into a special idiom of word and tone. The evening hour seems an objective description. But the pre-nocturnal languor of it washes in into the yearning, nostalgic mood of Praneshacharya. Are the lamps lit, are the cattle fed, are they bathed and milked in the village? And the plaintive-ness of his reflections seems to take voice from the careless, sovereign splendour of the evening.

This layered narrative tone unifies as the passage goes on. The enriched voice of Praneshacharya prevails as he rehearses to himself the act of self disclosure he is going to make in the wastershed hour of midnight. It is the persona behind this composite, far-seeing voice that sweeps out to the liquid beauty of the line from Jayadeva's song, clasps the untouchable cart man in a flood of 'solla mudiyada dukham'[37] and 'anbu surandadu'[38] ('uncontainable sadness' and 'overwhelming, flowing love'). And finally, it is this purified, catharsized being, who, seated in the carriage going towards Durvasapuram, awaits the hour of his confession with 'expectation, with keenness'.

The story of Praneshacharya, one feels after this last line in the book in the Tamil rendering, starts anew, afresh. This interaction at the level of the onlooker's voice and the agitatedly involved voice of the main character operates at a lower pitch in the English version. But the interaction is there, and that is important. The language, steered by the translator, reaches out to the non-English original, runs its feelers into its grooves of sound, probes its seams for tissues of connection between the level, onlooker's voice and the involved, subjective voice of the main character. Consider the line, 'The colours of this moment fading the next, the sky grows bare.'[39] In the Tamil, there is a fullness, a roundedness of emotion in that sentence. Between the two moments—the moment now and the moment after—we sense a continuity, a fluidity of time despite the break. And this rounds out to a poetic seamlessness in the latter half of the sentence, '...the sky grows bare'. In the Tamil, the homonymous words 'vaanam' meaning 'sky' and 'nirvaanam' (the second 'n' thickened, produced by striking the tongue against the roof of the mouth) make the whole image of the sky growing bare a vivid, clean-swept happening. But there is a crafted quality to the English that wakes you to the voice ensemble in the passage, to the alternating and also united voices of the narrator and Praneshacharya. This crafted quality touches a creative height in the phrase 'the naked quick of life,'[40] a few sentences later in that passage. This in-depth translation—a trans-creation, one may call it—is for the Tamil phrase meaning '(standing) like one who, to the frightened eyes of the Brahmins seemed as one who had withdrawn from this world (I shall become)...' The extended negative of that phrase in Tamil has been shortened and reexpressed as a taut positive. The Tamil evokes the image of a man as yet querying, gauging the hearts of his interlocutors. It evokes the eyes of the Brahmins dumb with fear at the sight of a man who has moved away to another realm. The English cuts down on the imagery and makes the condition of going away from the everyday world a state of being in its own right. It says, 'In full view of the frightened Brahmins I'll stand exposed like the naked quick of life.'[41] The sense of the freezing of motion that the Tamil conveys is absent here. The phrase 'full view' gives the sentence a living, speaking quality, a face-to-face quality. The frightened eyes of the Brahmins are not speechless with fear, even if they are not speaking. Their frightened eyes speak, communicate their fear, look for response. The phrase 'the naked quick of life' autonomizes the phenomenon of life, irrespective of the vagaries of personal decisions or impulses. Further, '*I'll* stand exposed like the naked quick of life' is an I-statement in the square, level-eyed and objective way possible only in English, in which the I-word has undergone a consistent ideological empowerment and dignifying.

Of course, the Tamil is also in the first person. But how different is this first person! He is modest. Even his resolve to make a clean breast of his heresies has an inward-looking, self-effacing, subjective air. He will in all likelihood be a totally isolated man after his confession, and he is quietly prepared for it.

The English first person, on the other hand, is more than an ago-nized, isolated figure. There is a marked vein of pride in his I-hood. He seems to have an invisible but palpable backing of historical forces. He gets a context and he can objectivize himself, can liken himself to other things, stand outside of himself and regard himself in a more cool, collected way than the Tamil first person. It is this exteriorized vision of himself that he is capable of having which makes him liken himself to the naked quick of life, like the first, primal beginnings of human life, he means. Driven by these impulses deep within, he will turn into a new man at midnight, he says. There is a quiet firmness of tone here, to this English 'I', in contrast to the quaver that the Tamil 'I' just manages to hold down.

The Tamil for 'new man' is an irreproducible, alliterative phrase— 'puttam pudiya'—meaning 'new as new', which infuses the quivery tone of the Tamil-I with a lyrical intensity, heightening its pathos. This effect is not producible in English, at least not through any alliterative process. But the concrete-seeming 'I' of the English translation—the 'I' that is 'like the naked quick of life'—undergoes further streamlining by the two short, clipped monosyllabic words, 'new man'. This new man, aware of his newness, more controlled in his emotions than his Tamil counterpart, is still no less poetic. 'Lalita-lavanga...' (delicate vines of clove...), the refrain from the *Gitagovinda* goes up in the new man's ear. It is an exquisite aesthetic moment. His clairvoyant awareness of impending rebirth and the liquid beauty of Jayadeva's poetry combine to breach the barricade stemming his emotions, and they spill out of him. It is in this liqueous state that he reaches out to touch Putta on his back

This physical contact with the untouchable is a milestone in Praneshacharya's evolution to a new state of being, a rite of passage he has performed. And any writing, original or translation, has to communicate the momentous-ness of this event. For, it is this internally overhauled, reconstituted man that we are to see in the end, journeying back to his village. The paragraph depicting that event connects dramatically with the description of the evening hour when Praneshacharya stabilizes after his frenzied rush out of the dining hall. The two descriptions, apart from each other by three pages and several paragraphs, need to be seen together for their inner dramatic continuity. Obviously, then, both have to be of matching strength to complement each other. And for this merging to take place, the event of Praneshacharya's physical contact with the low born Putta has to break in on the reader with the right impact. The decisive turn to Praneshacharya's personality denoted by the contact is the link between the two evening hours and the onward momentum that the story receives from this integrated push.

The Tamil is forthright. 'Sadness inexpressible sluiced out of Praneshacharya. Love seeped from him. Upon Putta's back for the first time he placed his hand. Drew him close...' [Author's translation]. The essence of a sadness inexpressible and sluicing out, of love seeping from the pores of his being, come across in an intimate, flesh and blood way, with a pang. The narrative voice undergoes the ache and yearning of Praneshacharya with no less intensity than does Praneshacharya himself. This kind of total blending of narrative, character and emotion—an extreme synthesis—is, one feels, alien to English. English has an objective thrust, a no man's land is always in operation, is mandatory, between the narrating voice and the narrative. But even granting this, the English translation of Ramanujan seems prosaic here. Way below the Tamil, and also way below the power his translation shows just a few lines earlier, when Praneshacharya sees himself standing like an accused in front of the Brahmins. The inventiveness of those lines is absent here. Consider the line, 'Praneshacharya was quite moved. Affection moved him. He put a hand over Putta's shoulder and drew him close.'[42] 'Quite moved' is for 'sadness inexpressible sluicing out of him', and 'affection moved him' is for 'love seeped from him'. Understatement and paraphrasing, of course, are methods allowed in translating into English. But surely not at the cost of reduced intensity? This flatness is difficult to understand in a translator so alive otherwise to the angst of Praneshacharya, is able to express this in his medium in words that invoke the original.

In the Hindi, the inner voice of the words, the free flow of the stream of thought within them, is impeded by unnecessary prepositions that block the formation of mood. It runs as:

Ek taptey din kee lambee see shaam. Paschim ke akash mey raktim aabhaa. Safayd pakshion kee kataron par kataarey apney ghoslon ko laut rahee hain. Neechey, taalaab ke kinaarey khada ek bagula gadgadaa raha hai. deepak, candeel jalaney ka praaya vakht ho gaya hai.[43]

Let us take this sentence by sentence. Could not the word 'ek' and the sub-word 'see' have not been there? Does not the quick trot of—'*Taptey din kee lambee shaam…*'—go better with the keen, short-breathed quality of Praneshacharya's thoughts and his anguished body language? Connect these descriptive sentences to his just preceding physical gesture: his looking up. The English says just that, 'Praneshacharya looked up.' So does the Tamil. Just a sentence of three words each in both the translation. The Hindi is long-winded, needlessly explicit, '*sir oonchaa uththaa kar Praneshcharya ne dekhaa.*'[44] Why? The same tendency to pad out action marks the other sentences in that segment. The tendency is curbed in the sentence, '*pachim ke akaash me raktim aabhaa.*' In the two other translations, the red of the sky is described in active, kinetic terms. The Tamil is a tight knit sequence of composite words, not easily translatable. 'In the west, red luminescence lay spattered' approximates to it, perhaps. The English is terse, economical and mood-evoking in 'streaks of red in the west.' 'Streaks' here is a noun-and-verb combining word. The Hindi is a concentrated adjective, 'raktim aabhaa' (blood-red glow). It is a powerful phrase. 'Raktim' weds the violence of blood to the sensuousness of the colour red. And this artefact of violence and sensuousness conjoins the word 'aabhaa', qualifying it and being qualified by it. This deviation of the Hindi from the other languages is enjoyable, fully in keeping with the individual translator's autonomy. But why 'pashchim ke aakaash mein'? Would just 'pashchim' not have been enough? The two 'm''s of 'paschim' and 'raktim' are too close. It sounds unmusical. But devices exist for getting round problems of that sort, such as, a dash after 'mey'!

It is astride this overdone prose that Praneshacharya is brought to the all-important monologue which culminates in Jayadeva's song ringing in his ear, impelling him to clasp the cartman in a blind yet historic act of breaking the barrier of touch. How do the lines in Hindi tackle this stage in Praneshacharya's evolution? As in the Tamil and English, in the Hindi too, the first person voice is made explicit, and we hear Praneshacharya talking to himself in low discreet tones, as:

'*Yadee mai isi vakht chalnaa shuru karun to aadhee raat tak agrahaar, is duniya se kitnee dur, pahaunch jaungaa. Un bhaybheet brahmnon ke sammukh me maano bilkul nishank, nanga hokar khada ho jaunga: tab mein un sabsey jyeshth, us aadhee raat ke pal apnaa naya vyaktitva paa loonga.*'[45]

Where, in these lines, is the controlled passion of Praneshacharya that we sense in the Tamil and the English? Is not this feel of passion-held-in-leash closer to Praneshacharya's state of mind than these sedate, un-anxious reflections of his? Why is there no quickening in his voice when he soliloquizes about showing himself defenceless and uncloaked to the Brahmins, and becoming a renovated man at the crack of dawn? And lastly, where is the control when Jayadeva's line rings out in his ears, making him lunge forward and clasp Putta by the shoulder? The sentences are too symmetrical. Between the narrating 'I' and the 'I' visualized by the narrating 'I', there is no tug and pull of a shared pulse. There is no sense of a wrench being felt by the narrating 'I' to slide out of himself and transform to the 'I' he is visualizing. Not surprisingly, then, this slow-paced, even-voiced being lacks the drama necessary to imbue with significance his revolutionary act of clasping Putta. '*Praneshacharya bhaavaatirek se gad-gad ho gaye. Unmey anuraag umad aaya.*' What ornate, literary words! 'Bhaavaatirek' is just too much of Sanskrit, too florid, for saying 'overcome with feeling'. 'Gadgad ho gaye' again, is an overstatement, too stilted, for 'swept by emotion'. And 'anuraag?' Would not 'prem' be enough, simpler and quicker? How can intensity be conveyed through over-Sanskritized, polysyllabic words?

The final image of Praneshacharya we have is of a man shed of a whole lot of outworn spiritual baggage. Let us recapitulate the shedding. He has broken the taboo of touch, the major instrument of Brahmanism for enforcing and retaining overlordship. He has cohabited with Chandri, the untouchable of classic beauty. It has sublimated him. She and the earth on which he lay with her have become one, become one timeless female figure, an ever present enveloping femininity. And with Putta, he strikes up an easy male camaraderie of free flowing, wide ranging conversation that becomes heart-to-heart, risen above caste. He has, in effect, given himself a new parentage, a new pedigree. Wiped clear of the tattoo marks of orthodoxy on his being, minted anew, he sets forth on his journey back to the Brahmins, to whom he will declare himself.

As if gauging the hour for that event, he looks up at the sky. Four or five hours more of journeying. A sudden roll of temple drums goes up. Yellow circles of torch fires shine here and there. The hard breathing and puffing of the bullocks moving up-hill, the tinkle of their bells agitate the air.

The slender yet tough fibre of stability amidst flux that the scene projects is what the translation has to evoke.

The sentence that balances the two realities in that paragraph is, 'Over. Just four or five hours of travel left.' It is repeated twice. And here, perhaps, we might note once again, the variations that creep into translations, variations that do not affect the theme and text but do make us wonder how they happen. The English and the Hindi have this sentence the first time as the last line of their respective paragraphs preceding the paragraph under discussion, which is the last but one paragraph of the novel. In the Tamil, it is the opening line of this last but one paragraph. It repeats itself as the last line of this last but one paragraph. The English and the Hindi also repeat the line in this paragraph, but add a short line after, 'Then, after that, what?'[46] ('*Phir, uskey baad kyaa hogaa?*[47]).

This difference in placing does not matter, of course, for the importance of the sentence is felt uniformly in all the three renderings. But it draws attention. The first time that the sentence occurs is in the wake of the fears of being spotted by other Brahmins that have broken afresh in Praneshacharya's mind. Exhausted, benumbed, seated in the carriage that is to take him to his destination, he nods farewell to Putta. And in the hurl forward of the carriage, the thought goes up in slow motion in his mind, 'Over, that's over. Four or five hours of journeying more to get through. Then?' It is the voice of a man not yet broken free of the web of his present. It is a face with the eyes not in focus with themselves.

This shaken, as yet unsteady being looks up at the sky, seated in the carriage, and registers the nightscape: the thin second moon quivering towards fullness, the throb and pulse of life become sharper in the enveloping darkness. The onward, ever onward, course of life floods his awareness. Mounted again on the steed of life by this awareness, the thought speaks itself into his mind once more, 'Four to five hours of journeying.' It is a firm voice now, belonging to a man come clear of the tentacles of his present. He is a man with eyes fixed ahead, freed of their backward tug. The Tamil captures the two facets of the sentence beautifully. The first time it begins with a single word 'aayitru', which just means 'over' with a suggestion of 'so that's that'. You read it in conjunction with the preceding sentence which shows a Praneshacharya patient, long-suffering and limp at the prospect of Putta's unbreakable seeming company. 'So that's that. Some four or five hours of travel more', he seems to be saying with a sigh, a helpless shake of the head. In the lines of scenic description that follow, this heavy lethargy drags along. He sees as faraway fixtures the slice of the second moon, the stars and the constellation of the seven sages. In the very next sentence, the static mood is dispelled. 'Suddenly, the tumult of temple drums' [Author's paraphrasing into English]. The decisive word here is 'irundaapalirindu' (suddenly). Without this sense of an abrupt burst into motion that this word conveys, 'tumult of temple drums' by itself would not have got activated. 'Suddenly', then, the burst of drums, the sweep of torch flares, the hard, rhythmic breathing of the bullocks climbing uphill. The slow, steady vitality of these movements and motion flow into Praneshacharya, and he says it again, 'Four or five hours of travel'. He attaches no prefix, no suffix, to that statement, as do the English and the Hindi.

This contrasting use of the sentence 'four or five hours more of travel', and the diverse moods produced by the usage, felt so strikingly in the Tamil, is noticeable, is far from absent, in the English too. But the throbbing intensity of the Tamil is replaced by a more controlled, more considered use of language. Each detail of the night scene is set down in photographic clarity. Each is distinct, stays put in its place, not ramming into the other. Stars and moon, drums and torch lights, the bullocks' breathing and the bells round their necks: these do not amalgamate into a compound of sense impressions, as in the Tamil.

The result is a prose of tranquillity. The lines read themselves out in pace with the reader's reading of them. The fever and the groping, questing quality of Praneshacharya's saga of journeying forth, rise afresh from this fusion of voices, the voice of the lines and the voice of the reader reading them. In this stirred yet critically demanding atmosphere, you read the recurrence of the sentence, 'four or five hours more of travel.' In the Tamil, as said, the sentence recurs without any qualifying word before or after. And it rings out as Praneshacharya's voice, a Praneshacharya come clear of the anxieties that were tormenting him when he calculated the hours of travel left, just a while ago. In the English, this conversion of the narrative tone into the first person voice of the protagonist does not happen. Praneshacharya's remains a third person voice. But we feel his nearness, feel the stirs and tremors of his personality as the descriptions of the night scene draw him to the foreground and make him seem the describer. The serenity and perenniality of the sounds and movements filter into him. 'He will travel, for another four or five hours. Then after that, what?' says the narrative. The inquiring tone levels off into soft, mellow moods as it merges with Praneshacharya's personality. Made serene by the serenity of his surroundings, Praneshacharya considers his way ahead with composure, the ghosts of his past laid low, at least for the time being.

In the Hindi, this sense of a watershed of time and mood is not evoked by the repetition of the sentence, '*Unkee yaatraa—abhee chaar paanch ghantey aur beetney hain. Phir uskey baad kyaa hogaa?*'[48] ('Four or five hours more of his journey left. Then after that, what is to be?'). Praneshacharya does not seem energized into a keener, more settled state of mind with the asking of that question. The change of mood takes place, as we saw in the other two translations, with the sweep of the night scene into Praneshacharya's innermost senses, as his carriage rumbles along. Obviously then, the sixteen or so lines of description have to be powerful enough to awaken Praneshacharya to the mystique of the phenomena being described, that reshape his mood. The lines lack thrust, the palpable thrust towards the turmoil raging within Praneshacharya, which the Tamil and English versions have achieved in their own ways. For the hot-breathed intensity of the Tamil, we have the judicious steering of language in the English version, making for its own compelling quality. In the Hindi, the reader does not feel this pegging of the language to the emotional hub of the story. The objects described seem like items in a list. This lack of flow is ascribable to the formal, grammar-bound prose of the Hindi that we notice all through the translation. This is how the Hindi of the lines being considered here, goes:

Askaash taron sey bharaa huaa thaa. Ek koney mein dwitiya ke chaand ka tukdaa. Ek taraf saptrishi mandal: achaanak kaheen se dhol bajney kee awaaz aayee. Jahan tahan mashaalon ki roshnee. Pahaadee par gaadee khenchte hue bailon ke saans-usaas kee oonchee awaaz. Unkey galey mein bandhee ghantiyon kee runjhun. Unkee yatra—abhee chaar paanch ghantey aur beetney hain. Phir uskey baad kya hogaa?[49]

Why 'bharaa huaa thaa'? Does not the 'thaa' make for a fussy precision of tone and place? Does it not affect the timelessness intended in the description, the timelessness that sweeps into Praneshacharya and composes him? In the next sentence, *'ek koney mein dvitiya ke chaand ka tukdaa'*, are the words 'ek' and 'ke' necessary? Why not just *'koney mein dvitiya chaand ka tukdaa'*? Does not the clipping strike better the intended mood of detached involvement? And, *'ek taraf saptrishee mandal'*? Why not 'sapt rishi mandal—us taraf'? 'Achaanak kaheen sey dhol kee avaaz aayee' is a disaster. Could not 'kaheen se' have been better placed? Would not the sound of dhol be coming from *some* direction any way? Why specify it? Why not *'dhol kee avaaz, achaanak kaheen sey'*? Does not the sense of space and direction blur in this construction and become more intense in the blurring? *'Jahaan tahan mashaalon kee roshnee'* is all right, but immediately after is the full blown, full-fledged line, *'pahaadi par gaadi kheenchte huey bailon ke saas-usaas kee oonchee avaaz.'* The specific quality of it mars the sporadic and suggestive quality of the sentence before. Would not *'bailon kee oonchee saas-usaas, gaadee kheenchtey huey'* have sufficed? And then *'unke galey mey bandhee ghantion kee runjhun.'* Why 'unkey'? Would not *'galey ki ghantion kee runjhun'* have been enough? And finally come the two lines *'unkee yaatra—abhee chaar paanch ghanatey aur beetney hain. Phir uske baad kya hogaa?'*

Again, the word-load seems too much. If rendered as *'Yaatra— abhee chaar paanch ghantey aur. Uskey baad?'*, would not the deletions emphasize the aspects of who, what and how long, present in the sentence, give it the concentration necessary for establishing the required mood?

Praneshacharya does not seem rejuvenated enough by the spiritual essence of the night scene unwinding before him. That he is affected is made clear in the concluding sentence of the rendering, *'Praneshacharya utsuktaa se, udvignata se, aashaa se, us ghadi kee prateekshaa kar rahey the.'*[50] Again, how faint in it is the element of yearning that characterizes the versions in Tamil and English! We get it from the narrator's say-so rather than from the charged mutation of the narrator's voice into words voiced by Praneshacharya himself. This synthesis is central to the novel. It manifests itself in it all along and is among its major refrains. In not achieving it, the Hindi rendering, sadly, emerges as an anti-climax.

Notes

1. Anantha Murthy. 1965. *Samskara*. Banglore: Kavya.
2. Sadasivam, T.S. 1993. *Samskara*. Hyderabad: Orient Longman. Trans. of. Anantha Murthy, op cit.
3. Ramanujan, A.K. 1978. Afterword. *Samskara: Three Crowns Series*. New Delhi: Oxford University Press, p. 139. Trans. of. Anantha Murthy, op cit.
4. Ramanujan, p. 17.
5. Kusnoor, Chandrakant. 2005. *Sanskaar*. New Delhi: Radhakrishna Paperbacks. Trans. of. Anantha Murthy, op cit.
6. Kusnoor, p . 45.
7. Ibid., p. 157.
8. Ibid.
9. Ramanujan, p. 127.
10. Ibid., p. 114.
11. Ibid., 114–15.
12. Ibid., p. 115.
13. Ibid., p. 131–32.
14. Ibid., p. 135.
15. Ibid., p. 83.
16. Kusnoor, p. 101.
17. Ibid.
18. Ibid.
19. Sadasivam, T.S. 'En paarvayil Samskara'. Trans. of. T.R. Nagarajan's Introduction in Kannada.
20. Kusnoor, p. 101.
21. Ramanujan, p. 114–15.
22. Ibid., p. 114.
23. Kusnoor, p. 140.
24. Ibid.
25. Ibid.
26. Ibid.
27. Ramanujan, p. 114.
28. Sadasivam, p. 118.

29. Ibid.
30. Ramanujan, p. 128.
31. Sadasivam, p. 118.
32. Ibid.
33. Ramanujan, p. 128.
34. Kusnoor, p. 158.
35. Ramanujan, p. 132.
36. Kusnoor, p. 164.
37. Sadasivam, p. 124.
38. Ibid.
39. Ramanujan, p. 134.
40. Ibid., p. 135.
41. Ibid., p. 135.
42. Ramanujan, p. 134–35.
43. Kusnoor, p. 166.
44. Ibid.
45. Ibid.
46. Ramanujan, p. 138
47. Kusnoor, p. 171.
48. Ibid.
49. Ibid., p. 170.
50. Ibid., p. 171.

Chapter 6

The God of Small Things: A Wrong Book to Translate

The language of *The God of Small Things*[1] is overpowering. For the translator, this strong, foregrounded presence of the parent language creates problems. Its language, however, is not the exclusive factor for the power and impact of the novel, it should be mentioned. The deeper bearing on Neelabh's translation[2] of this near but not exclusive sway of language in the original will become clearer—I hope!—as the analysis goes on. The immediate effect on the translator of this thrust of language is that it thwarts him from sufficiently distancing himself from it, and focusing on the thought/thoughts behind it. Such distancing is a necessary step in all translation exercises. The aural incursion of the source text has to somehow get toned down sufficiently, to enable the translator to go past it and make contact with the cerebral-cum-psychic propellers behind the cascade of voice and tone.

Roy's spell-binding text complicates this necessary and instinctive move of the translator, equipped as he is, with the counter weapon of his own rendering language, and dutybound, so to speak, to demonstrate its equal virtuosity. For most of its narrative stretch, Neelabh's rendering responds and reacts more to the verbal magnetism of Roy's text. He does this with gusto, it must be said, and does it with what seems a devotee's adulation of her prose. For instance, consider this passage:

> He didn't know that in some places, like the country that Rahel came from various kinds of despair competed for primacy. And that *personal* despair could never be desperate enough. That something happened when personal turmoil stopped by at the wayside shrine of the vast, violent, circling, driving, ridiculous, insane, unfeasible public turmoil of a nation. That Big God howled like a hot wind, and demanded obeisance. Then Small God (cosy and contained, private and limited) came away cauterized, laughing numbly at his own temerity. Inured by the confirmation of his own inconsequence, he became resilient and

truly indifferent. Nothing mattered much. Nothing much mattered. And the less it mattered, the less it mattered. It was never important enough. Because Worse things had happened. In the country that she came from, poised forever between the terror of war and the horror of peace, Worse Things kept happening.[3]

Before taking up Neelabh's translation of the above paragraph, it might be helpful to consider the special features of the original, and thereby, the variations deriving from it. Firstly, that whole passage is an encoded and anguished statement of political import. It rises from an involuntary expression of unbridged, unbridgeable differences between not only different cultures, but more importantly, more urgently, between segments of the same culture, the same country; that of Rahel's, the girl proxying for the narrator. It sways between the two extremes of the 'Small God' of this country and culture signifying the impertinent growth of personal ordeals, and its 'Big God', signifying the immanence and rooted strength of the body politic, of land and country. With taut, sibylline utterances, the narrative voice details the tragic–comic, yet grim, deadlock that results when the Small God tries to dislodge the Big God. No David and Goliath story results from the bout, the narrating voice says. The Small God remains small, a defeated and defiant loner, homing in into people's eyes and freezing there as an inscrutable look. 'He climbed into people's eyes and became an exasperating expression,'[4] is how the Small God is described in the next paragraph.

Secondly, we can divide that passage into three clear segments. There are, firstly, the two classic segments of Thesis and Anti-thesis that comprise a proposition. There is, secondly, the Thesis of the Big God: immanent, invincible, supreme. The Small God, the god of personal despair crossing sword with the Big God, is the Anti-Thesis. The third segment, comprising the classic summation of a proposition, Synthesis, is signified in that passage by the near total subsuming of the Small God by the Big God. *Near* total, not total. The passage transcends or breaks out of the formal pattern set for a syllogism by the rules of formal logic. The two segments—major premise and minor premise, to use the terms of formal logic—or Thesis and Anti-Thesis, symbolized by the Big and Small Gods stay apart in their respective spheres in uneasy proximity, liable to come to blows, tethered to their tethers. The passage, in effect, leaves behind semantics for the natural poetry of free expression.

The question now is, do we get this sense of a beauteous construct of semantics and poetic fervour from the Hindi translation? At first, the Hindi phonetics trip you up in the leap that you as a reader—and perhaps a potential translator—need to make to get to the lull behind the words, to get to the word-quietened, evocative essence of the prose, in order to grasp its underlying statement. You tend to read the Hindi simultaneously with the English, letting yourself into a scramble of languages. The irony here does not escape you. For, scrambling up the language is a prominent feature of Roy's prose style and form. But the scramble you come up with, alas, is devoid of the method gone into Roy's creative scramble!

Anyway, you persist, and persistence pays, as always. The English intrusions die out, leave the field clear for the native genius and tonal dynamics of the target language to wash into your ear. Made receptive, objective, you register the adequacy of the translation. You wake to the close, analytical attention paid by the translator to the choice of words in the original, and his painstaking, disciplined search for words of matching import and impact. Take, for instance, the long, high-decibel, adjective-ridden concluding phrase, 'vast, violent, circling, driving, ridiculous, insane, unfeasible, public turmoil of a nation.'[5] The English ends with 'public turmoil of a nation'. The translation takes this end as the opening parts of its rendering. It runs, '*Rashtra kee vishaal, prachand, chakkar khaatee....*'[6] Other displacements also occur. The opening phrase of the English, 'That something happened...'[7] comes at the end of the Hindi rendering. In the English, the two phrases 'That something happened' and 'when personal turmoil' are joined, made consecutive. 'Dropped by at the wayside shrine of ...'[8] immediately follows this conjoined phrase. The three parts then unite and brace to meet the barrage of adjectives that breaks out immediately after, '...vast...insane...unfeasible...' And this swinging, swaying complex of mutually sustaining phrases allied with high-spirited adjectives is halted by the slow, measured gait of the concluding phrase, 'public turmoil of a nation'.

The Hindi, as said earlier, changes the order of the sentence, almost inverts it. 'That something happened', followed by 'when personal

turmoil' is broken into two separate phrases, placed at the beginning
and end in reverse order. The full sentence reads, '*ki jab niji uththal-
puththal ek rashtra kee vishaal, prachand, chakkar khaatee, ayed lagaatee,
haasyaaspad, unmathth, asangat, saarvajanik uththal-puththal kee sadak
kinaarey banee samadhee par pahunchtee to kuchch ghatithth hota.*'[9] The
reordering does not bother you though you do wish for and work out
alterations, in a kind of word game. How about, for instance, '*kee
kuchch ghatithth hota jab nijee uththal-puththal rashtra kee vishaal,
prachand, chakkar khaatee, ayed lagaatee, haasyaaspad, sadak-kinarey
banee samaadhee par pahunchtee?*' Do not the six concluding words in
this order highlight better the dramatic impact of the act of stopping by
at a wayside shrine? You wonder, speculate. But the speculations fade;
and speculations can be endless. Solid workmanship is unmistakable
in that line. To revert to the English for purposes of comparison, we
find that each adjective in the English has a point of convergence for
its vowel compound. The voice is expelled with force from this point
into new vowel shapes that give the adjective a solid, noun-like feel.
In 'violent', for example, the speech stress first homes in on the 'i'-'o'
vowel compound, and then springs out on the weaves and turns of the
succeeding vowel 'e', such that you feel the violence of the 'violent'.
The same principle of inward and outward motions of sound-fall is
discernible in the Hindi words. In 'prachand' (for 'violent'), the voice
gathers in and bounces out on the tracks of the successive 'a' sounds
of the word. More. The consonant 'pra' preceding the first 'a' sound,
and the consonant 'nd' that succeeds the second 'a' sound exert their
own pressures of sound and evocation on the vowel, giving the word
a special feel of solidity. 'Prachand' (violent) expands as 'prachanda-ta'
(violence): adjective becomes noun. A special, inner assonance of
articulation caused by some ground rules of speech articulation brings
the two languages on a fraternal level. Add to this the diligence you
cannot help but notice in the translator's choice of words: you reread
the passage as writing in its own right.

The English subsides in your field of attention. The Hindi appropriates sound and sense, gains ascendancy. The prose carries you
along. The line of thought, reasoning and argument engages you.
The imagery comes as novel, bold, paring the language to re-contour
it, recode and reconstitute its silences. At the end of the exercise, you

sit back, awash with the contentment that a well-proportioned, well-rounded product of literary effort arouses in a reader. But a sense of incompletion persists. The context beyond the context created by words and meaning, does not break into the reader's awareness with the unambiguous clarity of the English original. The three elements, one, the immediate context, two, the context beyond, and three, the words, stay in a working coalition, each distinct from the other, brought together under the pressure of the narrative voice. In the English, the feel of a nation sprawling, tempestuous, a mastiff unchainable (the Big God) and of the hardened, veteran survivor of life-long strife and privation (the Small God) unfurls genie-like from the pulse of the prose-narrative. The image, shadowy yet firm of feet and solid, anchors the rush of thought in that passage. The dead serious political statement that is contained in the characterization and alignment of the two gods, Big and Small, with Rahel the Indian girl, of Larry McCaslin, the American with Rahel, the Indian, rings out from the inner construct of the passage.

This audibility of the unsaid, this immediacy and life-like presence of a reality presented not frontally but in silhouette, is not a feature of the Hindi. A translation which compels attention from its sheer reproductive élan, a translation which carries the reader along on the momentum of this élan, a translation of this calibre fails this litmus test set by the English original. Why? One cannot help wondering. Is it something to do with the shaping agents that have gone into the physique of the language? It may well be so, one cannot help feeling. Let us take some key phrases and sentences from the English original of that passage. Country and nation emerge as vivid, ineffaceable realities from them. '...in some places, *like the country that Rahel came from* various kinds of despair competed for primacy' (emphasis added). The italicized phrase acted upon and spotlighted by the preceding and succeeding phrases '...in some places' and 'various kinds of despair', simply condenses into the country meant. The term 'India' flashes on like a neon sign in the corridors of the reader's mind, and stays lit. The whole sentence mutates and metamorphoses into one particular place, like a leaf turning to flower.

One looks for this kind of transformative energy from the Hindi equivalents of those phrases. '*Kuchch jagahon mein, maslan Rahel jis desh se aye thee, hatasha kee alag-alag kismen avval rahney ke hod mein shareek rahteen thee.'* Now, to repeat what has been said before, the Hindi of course has to be read with the mind purged of the spell of the English. It has to be read as a text in its own right, even though its reproductive verve is what gives it its stature. But at this point in our analysis reproductivity is not the issue. The issue is the realm beyond. '...*Rahel jis desh sey aayee thee*' is alerting. You connect 'Rahel' with 'jis desh sey aayee thee' and sense the phrase contracting to its hard, implicit essential. But the qualifying phrase '*hataashaa kee alag-alag kismen avval rahney kee hod mey shareekh rahtee theen*', does not merge with the initiating phrase in the metaphorizing and metamorphosing way it does in the English. It does not condense, does not essentialize the sentence into the emotive one-word, India. Once again, why? The words are apt and faithful to the nuances of the original. But the magic synthesis of the original does not take place amidst all this verbal proficiency. Why? Forget the sprawling and over-loaded feel of the phrase. The English is taut and quick-footed. It is verb-based, action-based—'various kinds of despair competed for primacy'—it goes. The Hindi, almost double the word-load of the English, from 'hataashaa' to 'shareekh rahteen thee' sags under the strain of grappling with the pithy, quick-off-the-tongue quiver of the English. Compare the two. 'Hataashaa', the operative word, takes quite a while to connect and fuse with 'alag-alag kismon', denoting variedness. In the English, the connection is instantaneous, no sooner said than there. In 'alag-alag kismon' for 'Various kinds', 'Alag'alag' is the main culprit. Say it fast or say it slow, for the significance of 'alag-alag' to register; say it anyhow. But 'various' releases into the mind its sense and sound with the utterance. And then there is the phrase '*avval rahney kee hod men shareekh rahteen theen*', for the three-word English phrase 'competed for primacy'. The English is lighter, lither, fleet-footed, discharging into the mind the sense and import of the words with the sound. Forget all this. They are secondary and can be overlooked. Forget also the possibility that the inversion in the placing of 'despair' and 'various kinds' in the Hindi could be part of the reason for its ineffectiveness. What if it had been 'alag-alag kismon kee hataasha'? Would it not have compressed the phrase into the required tautness? Would it not have absorbed better the eight-headed monster, '*avval*

rahne kee hod men shareekh rahteen thee' for 'competed for primacy'?
Perhaps. Perhaps not. Perhaps yes. Perhaps, perhaps...

It is not verbal recasting that is the issue here. It is something bigger,
more basic. The synthesis does not take place because the nuances of
the original, its suggestions and semi-suggestions, issue from a full-
fledged image-compound present in the first writer's mind. Because
this image-compound itself has been thrown up in the first writer's
mind from the slow churning of concepts formed in her mind much
before the writing. Because the resonances, the metaphysical and
allusive vein, the undertones and overtones of this vein that combine
to give the language its strong personality and distinct orientation,
are effects of a cerebral–emotional exercise undergone by the writer
before she commenced writing the novel.

The translator, of course, cannot be expected to undergo or to have
undergone the same inner dialoguing. But he *is* expected to connect
with the wavelengths of the first writer's thoughts and feelings. Either
through self-suggestion or auto-suggestion or what you will, he has
to vibe with the author. On this score, that of vibing, Neelabh, as we
have seen, gives no ground for, complaint; far from it. This brings
us back to the question being considered here: why, even a most
sensitively wrought verbal similitude like Neelabh's, fails to match
the power of signification that Roy's novel has. One reason could be
that the signifying powers of languages differ in quality: that no two
languages signify similar objects or similarly.

Let us take again, one last time, even at the risk of rousing boredom,
the sentence we have been considering: 'In the country that Rahel
came from, various kinds of despair competed for primacy.' You see
smoky, surrealist outlines, while the word 'India' tattoos faintly in
the voice-box of your understanding. Alongside, the word 'despair'
sets off a jumble of images, sprung from anterior images of poverty
and disease. In 'despair', you read and hear the word; watch a mad
jig of cholera, hunger, penury. The word 'India' tolls again from
this montage, superimposes upon it as a steady, cognizable presence
of face and form. This drama of signifying is much less dramatic in
the Hindi as compared to the English. Here is the translation again,
to repeat it here for quick and easy reference, *'Rahel jis desh se aayee
thee, hataashaa kee alag alag kismen avval rahney kee hod mey shareekh*

rahaatee thee.' Except for the word 'desh', individual words do not fold in and unfold into a major reality. 'Hataashaa' does not have the hard, well-defined feel of 'despair'. It sounds fluid, evokes a state of generalized, unfocussed unhappiness. The phrases 'various kinds of despair' and 'hataashaa kee alag-alag kismen' do not evoke the same sensation. The clipped, compact and staccato quality of the English is very different from the vowel-centric, sprawling phonetics of the Hindi. This sense of an uncondensed centre to the words continues, is carried over to the succeeding words, till the whole sentence gets a swinging quality of perpetual motion. Motion and motility are held in leash in the English. Words harden, centralize, mutate and transform into deeper, metaphysical implications.

Why does the Hindi fall short of this final turn? Why does not a direct and taut link, a current of instantaneous, mutual recognition get established between the narrating voice and its narrative? One reason could be the rather obvious one, that the parent narrating voice has an umbilical connection with the well-springs of its narrative, rises from the underbelly of its rationale and semantics. In a translation, this organic connection of the narrator with his narrative is, of course, not possible, as pointed out before. But the interlock this connection denotes remains the test for the successes and failures of a translation. The failure of Neelabh's commendable translation to bare the unverbalized yet unmistakable vibrant presence of the statements behind the words, thus, can only be attributed to the chanciness, to the hit-or-miss element inherent in the translator's craft, inherent in the translator's deliberate, necessary act of fitting the original writer's nerve cords of feeling to his own mode and range of cognition.

Let us turn now to those instances in Neelaabh's rendering where chance works in his favour, where his professional endeavour of chiming with the original writer has paid off. We see it in his rendering of a nursery rhyme. Here is the English, 'There's a sad sort of clanging/From the clock in the Hall/And the bells in the stee/ple too/And up in the nursery/An abs-urd/Litt-tle Bird/Is popping out to say…'[10] Neelabah's rendering is, '*Galiarey mey khadee ghadee kee ghantee bole tan-tan/door charch kaa ghantaa baajaa/madhdham sur me ghan-ghan/khidkee par aakar chidiya ne/ooncheetaan lagayee/baith ghadi ke bheetar koyal…*'[11] Some material differences between the two catch the attention immediately. There is only one bird in the English whereas there seem two in the Hindi: the 'chidiya' (bird) in the 'khidkee' (window), and the koyal 'ghadi ke bheetar' (within the clock) seem two different birds. And there is nothing like a bird on a high note in the English (*'chidiya ne oonchee taan lagaayee'*[12]). There is no window, no 'khidkee', nothing like a bird coming to the window. In the English, the 'clock in the Hall' goes up in a 'sad sort of clanging'. In the Hindi, the clock comes out with just 'tan-tan'. The onomatopoeia does not evoke sadness. And nowhere in the English do the church bells peal in a 'madhdham sur' meaning medium scale. But another reading of 'madhdham sur' is possible, you realize. 'Madhdham sur' could be meant to convey the idea of plaintiveness present in 'sad sort of clanging'. It denotes a mood couched in the terminology of music. But even granting this, a distinct difference is perceptible in the two versions. The English has a languid, lingering tone of the blues, become catchy with the lilt of a children's jingle. The Hindi is just sleepy-eyed. No undertones of a sad strain quiver behind the words. And yet, despite its a-tonality, its lack of an inner dimension, the Hindi rendering captures the reader's attention in a sweeping, disarming way. It gives a spell of sheer aural pleasure, inlaid with the primal fancies of a childhood re-awakened. Even more, it makes you sway back to the context in which the nursery rhyme is being sung. Makes you visualize the scene, visualize the characters and circumstances that make for this incursion of a nursery rhyme in their midst. It makes you, in short, reread, reconsider the two texts, takes you deeper into the cross-currents of translation. For those few trance-like seconds that come from the reading of good writing, you hear, feel and live the being-ness of the characters: you rock with their bickerings and squabbles, their face-offs. And most importantly, you feel the throb of their turbulent, inherent bilingualism.

Bilingualism is more than *knowing* two languages. It is an intimacy with the speech sounds of two languages, giving the bilingual a manoeuvring capacity between them. The bitonal quality that this kind of flesh and bones bilingualism can lead to is vivid in Roy's text. It is basically an English text. The non-English, Malayalam inflexions injected are into this English body. For instance, consider the following dialogue:

'Nothing specifically as such', Comrade Pillai said. 'But see, Comrade, any benefits that you give him, naturally others are resenting it. They see it as a partiality. After all, whatever job he does, carpenter or electrician or whateveritis, for them he is just a Paravan. It is a conditioning they have from birth. This I myself have told them is wrong. But frankly speaking, Comrade, Change is one thing. Acceptance is another. You should be cautious. Better for him you send him off....'. 'For you what is nonsense, for Masses it is something different.'[13]

If a Hindi translation evokes the bitonality of an English framework, it would be no mean achievement. For the most part, Neelabh's translation does not achieve it. The right linguistic field or balance is not available to him. His rendering of the passage quoted above is bereft of the comedy in the English original produced by the juggling with two speech idioms, and the parodying of the variant form. Here is Neelabh's rendering:

'Naheen, aisi koi khaas cheez nahin,' comrade pillai boley. 'lekin dekho, kaamraid, jo bhi suvidhaaen tum usey deytey ho kudrati taur par doosrey uska bura maantey hain. Vey isey ek tarafdaaree kee taur par dekhtey hain. Aakhirkaar, kaam voh jo bhee karta ho, badhaigiri ya bijli mistri ya jo kuchch bhee, unkey liye voh sirf ek paravan hai. Yeh sanskaar unmey janm sey hoten hain. Yeh mein khud unhey bata chukka hoon ki ghalat hai. Magar saaaf-saaf kahen to, kaamraid, parivartan ek cheez hai. Usey sveekaar karnaa doosri cheez. Tumhey hoshiaar rahanaa chaahiyey. Usee ke liye behtaar hai ki tum usey kaheen ravaanaa kar do...' 'tumhaarey vastey jo ek bakvaas hai, janta ke liye voh ek alag cheez hai.'[14]

All the comedy, all of Roy's tongue-in-cheek showcasing of a mutant idiom, have been wiped out of the rendering, leaving it flat. 'Others are resenting it'; '*a* partiality' (emphasis added); 'I myself have told them'; 'Better for him you send him off'—are typicalities of a certain idiom of spoken English grown amongst us. Such dramatizing of a group idiom is among the reasons for the exceptionally strong aural dimension of Roy's novel. And then there is the jammed up word 'whateveritis'. This word compound, constructed from the particular tone-fall of Comrade Pillai's way of speaking, sets his voice and vocal inflections ringing in the ears. It evokes the ethno-culture of Comrade K.N.M Pillai.

In addition to these absences of speech variations evoking ethnicity, the absence of capitalized letters—not possible in Hindi—affects it further. Words like 'Change' and 'Masses' acquire an intended comic/heroic twist from the capitalizing of their first letters carried out in the English. Roy's prose style has a visual feel, a visual presence, as well as an aural, let us not forget! But in the verse sections that Neelabh tackles and which abound in the book, these innate non-presences are not felt at all. A harmony of voice and word gets formed, a harmony of narrative voice and narrated words, in a kind of sporting contest, a sparring, with the English. This rejuvenation is felt, to begin with, as a change in the timbre of the narrative voice, a sudden heightening of it. At first, the objects and events figuring in the verses seem alien, unconnected to the translating language, and you balk at this alien-ness. The cuckoo clock, for instance, in the verse we dealt with a little earlier, or the church bells chiming in the distance, are not features of the Indian milieu-scape. Take this verse, for example: 'O Esthappaappeechen Peter Mon/Where, oh where, have you gone? We seek him here, we seek him there/Those Frenchies seek him everywhere/Is he in heaven? Is he in hell?/That demmedelusive Estha-Pen?'[15] The corresponding Hindi is: '*O esthaappappeechen kutappan peter maan/Kahaan haan kahaan gaye tum jaan/ham dhoonden yahaan ham dhoonden/vahaan/franceesee dhoonden yahaan vahaan/ voh nabh main hai ya gaya paataal/voh mahachchali estheppen lal?*'[16] We note, to begin with, the absence of capital letters in the Hindi as we did in Comrade Pillai's speech. And we feel again that the words have been reduced or truncated in some way. The whole text has a sunken, curtailed look. (We *see* Roy's text too, don't forget!) About 'maan' and 'jaan', and about the whole of the succeeding line—about the whole versifying, in fact—you feel something forced about the rhyming and the rhythm. In the second stanza 'ham dhoonden... dhoonden', that veers away to the 'Frenchies' and evokes the lore of the Scarlet Pimpernel, this sense of laboured craftsmanship deepens. For the slang 'Frenchies', no matching Hindi slang has been sought or attempted since none exists. But the gains that the Hindi registers despite these lacks are not dismissible. The whole of the first line, even in its undifferentiating, uncapitalizable nagari script does look and sound like the nonsense words of a children's jingle in Hindi. Yes! The Hindi text too does acquire a visual quality, over and above its alphabet and letter formation. This is one of those inexplicable, alchemizing processes by which words read gain an aural materiality, and this aural mass reconnects with the sense of the words, giving the words a kaleidoscopic animation. The overall rhythm stays firm and the words 'dhoonden yahhan, dhoonden vahaan...' rise newly minted from its beat. Their brevity, tailored to the beat and in tandem with it, immunizes the Sanskritic strain in the rendering, 'nabh' (sky), 'paataal' (the nether world), 'mahachchali' (the great trickster), to charges of pedantry. This friendly, approachable Sanskrit conflates with the uncolloquialized word 'franceesee', (for 'Frenchies') and creates a piquant 'firang' ambience that evokes the multicultural, multilimbed body of the novel.

A similar evocation of the multilingual, multicultural essence of the novel through a kind of occidentalism occurs in the translation of another form of versifying prevalent in it. Here, the last letter or syllable of a word links up with the first letter or syllable of the next word, in a faithful, well-observed parody of speech habits. Here is an example in the English and the Hindi. 'O young lochin varhas scum out of the vest/Through wall the vide Border his teed was the bes:/ Tand savis good broad sod heweapon sadnun.'[17] In normal English, it would be, 'O young Lochinvar has come out of the west/Through all the wide Border his steed was the best/And save his good broadsword he weapons had none.' The Hindi is no less of a hilarious garble. Here it is, '*lo, yuva lokin vaarnikla paschim se ho kar/saaesee maaprant me us kaashva thaam nohar/rar khada chchodus kepaas nahinththaha thiyaaar/ aurchala oh nishastr akelaghode parsavaar.*'[18] In ungarbled Hindi, it would be, '*/lo, yuva lokinvaar nikla paschim se hokar/saare seemaprant mey uska ashva tha manohar/aur khadag chchod uskey paas naheen ththaa hathiyaar/aur chala voh nishastr akeley ghodey par savaar.*' And here again—as with the translation of the rhyme about the clanging of clocks and church bells noted earlier, and thus testifying to the success of the translation—the reader's attention winds away from the crafted, arresting senselessness of the garble, to the essentials of the novel, in a recapitulative consideration of the why and whence of the creation of the garble.

Another small and utterly delightful euphonic translation: this one is un-versified. The context is of Rahel and Estha pleading with

Velutha's brother, Kuttappen, to repair their boat. Here's their dialogue:

> 'First we'll have to find the leaks,' Kuttappen said. 'Then we'll have to plug them.'
> 'Then sandpaper,' Estha said. 'Then polish.'
> 'Then oars,'. Rahel said.
> 'Then oars,' Estha agreed.
> 'Then offity off,' Rahel said.[19]
> Here is the Hindi:
> *'pahely hamey chched dhoondnen honge,' kutappan ney kahaa.*
> *'phir regmaar,' estha ney kaha. 'phir paalish.'*
> *'phir chappoo,' rahel ney kahaa.*
> *'phir chappoo,' Estha ney razamandi kee.*
> *'phir chalchalachalchal', rahel bolee.*[20]

'Chalchalaachalchal'—'Offity Off'. The Hindi with its very different phonetics produces the same mood of a skipping, fragile joy as the English; a fragile joy miniaturizing the evanescent high spirits of the Small God that pervades the novel.

But are these occasional sweeps into the inner signifiers of the novel enough to create a translation equalling its mass and weight? We raised this question in the beginning and answered it in the negative. Let us see, taking the following passage as an example, if we have to retain the negative or withdraw it, 'The candlelight accentuated her rouged cheeks and painted mouth.. Her mascara was smudged. Her jewellery gleamed.'[21] Here is the Hindi, *'mombataaee kee roshnee uskey surkhee lagey gaalon aur rangey huey honton ko aur bhee numayan banaa rahey they.'*[22] The difference from the English gets very well illustrated here. There is no intimacy, no direct link, no bond, between the character and the description of her by the narrative voice. The use of the word 'uska' or 'uske' for 'her'—however correct linguistically—has an inexplicable, distancing and impersonalizing effect. Baby Kochamma, the character figuring in that paragraph seems a figure seen from a distance, seen from the outside, by the describing voice. She becomes a third person presence, which she does not in the English, despite the third person terms in which she is described. The English is verb-centred. And it has adjectivized nouns such as 'rouge-ed', 'paint-ed', which make quick connections with the pronoun 'her'. This halts and reverses the distancing capacity of the third person pronoun.

Perhaps the pronouns 'uska', 'uske', could have been avoided altogether as, '*Mombattee kee roshni surkhee lagey gaalon aur rangey huey honton ko aur bhee numayan bana rahieen thee. Kajal phail gaya thaa. Gahney chamak rahey ththey.*'[23] Even assuming that these deletions echo the original they still are only minor changes, minor verbal adjustments. The problem with Neelabh's work is bigger: that even when linguistic faults cannot be cited—and for the most part, as we have maintained, they cannot be—it yet misses making contact with the life-giving lungs of the words. And it is this shortfall that this analysis has been attempting to explore and fathom.

Let us consider the paragraph describing the path leading to Velutha's hut. Velutha, let us keep in mind, is the god of small things. The passage reads:

> The path, which ran parallel to the river, led to a little grassy clearing that was hemmed in by huddled trees: coconut, cashew, mango, bilimbi. On the edge of the clearing, with its back to the river, a low hut with walls of orange laterite plastered with mud and a thatched roof nestled close to the ground, as though it was listening to a whispered subterranean secret. The low walls of the hut were the same colour as the earth they stood on, and seemed to have germinated from a house-seed planted in the ground, from which right-angled ribs of earth had risen and enclosed space. Three untidy banana trees grew in the little front yard that had been fenced off with panels of woven palm leaves.[24]

The line that springs out from that passage, and hoists the reader's attention over its full range back and forth is, 'The low walls of the hut were the same colour as the earth they stood on, and seemed to have germinated from a house-seed planted in the ground, from which right-angled ribs of earth had risen and enclosed space.' The imagery of walls sprouting from the earth and coated the same colour as their parent, walls nestling close to her, angled like her inner shape and architecture, invokes the subsistence-level life of the inhabitants of the place. They are the sons of the soil, the gods of the small things, the trees and vegetal life that grow from the same belly from which they themselves have grown. The unassuming yet seething, rumbling energy of these gods, perennially fed by the saps of the earth goddess, is a standing statement in the polemics of the novel. And the sense of a close, unbreakable physical union between these gods and the earth mother that this statement and the imagery suggest, finds reiteration in the preceding line about the roof of the hut 'nestled close to the ground as though it was listening to a whispered, subterranean secret.'[25] The first and last line of the paragraph, foregrounding the growth of trees and the chancy supplies of food they make, completes the statement of the precarious and explosive living conditions faced by the inhabitants—the Paravans, or the Untouchables—that the novel makes.

The Hindi twins the original. Neelabh *hears* the words he translates. He is dedicated in his endeavour to gather into his rendering all the tremors or meaning and association in the English. In the passage being considered here, the Hindi words are not only equivalents, thy also replicate the stress-tones of the original. The Hindi runs as, '*Raastaa, jo nadi ke samaanaantar chaltaa ththaaa, ghaas ke ek chchotey, khuley ahaatey tak gaya ththaa, jo sataa kar lagaayee gayeen peydon ke jhurmut se ghira thaa.*'[26] The stress words and phrases in that sentnce, 'samaanaantar', '*jo sataa kar lagaaayee gayii peon ke jhgurmut sey ghira thaa,*' diligently echo the risen, descriptive tone of voice we register in the English at these points. The whole paragraph is animate with these spells, of sharpened narrative voice. The sharpened quality is present unfailingly in the key sentence we discussed above in our analysis of that passage in English, '…*lagtaa thaa ki veh dharatee me boey gaye kisi ghar ke beej se ankurit huey they, jisse dharti ki samkon pasliyon ne phootkar jagah ko gher liya hai.*'[27]

Now there is, admittedly, something freakish about this yoking of an imagery that sounds remote to Hindi. They do not seem to be in harness, do not seem to be in any engagement with each other. Nonetheless, the imagery attracts the attention. Its strangeness compels, and drawn by it, you settle down to the comparative study of the words. You do not come out fully satisfied with the exercise. 'Ghar ke beej' for 'house-seed' is misleading. It seems to mean 'seeds belonging to the house,' and not 'seeds of house'—like the seeds of the peepal tree or the banyan—which is the sense in which the words are used in the English. '*Jissey dhartee ki samkon pasliyon ne phootkar jagah gher liya hai*'[28] takes a while to settle down and disclose the picture the words hold. The English equivalents nudge you—'Ankurit' ('Germinated'). 'Germinated' ('Ankurit'). *'Samkon pasliyon ney phootkar jagah gher liya hai'*: 'right angled ribs of earth had risen and enclosed space.'[29] 'Right angled ribs of earth had risen and enclosed space': *'samkon pasliyon ney phootkar jagah gher liya hai'*—back and forth you say the words in a Babel of English and Hindi, Hindi and English. 'Samkon pasliyaan' for 'right-angled ribs' do not quite interlock. 'Samkon' used for 'right-angled' has a smooth, rounded feel to it, made, you feel, by the 'm', 'n' nasals. 'Right-angled' is hard, crackling of tone, with its 't' and 'ngle' sounds making it solid, throaty.

But you do not give up. You cannot. Neelabh's translating élan cannot be set aside easily. Eventually, the linguistic din and disunity quiet down; the Hindi words stay poised over their store of imagery, legitimized. Yet a sense of the disconnectedness persists. Word and image do not seem organically connected, the one does not unfurl on the dot to disclose the other within itself. But it is not words that can close this gap, you realise, even as you register and acknowledge again the handpicked, thought out quality of the words. The sentence and its imagery do not radiate and floodlight the entire paragraph above and below, as its English precedent text does. It does not conflate with the sister image in the preceding sentence that delineates the low roof of Velutha's hut, so low that it seems to have its ear glued to a secret message from the earth. And it does not drive home, with sphinx-like, mock-smiling seriousness, as the English does, a founding statement of the novel, that it is, always has been, a dog's life for the paravans, and perhaps always will be despite the communists' drumbeating.

This lack of recapitulative, retrospective vigour in that passage remains a feature of the translation all through. It cannot be ascribed to the language, as we said. The language mirrors the original with devotion and verve. But it does not spring from the passionate concern for the underdogs of society, from the passionate rage at discriminations over and above those bred by caste, that vibrate in the narrative voice of the English. The Hindi's inspiration is from the English text. Its narrative energy is text-derived, not idea-generated and imagination-driven as the English is.

And so, eventually, this under-muscled, un-veined idiom moves up to tackle the scenes of Ammu and Velutha's lovemaking. The Small

Gods, touchable Ammu, and untouchable Velutha, rise against the Big God of History in a desperate supreme act of defiance. History is braved by its own offspring. Where can the lovers hide? History is immanent. It is of rarer substance than the earth on which it is made. This earth, colonized by History, cannot give the lovers asylum. They are the cast offs of both History and earth. Water holds out hope. Velutha swims or rows across the river Minachal to reach Ammu on the other bank. But water is transparent. It cannot keep secrets. Boat, oarsman, swimmer, tryst-on-the-bank: all soon to become public, each object outlined and thrown into relief by the undulating action of the water.

The censuring eye of the public and the freezing gaze of history—the Big God—are looming absent presences all through the thirteen nights of Ammu's and Velutha's tryst. The lovers expand within, as their bodies converge and root into sensations never known. Simultaneously, the spaces outside them contract, become menacing with the hot, panting breaths of History and its minions closing in. The simultaneous projection of opposites, which is the main narrative strategy of the novel, reaches its peak in these sections. The fleecy, spring-time symphony of the lovers' union is shot through with the heavy, approaching roll of enemy drums. Consider this passage:

> Biology designed dance. Terror timed it. Dictated the rhythm with which their bodies answered each other. As though they knew already that for each tremor of pleasure they would pay with an equal measure of pain. As though they knew that how far they went would be measured against how far they would be taken.[30]

Does the Hindi project the binaries of pleasure–pain, terror–anti-terror, distance–nearness that form the brickwork of that passage in English? Does it secondly, move on from the binarian method to consolidating the binaries and bringing back into attention the parent proposition, or, as it were, the bear hug of History on human beings? The Hindi runs:

> *Shareer ke vigyaan ney nritya ki roop-rekha banaayee. Aatank ney taal nirdhaarit kee. Us laya ko nirdeshit kiyaa jissey unkey jismon ney ek-doosrey*

ko uttar diya. Maano unhey maaloom ththaa ki sukh key har spandan ke liya unhe usee maatr mein peeda sah kar keemat chukaanee hogee. Mano unhey maaloom ththaa ki jitnee dur veh jayengey yeh us par nirbhar karega ki unhe kitnee dur tak ley jaayaa jaaney vaalaa thaa.[31]

Once again, the careful, crafted word-conscious quality of the prose catches the attention. Deferring to its claims, we turn a deaf ear to the speed-breaking circularity and multi-vowelled phonology of the Hindi. We reach out, instead, to discern in the marrow and after tones of the words, the founding statements on history that the novel makes and sustains. We do not get it except in faint echoes. Disturbed by the lacuna, we revert to the English and try to imbue fullness into the Hindi. We try to draw fullness from the translation by rereading into it the image of retribution biding its time, of a menacing immanence, thrown up by the English.

Why does not the Hindi, word-perfect as it is, have the retrospective sweep of the English? The question nags us again. And in its wake other limitations of this word-perfect translation come bristling in. Why do Ammu and Velutha seem distant from the narrative voice? Why do they not seem like the close kin of the narrator they do in the English? Why is there no sense of a blood tie between them? Why does the narrator seem an outsider, not the participating insider as in the English? Strictly speaking, this lack of intimacy between the narrator and the narrative ought not to be considered in absolute terms. The writer of the original, and the translator, *are* two different people, separate, however much the translator assumes the original writer's mien. And readers do make allowances for this separateness. But the translator cannot get this indulgence from *The God of Small Things*. The book's very being springs from what seems an umbilical connection between the narrator and the narrative. Call it autobiographical, if you like. Call it anything. But all its characters—Estha, Rahel, Mammachi, Baby Kochamma—seem like intimates of the narrator, genetically connected to her. All its events seem like tests of fire gone through by the narrator. Its searing quality comes from this knife-edge closeness. A closeness paralleling this cannot be established by the translator, however conscientious his pursuit of the word.

Neelabh just chose the wrong book for his skills.

▌ Notes

1. Roy, Arundhati. 1997. *The God of Small Things*. New Delhi: IndiaInk.
2. Neelabh. 2004. *Maamoole Cheezon Ka Devta*. New Delhi: Rajkamal Prakashan. Trans. of. Roy, op cit.
3. Roy, p. 19.
4. Ibid., p. 19.
5. Ibid., p. 19.
6. Neelabh, p. 32.
7. Roy, p. 19.
8. Ibid., p. 19.
9. Neelabh, p. 32.
10. Roy, p. 87.
11. Neelabh, p. 100.
12. Ibid.
13. Roy, p. 279.
14. Neelabh, p. 299.
15. Roy, p. 182.
16. Neelabh, p. 201.
17. Roy, p. 271.
18. Neelabh, p. 291.
19. Roy, p. 210
20. Neelabh, p. 230.
21. Roy, p. 296.
22. Neelabh, p. 316.
23. Ibid.
24. Roy, p. 205.
25. Ibid.
26. Neelabh, p. 224.
27. Ibid., pp. 224–25.
28. Ibid., p. 225.
29. Roy, p. 205.
30. Ibid., p. 335.
31. Neelabh, p. 354.

Index

About the Author

Raji Narasimhan, born in 1930, took to full-time writing in the late 1960s, after quitting journalism (*The Indian Express*, New Delhi). She writes fiction, literary criticism and translates from Hindi and Tamil into English. Her book *Sensibility under Stress: Aspects of Indo-English Writing* (1976) was shortlisted for the Sahitya Akademi Award. The second of her five novels, *Forever Free* (1979), was also shortlisted for the Sahitya Akademi Award, and was on the English Literature syllabus of IIT, Delhi, all through the 1980s and part of the 1990s. She has two collections of short stories: *The Marriage of Bela and Other Stories* (1978) and *The Illusion of Home* (2007).

Her translations include *Unarmed* (1998) of Rajee Seth's Hindi novella *Nishkavach*, *Alma Kabutari* (2006) of Maitreyi Pushpa's Hindi novel of the same title (shortlisted for the Crossword Translation Award in 2007) and *Not Without Reason and Other Stories* (2012) of Rajee Seth's Hindi stories *Akaran to Naheen*.